BROKEN FEVER

BROKEN FEVER

REFLECTIONS OF
GAY BOYHOOD

JAMES MORRISON

ST. MARTIN'S PRESS
NEW YORK

www.stmartins.com

"Saved" was published in the anthology *Wrestling with the Angel* (New York: Riverhead, 1995); "Practice" was published in *The Massachusetts Review* (Fall 1999); and "The Animal's Glance" was published in the *Santa Monica Review* (Spring 2000).

BOOK DESIGN BY CASEY HAMPTON

Library of Congress Cataloging-in-Publication Data

Morrison, James.
  Broken fever : reflections of gay boyhood / by James Morrison.—1st ed.
    p. cm.
  ISBN 0-312-26129-2 (hardcover)
  1. Morrison, James 2. Gay men—United States—Biography. 3. Gay youth—United States—Case studies. 4. Gays—Identity. I. Title.

HQ75.8.M67 A3 2001
305.38'9664—dc21   00-045970

First Edition: March 2001

10 9 8 7 6 5 4 3 2 1

FOR MY FAMILIES

I wish that for this hour I could swell into someone of importance, so as to do you credit. I suppose you had a melting for me because I was hewn out of one of your own quarries, walked similar academic groves, and have trudged the road on which you will soon set forth. . . . I would that I could put into your hands a staff for that somewhat bloody march, for though there is much about myself that I conceal from other people, to help you I would expose every cranny of my mind.

—J. M. Barrie, "Courage" (Rectoral Address delivered at the University of St. Andrews, 3 May 1922)

CONTENTS

BROKEN FEVER

How intensely people used to feel!

—James Merrill, "The Broken Home"

HE WASN'T THERE
AGAIN TODAY

Exhibits—A and B.
Exhibit A: First this poem:

> *As I was going up the stair*
> *I met a man who wasn't there.*
> *He wasn't there again today.*
> *I wish, I wish he'd stay away.*

I'm nine, and trembling with happiness as I read this poem into the slender microphone, whose little steel-plated head is studded with the tiny holes that will absorb my voice magically, take it in, and then give it back to me, recorded. Months from now, after the glow of its novelty has faded, I'll filch the mike, this sleek plastic tube, because it looks like a gun, and sure nobody will ever miss it—for even wonder always turns ordinary—I'll put it to new uses as my nifty weapon, much coveted, in neighborhood games of cops and robbers. (I'm the robber, or else I won't play. I don't need them. There's always TV.) But now it is still new, and the four of us—mother, father, sister, self (my other sister comes along a little later)—loll around it, on the aquamarine couch with napless texture of plastic and spindly arms of deal. A wire coils from

the mike and taps into the whirring body of the tape recorder.
It is new, it is still all new.

It is new in more ways than one. The Pandolfs, down the block,
own a tape recorder, and it sits on a makeshift mantel in their
dining room, which is really a kitchen with a table crammed in
it. (Our houses are small.) Two big wheels, like the reels of the
film projectors at school when they show movies about the history of the country or the mysteries of the bloodstream
("Hemo the Magnificent"!—my favorite), trade endless lengths
of fawn-drab tape that stream through a little steel tunnel on
the way from one spool to the other. On the strips of film at
school, you can see little pictures, one atop another, like a totem
pole, but the surfaces of the tape—tilt your head and you can
see them, though you cannot tell where the sound comes from—
are as blank and as slick as the texture of the aquamarine
couch. Our tape recorder, though, is a *cassette* player. It is new.
At once the cumbersome heft of the reel-to-reels becomes out-
dated. How ridiculous, to keep that big silly-looking machine
about the house! You might just as well have an old-fashioned
phonograph cluttering up the place, complete with arcing meg-
aphone ("His Master's Voice"), or you might as well tool about
the streets of town in a Model T. Soon, though not as soon as
you'd think, the old reel-to-reel disappears. It is replaced on the
Pandolfs' shelf by an assortment of framed photographs. That's
progress for you! The cassettes *improve*: to get smaller does not
always mean to dwindle. *Compact:* not a new word; I loved my
mother's compacts—the pinkish cakes of makeup, and the glinting
mirrors, and the scruffy brushes, removable as pearls from oysters'
hearts. The world changes, in my lifetime. Everything gets better,
better, better, better.

But the cassette recorder was not just a new kind of thing. It
was newly acquired property. A different kind of new: we'd never
bought a *brand*-new car, but the *used* cars always still sparkled with

novelty, so long as they were new *to us*. We had no earthly need of a tape recorder. Maybe my father thought he might need one, since he was about to go into Business. What *kind* of Business? Who knows! First he was a "draftsman," then he was an "engineer"—but not the kind that drives the trains. It is amazing, what I did not know then, and what I did.

Into that docile but receptive mike he read this poem: "O Captain, my Captain, our fearful trip is done. . . ." My mother read: "Johnnie Crack and Flossie Snail / Kept their baby in a milking pail." Or else: "It was many and many a year ago, / in a kingdom by the sea. . . ." My sister read: "I think that I shall never see / A poem lovely as a tree." Or else: "Whose woods these are I think I know. / His house is in the village, though." We played the tape back. The voices—muffled, but recorded—were ours. The other three voices sounded, albeit transformed, like theirs. The fourth voice did not sound like mine. It squeaked and trembled. I did not expect my vivid happiness to be so known. I blushed, and that too shamed me, the blush of my face like the tremor of my voice—a giveaway. Still, I was happy—shame and joy not opposites. The voices were fixed, what we had read, what we had done, just a minute ago, fixed invisibly to the tape. That voice could not be mine, yet it had to be. For weeks we read our poems into that tape recorder, new recordings over old ones. What is fixed is still not permanent. My father always reads the same poem. I usually read the same one. Mother father, sister—and soon, another. How I love them all.

What is left, since stark posterity neglected the tapes themselves, is the poem, and that only in memory:

> *As I was going up the stair*
> *I met a man who wasn't there.*

He wasn't there again today.
I wish, I wish he'd stay away.

An early foray into paradox: How could you meet a man who wasn't there? And how could such absence translate into recurrence? And why should it stir deterrence? Maybe the problem was not that the man *wasn't* there but that he really, somehow, was. But what was he doing, anyway, lurking and skulking about the stair, instead of making up his mind and going either up or down? To those who attend to their proper business, not to mention their well-watched p's and q's, stairways are not havens but mere passageways. If the one who was going up the stair—a boy, I never doubted for an instant—was going *up* the stair, then the man who wasn't there must have been coming *down* the stair. Maybe there were different ways of not being there. There was something creepy in the poem, under the exacting cadences of the nursery-rhyme whimsy. And what was all this nonsense about a stair, anyway? However many steps a particular case might yield, I always called them *stairs*. On the other hand, it sounded English, to call it a stair, and I wanted to be English. I liked the way they talked. It was so civilized.

I did not like the way I talked. Hearing my voice played back on the new tape recorder, reading the poem about the man who wasn't there, I felt as if I were meeting myself as another. How was it possible that I could not know myself, conditioned by every day's proofs? Yet how could I claim to do so, if the voice that was mine sounded so insuperably strange to me? Yet the truth was, the strangeness of it came in large part from what it revealed, the tremor of my happiness, that I'd thought secure, hidden. Was it strange, then, because there was too much of me in it? I was there, in it, and not there, only too much there.

Exhibit B: A stuffed monkey with white marble eyes, a red felt tongue protruding from a fixed grin, and thickly matted fur the color of apricot. The tail has been torn, and a few gray filaments of stuffing stick out of the raggedy rip. The animal smells of dirt, a safe, comfortable smell. Beyond a certain point the smell never changes, and cleanliness would only usurp it. That is why I will not allow the animal to be washed. At times it gets washed anyway, behind my back, causing a temporary rift in my relation to it— and to the washer, reluctant but vigilant usurper—until the dirty smell starts to come back, the laundered smell to fade. The animal's name is Monkey. A name need not be fancy. It only has to define the thing it designates, and some things could not be named at all. Monkey has a companion, a bear twice Monkey's size, with stumpy limbs and a hairy pot of a belly, and squinty eyes that might be scary but for the low, folksy rumble of Teddy's well-known, soothing voice. In truth, Teddy, who always sounds like he has a cold, is kind and generous, and maybe a little slow on the uptake, like Baby Huey, but basically lovable. Teddy looks after Monkey. The two of them, Teddy and Monkey, go on numerous adventures. Monkey's voice is high and squeaky, an exaggerated version of my own voice. In fact, it is my own, since Monkey speaks through me, but Monkey is not quite me. Exaggeration may be a form of knowledge. It can let others know you know they know.

Teddy speaks through my sister, but while Monkey's voice is congruent with my own voice, Teddy's voice is nothing like the voice of my sister. The huskiness of the voice, and the burliness of Teddy himself, make it very clear that Teddy is meant to be a boy. So clear is this, indeed, that it is never spoken of. The obvious has nothing to prove. In the course of their adventures, however, Teddy frequently raises the question of whether Monkey is to be understood as a boy or a girl. Teddy is far too kind to raise this question with derisive intent. It makes no difference to Teddy. He just wants to know. Still, on the whole, Monkey would prefer that the question not be raised. For my part, I do not think Monkey is a girl, despite a voice even squeakier than my own, and despite faintly girlish features of face—like the delicate pink lips—but I do not exactly think Monkey is a boy, either. All in all, I don't want to talk about it myself, and though it is usually Monkey who speaks through me, it may be that I speak through Monkey on these occasions, when Monkey gently discourages Teddy's polite but robust inquiries regarding the matter. I'm not afraid of becoming a girl. The allegedly universal anxieties of castration never visit my conscious life. I'm far too comfortable, far too well protected, ever to entertain so horrific a prospect. I'm not even afraid of being a particular kind of boy, so long as I don't have to talk about it. I don't know exactly what kind of boy that would be. There is no name for it. I'm seven. It might have happened already. Maybe it is not even a thing that *happens,* in the ordinary sense of that word. I cannot help my voice. It is the one I have been given. Monkey gives me glimpses of what it might be like. That is why I love him—not as proof, exactly, but as evidence.

Conclusive evidence, I call it.

A child, in the famous case study, faced with the distressing absence of a parent, improvises this game: Hiding a toy, the child declares it "Gone." Then, revealing it again, the child pronounces it "Here!" A triumph over reality: what was gone is here again, and the child calls the shots. In the spectacular ecstasy of repetition compulsion, the dialectic is replayed, again and again: gone, here, gone, here! Or—if the parent stays away—here, gone, here, gone. Freud, the intrepid chronicler, deems the game the child's effort to master the parent's absence. Freud might better have recalled the loony wisdom of his berserk precursor Nietzsche: "You must

become a child, without shame." Only the presumption of innocence, that grown-ups' make-believe, wills the game to address
others, and the game's well-known variant, peekaboo—an invention of grown-ups—foists upon the child the very proof that the
child's own experiments test, in their own way. What does a child
care about innocence? Children know what they know, and even
Freud understood that children keep their made-up ideas about
sex long after adults' truths have surfaced to discredit their own
more complicated theories. They've been lied to so often by then,
why should they accept the sham truth of their parents, who
conspired to hide it from them for so long—not to protect their
children's innocence, but to guard their own cynicism?

Although from the vantage point of my present self, I do not
remember a time in my life when I was *not* "gay," I know that
the arrival at any avowed gay identity is always a complex process
of affirmation and negation, refusal and identification. It is just
this process, and the ways gay identity circulates before it is spoken,
that this book explores. In debates current with its writing, the
issues of identity the book addresses have largely been consigned
to the poles of a puny dichotomy, between identity as an *essential*
ground of existence on the one hand and identity as a *social* construct on the other. The dichotomy, I believe, is false, and part of
the elaborate system that will prevent us from comprehending
either of its terms. On the one hand, this book's premise relies
on the notion that there should be, in the first place, such a
thing—imagine!—as a gay child. In turn, this notion implies that
an identity putatively defined in terms of sexual desire may, in
fact, precede awareness, understanding, or experience of such desire. What happens then?

If, however, the rhetoric of self-affirmation requires us to think
that our selves cohere somehow within us, rather than simply
being inherited from without, it does not follow that this claim,

however empowering, liberates us from societal constraint. This book tracks a developmental narrative shaped by the regulatory mechanisms of many of the institutions of modern mass culture: those of education or medicine, those of the state, the law, the church. Yet again and again—for in the grandiosity and rawness of childhood, every phenomenon is new even at its thousandth coming—the story shows the systematic failures of these institutions, themselves so systematic, to regulate, to acculturate, "properly." The only triumph this book recognizes lies in the fact that our culture, so often bent on *eliminating* gayness, so often *produces* it, *enables* it. Freud himself may have been insufficiently attuned to the intricate relation between identities we long to claim as only and deeply our own, and the many mechanisms governed to constrict them. Maybe that was why he couldn't see that the absence being toyed with in the game he observed so acutely was not the parent's at all, but the child's own.

We do well ourselves, as responsible adults, to engineer games designed to convince our children that they exist, since we spend so much of our time, otherwise, denying their being. To advise the proprietors of the many voices always raised in wishing queers off the earth that, in these declamations, they are oppressing other people does nothing to stanch the chorus. Would it stop them, to tell these people they are also hurting children—children being, to such minds, distinct from people? It would not be an appeal to be proud of, if one were inclined to make it. But it is not one of a kind that these people themselves would be above, to achieve their own sorry ends. I wrote this book to know myself better, and maybe to help certain children, or the grown-ups who tend them, or the adults they grow into, to understand that they exist. But I also wrote it to answer the voices, the ugly clamor, of these people of whom I speak. You know who they are. They know who they are. If this—the book you are holding in your hands—

were a tract, I would name names, and I would have more, much more, to say about these people. But this is only the tale of a happy childhood, at the outset of an ordinary life.

I will now pass amongst you the aging, glossy Polaroids, to prove it.

I

SAVED

Fourteen years old, smack in the middle of the 1970s, and I thought that everything I knew, or needed to know, about religion could easily be contained, like a pair of quiescent worshipers in a big pew, in two sentences. *I believe in one God* was the first, intoned weekly in my Profession of Faith in a booming voice that then trailed off into the assured murmur of the following sentences—only, after all, less condensed versions of the all-important one. The other sentence was the pale underside of the leafy, bright, manifest first, its hidden mate, seldom spoken, always assumed, the deep principle of everything: *I am a Catholic.*

Yet even though I took these simple declarations as a sort of irrefutable basis for my self, I was aware from an early age of something not quite right in the strain of my Catholicism. During mass I was subject to dual impulses. I wanted to give myself up, to surrender myself wholly to rapture, and I could not understand why, if we really believed what we said on Sunday mornings, we should go on with our lives in the ordinary way the rest of the week. But we did, so I wanted also to resist my passions. Yet how I loved the flamboyant artifice of the mass, the resplendent escape, the exaggerated display! I could not help noticing, though, that I was not really supposed to love exactly these elements (yet, plainly, there they were!), or to love them in quite this way, or with quite this ardor. Something was obviously amiss, and religion came to signify for me a particular relationship to the ordinary. It was, itself, out of the ordinary: all that pageantry circulating, in a world of its own, with a kind of hysterical control, around the figure of a beautiful, doomed, naked man impaled on a cross. And at the same time my relation to it was not the ordinary one. Because I longed to be ordinary, I installed those two sentences as the cornerstone of my being, even as another, inverse sentence involuntarily formed itself within me, increasingly simplified, gradually stripped of equivocation, as the first two sentences grew ever more complex, sprouting modifying shoots. That sentence, the new one, I spoke finally when I was nineteen years old: *I am a homosexual.*

I had recently moved with my family from one suburb to another farther away from Detroit, better insulated from the city by distance and cost, and one of the many distressing effects of the move, I soon discovered, was that it made necessary renewed avowals of identity. Nobody in our old neighborhood needed to be told who I was, or what. I was known. I was "Jimmy," good-natured loner, spelling-bee champion, Catholic, bad in sports but too amiable to be mocked, a bookworm, a tease who in turn could take his share of ribbing except in certain well-known and carefully avoided areas: bad eyesight, thick glasses, freckles, general scrawniness giving way to increasing huskiness. This identity had grown within me like the white sap coating the inner walls of a dandelion's hollow mauve stalk—a charged image for my own mythologies of lost innocence, in memory of happy mid-spring hours spent decapitating yellow-headed weeds to suck their essence until the day Bobby Adams from down the block told me the white stuff was the flower's come. Then I had not had to think about who I was. Now we were leaving my best friend, a house I loved, teachers who already knew in advance how smart

I was, to whom I did not have to prove myself, in order to move into a new house, the lone structure in a still-unbuilt subdivision, surrounded by expanses of mud with here and there big rectangular holes, the basements of future houses, like craters in a lunar landscape. On top of that, I was expected to make myself known all over, or possibly even to remake myself, to endure yet again the humiliations of mutable but tenacious self-hood. During our first week in the new house I was riding my bike along a street in an established neighborhood next to our undeveloped one when a girl called to me from one of the porches. It was a rainy afternoon, and my slicker hung heavy on my shoulders, its yellow flaps concealing the shape of my body. My long hair fell in mid-seventies bangs across my forehead. The girl looked at me critically and tonelessly inquired, "Are you a boy or a girl?" I rode away without answering. This was not, I knew, going to be easy. I was going to have to start from scratch.

Is to speak one's identity always necessarily to reinvent it? If so, that would explain the existence of manifold structures through which the institutions we live by routinely keep even the most public facets of identity from being spoken. In elementary school, my identity as a Catholic was regularly made public, through regulations seemingly designed precisely so that I would never be called upon to speak it, so that it could be made to go without saying. On Wednesday afternoons, I and my fellow Catholics were excused from school early, whisked away without explanation, herded into buses, and transported the half mile to St. Cletus for what must have seemed to our classmates, left behind, the inexplicable, exclusionary ritual of catechism. *Election, communion:* these are common terms in the public rhetoric of religious affiliation, but what is seldom noted is how the exclusionism the concepts engender threatens the quality of unspokenness they are meant to guarantee. The ritual itself, whatever it was we did during those Wednesday afternoon disappearances, may have re-

mained undiscussable, mysteriously beyond the reach of those
social categories given to white middle-class suburban late-baby-
boom ten-year-olds. But its trappings came in for thorough public
scrutiny from the non-Catholics. For example, the bus that took
us to catechism was the special-ed bus, squat, squarish, half the
length of the normal bus with its big, sleek, rounded fenders. Our
status as catechism-goers was therefore linked to the outward signs
of abnormality, and Bobby Adams, irrepressible truth-teller, un-
leashed a gleeful weekly screed on the subject: "Retard bus, retard
bus, you're going on the retard bus, they're getting it all ready for
you, they're washing out the retard puke, hope you don't pick up
too many retard germs!" It was also Bobby Adams who first articulated the disquieting properties of the very word that named
this unknowable act, this hebdomadal vanishing, with its remote
but still distinct suggestions of kissing—evoking the kissing of
cats, of others, of other boys.

What Bobby Adams could not have known, of course, was that
though we may have felt called on to defend catechism, the word
was at least as disturbing to us as to them. For it could not be lost
on us that, in spite of the appearance of legitimation, a rhetoric
of shame attended our Catholicism. It was, in fact, a socially authorized intrusion on normality, on normal desire. Though sanc-
tioned by the school, it was understood as somehow ineffable,
deeply private, a facet of personal identity, an ingrained attribute
that, though chosen, was uncontrollable, seen as so profoundly
rooted as to render choice nugatory; and was necessarily associated, despite its apparent social accommodation as a simple fact,
with obsession, compulsive repetition, inner yearnings, ultimate
dispositions. More than once was I enjoined to be proud of my
Catholicism, and I saw that the injunction implied the previously
unimagined possibility of pride's opposite.

It was *weird,* a weird thing that was somehow accepted. And
my relation to it, to this weird thing, was not like other people's,

and so the weirdness was compounded. If common society ever finds a way of acknowledging or legitimating "alternative sexualities"—a possibility one can imagine only with ambivalence—that acknowledgment will probably in its early phases resemble this sanctioning of religious observance. What I knew then about inhabiting inverse identities, I learned from being Catholic.

But I was fourteen, and had only those two sentences to go by, the creed of an accepted silence. All I knew was that we were changing churches just as we were changing houses and schools. Like the other houses in our neighborhood, our new church was still under construction, so mass took place with folding chairs and portable lecterns in the cafetorium of the junior high school I attended every day. The name of the parish was St. René, and the nuns wore ordinary dresses beneath a chaste wimple. The priests did not chant their prayers but spoke them in a normal voice, and they told jokes during their sermons. A man with hair as long as mine played guitar during the hymns. People wore blue jeans to mass. How different this was from St. Cletus, with its aura of transcendent permanence and its otherworldly ritual, its exacting separation from the habits of daily life. To get to mass at St. René, even though we went in by the back door of the school that was named for a failed astronaut, we still had to pass the gym and the music room where my French class met.

Gradually I came to see that my experience with churchgoing would exist in a new relation to the idea of the ordinary. Where formerly I had been susceptible to a kind of effortless transport from the modes of everyday life in church, now I was surrounded by them, and what church would have to be about was the nexus between the ordinary and the extraordinary. During mass I watched one of the altar boys light the candles and prepare the altar. His face was angular and sharp-boned, with a prominent jaw and dark eyes that glowed with concentration as he moved slowly, ritually, extending a flame from elevated candle to candle. Then his air of solemn caution disappeared, and he drew back his staff, like a fisherman briskly drawing in his line, and blew out the flame at the end of it. He walked to his seat with an easy, loping gait. When he sat, easing his flattened hands palm down beneath his robed thighs, I saw that he was wearing corduroys and sneakers under his vestments.

All summer my mother said she was sick of seeing me mope around by myself. Mothers she was meeting as the neighborhood grew had boys my age, and she kept threatening to get me in on their ball games. But I refused. Deprived of the friends who had surrounded me all my life, I decided it was time that friendship, like other aspects of identity, became for me a function not of proximity but of choice. By the end of the first week of eighth grade, quirks of fate provided me with three suitable but very different friends. Kevin, my table mate in algebra, was a football player who looked like Robbie in *My Three Sons*. Ronny, my locker partner in gym, wore leather jackets that smelled of cigarette smoke; he had a ready, trilling laugh that sounded like an imitation of Cousin Itt. Craig was my chemistry lab partner, and the difficulty I had in placing him was explained for me in one of our first conversations when he spoke with conviction a sentence parallel to the one I recited so often by rote. "I am a Baptist," he said. The compartmentalized, hierarchic nature of junior-high culture made it possible to keep the three of them completely separate from one another. Faced with the challenge of reinventing myself, I saw each of the three as emblematic of a potentially separate destiny, and I wanted the freedom to explore each possibility in isolation, to see how it suited me in theory. Kevin was a Catholic like me, but the destiny he represented was by far the least likely one, that of jockhood. Ronny held out the promise of delinquency, with tales of bad trips, crime sprees, and sexual indulgence that always sounded remarkably like the plots of whatever movies were out that week. Craig was an intellectual companion, a fellow member of the chess club, from whom I could learn, who might lead me toward asceticism. No matter which of the three by turns equally appealing fates I finally accepted, I knew I wanted to go *somewhere,* and I knew I would have to be led there.

At that age I could no more invent the man I have become than I can now fully imagine the boy I was. From time to time I would try to do so, to foresee the cars I might drive, the jobs I might hold, the women I might marry, the children I might have. But whatever pictures of this domesticated future my imagination supplied always lacked fullness and conviction. They were like images in a child's gray plastic viewfinder: dim, distant, static, reduced. Should I have been able to imagine in more ample detail my possible adult lives? Were others able to do so? It certainly seemed so: Kevin was already able in rhapsodic tones to describe his wife and kids. What was it that prevented me from similarly being able to enter the world of projected time? Would this lack recede as I grew, as the very time I felt I could not invent for myself transpired, unstoppable, with purposes of its own? Or would I be crippled by whatever it was that was missing? Would I wear all my blighted life the outer marks of this lack—disproportionate limbs or the explosive scars of uncontrollable acne—unmistakable traces of a troubled transmutation into adulthood?

I can't say that these questions tormented me, if only because I wasn't then able to formulate them in exactly this way. But I began to glean, through the ways I *was* able to formulate them, that this growing sense of something missing derived from my having taken too much about myself for granted. Maybe the move would instill, in the end, the ambiguous benefit of self-consciousness. When someone in school asked me why I never said anything—for I spoke willingly only to Kevin, Ronny, or

Craig—I gave the stock answer that I remembered from the old neighborhood, what people used to say *about* me: "I'm just quiet." This caused the asker to roll eyes upward and say something to the effect of, "You are just so *weird!*"—the final epithet tortured into multiple syllables. I knew from such encounters that the old answers were no longer going to work. But I was still able, for a while, to cling to those two simple sentences: *I believe in one God. I am a Catholic.*

Spirituality presents itself as a transcendent answer to human desire, but it is also necessarily an analogue to desire. Miguel de Unamuno in *The Tragic Sense of Life* culminates a long tradition of describing faith as passion, as the only end of the unappeasable thirst of being, the hunger for immortality. The "vital longing for immortality" finds its closest fleshly incarnation in sexual desire: "Thanks to love, we feel all that spirit has of flesh in it." But that is not much. For Unamuno, love is as fully suffused with tragedy as any other earthly condition. In spite of the hopeful ardency of Unamuno's sermon on love—"Love is the sole medicine against death, for it is death's brother"—his bottom line is as starkly anatomic as Kant's description of marriage as a contract delimiting the use of a pair of genitals: "The species must renew the source of life from time to time by means of the union of two wasting individuals, by means of what is called, among protozoaria, conjugation." Sexual love, "the generative type of every other love," gives rise to suffering because it "seeks with fury, through the medium of the beloved, something beyond, and since it finds it not, it despairs."

In many spiritual traditions, it is recognized from the outset that what is sought, what is hungered for, can not be found, and spiritual quest must be seen as an end in itself: Seek, but do not find. Or, in Bonaventure's variant: Desire faith; desire not understanding. Unamuno concludes, with his characteristic gentle severity, that sexual love is an imperfect analogy for faith because it is really a form of pity, born out of an intensity of identification with one's fellow sufferers. Divine love eschews such identification: St. Teresa of Ávila addresses God erotically, not out of sexual hunger but out of an acceptance of her worldly state. Augustine imagines Adam's erections in the Garden of Eden with studious, not prurient, interest. I first read Unamuno at eighteen, when my inner life was already very different from what it had been four years before. I recognized, without perhaps yet being able to articulate it, that the highest forms of desire were believed to surpass identification. We love God not because He is like ourselves, but because He is not, *because* He is unknowable. In *Gravity and Grace*, which I read around the same time, Simone Weil teaches much the same lesson in her meditation on desire-without-objects: "We have to go down to the root of our desire in order to tear the energy from its objects." I thought I understood this lesson, and I took it to counterbalance some of my most powerful feelings of longing, fear, and emptiness. At the same time, I knew it did not account for more basic—even, as I would have thought then, baser—ones. The experience I had in reading Unamuno was just another version of those barely conscious feelings of intensity from my earlier life as a Catholic, like the experience of hungrily watching the altar boys during mass. Nowhere in Unamuno, as nowhere in the Church, was anything like this experience acknowledged. Yet the unmoored intensity of feeling there, the fevered invocation of passion, the refusal to distinguish absolutely between sexual love and other kinds, the submission of suffering to an ecstatic lyricism, the intimate address, all that yearning talk of brothers!—surely some acknowledgment of my own relationship to Catholicism, fraught as it was with an ever more disturbing amplitude of the prohibited identification, was to be found there.

Craig was as different from Ronny and Kevin as I felt I was, in my yet-unformed state, from all three of them. Kevin and Ronny represented distinct social types in junior-high culture, the jock and the burnout. Most of the time, I had the long hair of the burnout, but although this made me acceptable to Ronny, I let Kevin know it was more a sign of laziness than a gesture of solidarity. Nothing about me suggested even the raw materials of the jock, but Kevin thought I was funny, and my friendship with him allowed me marginally to penetrate that camp. I had not assented to social typology, and was generally regarded as a little weird, but I was in a minor way still able to traverse the classes.

My own position in junior-high culture may have been almost uniquely malleable, but what I admired about Craig was that he simply *had* no position there. He was not given to striking the same attitudes of superiority that certified outcasts fell back on, seeking lame revenge, as everyone instantly saw with the relentless gaze of the newly pubescent, for their own personal weirdness. Rather, Craig was above it all. The world of junior high with its rigid structures and social jockeying went on around him without attracting his notice. He was neither a player, like Kevin or Ronny, nor a vaguely tolerated reject, like me. I discovered with amazement early in our friendship that he didn't even know what a burnout *was,* and that, unacquainted with the word's subjection to metonymy, he thought a "jock" was what you wore in gym, though he preferred the even more literal "supporter." One Saturday afternoon his mother dropped us off at a movie, *Young Frankenstein.* After laughing uproariously through the first half, I noticed that Craig was sitting in perfect silence, his arms folded, a distant smile on his face. He was not bored, clearly, and he was even giving off a kind of genuine pleasure, but a pleasure lodged deep within him, the way a cat might express pleasure if purring were soundless. I felt chastened. I leaned back and folded my own arms, my laughter subsiding, and tried to imitate the quiet dignity of his demeanor. From time to time I still burst out laughing, but now the laughter brought with it the salve of shame, humility; at least I had come to know how worldly were my basest dispositions. On the way home Craig described the movie to his mother with invincible simplicity. "It was funny," he said.

A quality of purity was fully evident even in Craig's physical presence. The pressures of growth take their toll on most adolescents, and one reason that I was able to retain a certain hard-won equanimity amid the rank hysteria and casual cruelty of junior high was that I saw with clear eyes that, at least physically, no fourteen-year-old was much better than any other. For all practical purposes, my classmates constituted a richly varied gallery of physical freaks—even Ronny with his stunted trunk and incongruously sinewy limbs, even Kevin with his rubbery grown-up lips pasted in the middle of a boy's face—a procession of misshapen, acne-splotched figures caught in the protracted act of growing up. But Craig was possessed of a grace that pervaded his frame, which seemed otherwise untouched by the physical world. He didn't look like the strange hybrids surrounding him—part child, part adult, stranded painfully between irreconcilable conditions. Rather, he seemed to embody the line drawings of nude males I watched him sketch in the margins of his chemistry notebook during class lectures. The figures in these drawings, like Craig (as I knew from gym class), were fine-muscled and hairless. It did not seem unusual to me that Craig should be drawing such figures in his notebook. They were images of the saints, nothing but that, the saints in all their naked suffering. Yet I was conscious of the difference between his attitude as he drew and mine as I watched him draw. He drew with a kind of absent care, pencil grazing the page, stopping after every few strokes to jot a note from the lecture. The inattentiveness of his drawing was at odds with the intensity of my gaze as he manipulated his pencil with blithe agility. In spite of its frozen passivity, my gaze was voracious, as if the strokes of his pencil traversed some furrow in space-time to caress unknowingly, causing it to pulsate irresistibly, whatever part of my body corresponded to the one he drew—supple legs, sloping shoulders, small but precisely detailed nipples.

Craig's otherworldliness was not lessened by those frequent moments when he resembled other boys our age. He was *in* the world, necessarily, but not *of* it. Once he remarked how funny it was that the word *embarrassed* contained the words *bare ass*. Another time he suddenly asked, "Did you ever notice that asaparagus makes your pee stink?" I did not take these as lapses into standard adolescent crudity. I understood them as signs of a hallowed earthiness, like St. Teresa's, of a clear-eyed acceptance of the world from which he was inexorably turning away.

With this in mind, I was anxious about seeing Craig among his family. After all, my own impulses to asceticism were easy enough to sustain when I was by myself or at school, but they were routinely defeated the minute I returned to my family, with all their base earthiness, their constant jokes concerning farts, and all their other worldly dispositions. If I resolved in a solitary moment of spiritual intensity to subsist entirely on crackers and oranges, like St. Teresa, I could get through lunch, but at dinner I always fell victim to my reputation in my family as the Human Garbage Can, my plate a welcome receptacle for the leavings of my parents and my sisters, assorted items St. Teresa would no doubt have refused but that I could never resist. When Craig invited me to his house for the first time, I went in the hope that I would not be disillusioned, not find his home life too ordinary, too much like my own. The early signs did not bode well. The house was a ranch, just like the one we lived in, the only variation being in the color of its brick and the austerity of its furnishings.

The living room was uncarpeted and empty except for a single sofa. Craig's older brother Barry sat, bell-bottomed, against a wall, strumming a guitar. His mother greeted me with the platitudes of a sitcom mother: "I always enjoy meeting Craigy's friends" and "You boys just go on and make yourselves at home."

What I found out, though, was that Craig's way of relating to these ordinary circumstances was in keeping with what I knew of his inner life. As for me, I may have recognized keenly what I saw as the banality of my own circumstances and their distance from those of the saints on whom we were enjoined to model ourselves, yet in spite of this recognition I could not detach myself from the world as I knew it. I could only participate in it, help-lessly, convulsively—bickering passionately with sisters, desiring ardently all advertised goods, robustly consuming the boxed foods of a fallen age, the Sloppy Joes and Hamburger Helper. But Craig was no more a participant in the structures of the larger world than he was a cog in the hierarchies of junior high. He took me to the basement to play chess and to discuss the implications of the gift of tongues. He was heedless of the TV sets blaring from upstairs. He offered me Fritos but referred to them as "corn chips."

Yet, although Craig rejected the things of this world, he did so without ill spirit. Unlike me, he did not regard the materials of his everyday life as inexpressibly banal. Instead, he looked at them through eyes of cobalt blue that would have pierced if he had let them, and he saw there evidence of godliness. He did not regard the things of his daily life as obstructions to his spiritual life but as the conditions that made it possible. "Are you a Jesus freak like Craigy?" asked Barry, interrupting our talk. He stood with his guitar tucked under his arm, and when Craig looked from him to me with his familiar remote half-smile, I saw that he was in-terested in my answer himself. Before I could think of what to say, though, Barry lifted his guitar and sang in broken tones, "Jesus freaks, out in the streets . . ." Without transition he reverted to speech: "What are you guys fagging around down here for anyway? Why don't you come upstairs and muscle in on the real world?"

"If you're lonely," Craig said, "you can stay here with us."

Barry laughed. "I'm not lonely," he said. Then in a slow, deliberate gesture, he raised his guitar and lowered it gently so that the bottom of the sound box rested on Craig's head. "Kabong!" Barry said, trilling his voice to imitate the sound of reverberation. Craig only smiled. "What a nutcase," Barry said with a fond chuckle as he tucked the guitar under his arm and shuffled away.

"It's your move," Craig reminded me.

The event was trivial, but to me it was still revelatory. How adeptly—though without machination—Craig had resisted being drawn into his brother's wrangling! With what delicate perception he had seen past the contempt that would have infuriated me to the real need beneath it, refusing the imperatives of sibling rivalry without mundane condescension. I knew that if I tried something like this on my sisters, they would tell me to knock off the holier-than-thou stuff, or would sniff the air in front of my face and ask whether the smell was that of my brain frying. But there in his identical house, Craig's was a completely different life, a completely different way of being. When his mother said good-bye, I noticed that her sitcom-speak had edged off into a kind of sour, uneasy concern over the clear intensity of our engagement with each other. "What were you boys *doing* down there all that time?" she murmured. It was the kind of invasive parental question that, when my own mother asked such questions, made me flush with resentment, anger, and embarrassment—a reminder that I was after all only a boy in a fallen world. But Craig's tranquil smile persisted as I stepped out into the early dusk, starting home.

On a muggy night in early fall Craig and I slept outside in a little red pup tent pitched in his backyard. The moon was full, so the tent's sheer walls were palely aglow, crimson, holding in dense humidity. We lay side by side, inner arms touching, my left arm brushing softly against his right arm each time we breathed. "Do you think Christ knew He was God?" Craig asked. It was not a question I had considered before, and as always I was happy to listen to what he thought, hoping he would not notice the vacancy of my own responses. He laid out the issues carefully, with passionate reason, showing me why it was an important question without seeming to instruct me, without patronizing me. The son of God, Christ *was* God, yet He was expected to provide to men a model for faith, proving that faith can be found within the realm of the divine as well as in the world of the human. "It's not just that God *understands* faith," said Craig. "He made it, so of course He understands it, but even more than that, *He can share it*. He's what you're supposed to have faith *in*, but He has faith too, see? He wouldn't ask us to have what He couldn't share Himself. So He made Christ a creature of faith, who knew He was God only because He had faith, and who could even doubt, so God could know doubt. Like when Christ asked on the cross, 'Why have you forsaken me?' "

I listened raptly. I could tell from the rhythmic pressure of his arm on mine, each of its hundreds of minute hairs making me tingle with its glancing contact, that his breathing was regular, as even as his reason. I tried to control my own breathing, measuring it against an expanding sensation in my chest that compressed and shortened each breath. "I'm hot," Craig said suddenly, and then he was leaning over me, bristly knees pressed against my arm where his arm had been. He drew his gray tee shirt over his head. He dropped the shirt in a bundle in the only available space, on the other side of my head. His chest floated above my face. I breathed in its heat. His torso blocked the light from me for a second so that his chest was the color of darkness. The crucifix suspended from his neck hung before my eyes, glinting when it caught the light. The base of his palm, where it curved into his wrist, pressed against the tent's floor next to my ear, supporting his weight as he leaned over me. It occurred to me that he remained there, his body suspended above mine, a moment longer than was necessary. Then he settled down again beside me, naked. "Now," he said. "Where were we?"

I do not remember how the idea of conversion was introduced into our talks, but we began to discuss it soon after. Its appearance as a topic of our earnest conversations came by degrees, unnoticeable but somehow inevitable, like the slow appearance of the sun near the close of a cloud-choked day. Had he brought it up, motivated by the missionary zeal of the Baptist? If so, none of that zeal was evident as we talked about it. For him, the possibility of my conversion was simply an answer to a question, a step toward, not renewed, but *new* faith. I had recently had my confirmation as a Catholic, but Craig explained that confirmation implies a false equation between natural and spiritual birth in reaffirming in a state of knowledge the baptism that takes place in infancy. Regeneration, however, is chosen freely by a self-conscious penitent, and salvation follows without reference to anterior spiritual states. For Craig it was a simple matter. He wanted everyone to be saved; therefore he wanted me to be saved. For me it was simple too. I regarded conversion as a potential bond with Craig, a way of creating, by asserting, some elemental connection between us; or, to put it another way, of declaring that, through Craig, I had chosen asceticism as my destiny, so long as it meant I might spend occasional nights in tents with Craig's spectral body hovering, even for only a second at a time, above my face.

Salvation may be the final goal of spirituality, but asceticism is its medium, its intermediate goal. Salvation is the abdication of the self, surrendering it to God, even if it is sought, as it must be, in a wish to preserve the self. Asceticism is mastery of the self motivated by a longing to renounce individual identity. Both imply transcendent self-identity, a root where desire and action are one. According to Heidegger, only God has no essence because only God is completely identical to Himself. Asceticism depends not on the imitation of this divine self-identity but on a devotional assumption of it. Salvation cannot be earned through good works, say the Baptists, but only guaranteed by inner grace. Conversion—source of ascesis, path to salvation—paradoxically calls for imitation of outward action and, at the same time, avowal of an original condition. To circumvent this paradox, conversion narratives tend to be organized around the rhetoric of compulsion. Thomas Merton, in *The Seven Storey Mountain*, for example, and Richard Gilman, in *Faith, Sex, Mystery,* describe irresistible conversions forced upon them mysteriously rather than experiences they choose rationally. To convert is to speak a *new,* assumed identity while comprehending it as an authentic, originary one. "It may be a crisis experience," said one of the books I checked out of the library and hid under my bed. "But it will be definite." At night I lay in the bed under which these books were concealed and tried to make sense of my own fugitive impulse to conversion. Was it definite? Had I been born a Catholic by mistake? Was I really a Baptist without knowing it? Did that explain whatever needed to be explained about my relationship to faith? Would conversion fill the lack I felt when I forced myself to look inward, so that I might no longer fear such contemplation? I wanted to save my soul, but a more immediate longing, to be close to Craig, compelled me. Would anyone find that out? Was it sinful? Was it sinful to conceal the compulsion, or to hide books under my bed? A new street lamp had been put up outside my window and its dull yellow ooze seeped through the drapes at night so that even when I closed my eyes the darkness was edged with light.

The second time I attended a service with Craig converts were called forth. It was a weeknight, so only a few people were in attendance. Craig's mother dropped us off in their big blue van, Craig sitting in front next to her. The church was between the Farmer Jack where my mother grocery-shopped and an apartment complex where people I knew from school lived. It was brightly lit inside, and the pews and altars were made of plain, light-colored wood, oak, in contrast to the dun-colored or saturated-auburn and densely ornamented cherry wood of St. Cletus. Craig had explained to me that such services were intended to promote a greater sense of direct contact with God, unmediated by cere-mony. Still, the rhythms of the service were so loose and so ram-bling that I did not observe that converts were being appealed to until I noticed Craig looking at me with a beatific smile. Then I raised my hand.

I waited alone in a small back room. The room was in a style that I associated with schools, not churches. The linoleum floor was patterned in black spiraling curlicues meant to hide the dirt. There were three desks, chairs of white molded plastic, each with a single chrome arm extending from under the seat to support the attached Congoleum marbleized desktop. Tubes of white glar-ing light hummed in the paneled ceiling. When the door opened, I was surprised to see that the man who entered was the same man who had been conducting the service. He wore a business suit and had thin, bright-silver hair that was so close-cropped it appeared to be inset into his scalp, resembling the rough hewn coat of a mouse. In spite of his hair's lustrous monochrome, his eyebrows were a deep, bushy black. He shook my hand briskly and said his name was Mr. Brill.

While Mr. Brill talked I tried to keep myself from tapping

unconsciously on the floor with the toe of my shoe. Mr. Brill was saying the same things Craig said about atonement, conviction, repentance, perseverance. But these things did not seem compelling when Mr. Brill said them. He looked at the floor as he talked, and his hands were clasped together between clenched thighs. Even when he wasn't talking, he kept his mouth open, so I could see his irregular gray teeth, and between each sentence that he spoke, he moved the tip of his tongue back and forth behind the bottom row of teeth. As he went on talking, it seemed to me that he mumbled the important words and then gave sudden, explosive emphasis to the unimportant ones. Suddenly he was leaning toward me, with his still-clasped hands now in front of his face, thumbs supporting chin, index fingers pressed together, their tips against the isthmus of skin between his nostrils. "When you pray," he asked me, "what do you pray *for*?"

I was startled to be spoken to. I removed my own hand from in front of my face, where I had been unconsciously biting into it. A fine strand of saliva connected my hand to my mouth, stretching and glimmering and vanishing only when the hand came to rest on the desk. I was aware that some residual drool surrounded my mouth, but I did not wipe it away. For the poor, I answered. For the sick. For the starving. For the dead.

"For the dead?" One of Mr. Brill's husky eyebrows rose to a higher level than the other. "But surely the dead are past the need of human prayer."

"I pray that they'll be with God."

Mr. Brill nodded and leaned back. He placed his palms on the desktop, fingers curled. "Tell me how you understand the meaning of the Trinity."

I could tell him only what I had learned from catechism. I felt my face going red as I talked. I watched Mr. Brill's hands on the desktop. He methodically spread his fingers, flat now against the smooth surface. He reached with one thumb across the desk so that its tip touched the tip of the opposite thumb. "Of course," he said, "you don't mean there are three gods."

"No. No, no, no. There is one." My incantation, my simple sentence, was called for: *I believe in one God*. How is it that I did not speak it?

"There are three manifestations of God," said Mr. Brill.

"Yes," I agreed. "But there is only one God."

Mr. Brill looked both amused and contemptuous. "*Only* one?" he said. "When you think of God, what qualities come into your mind?"

"Goodness," I answered. "Love." I looked at the floor. The black curlicues were meant to hide the dirt, but I saw three footprints on the floor near my desk, the honeycombed shadows of big, cleated boots.

"Any others?"

"Goodness," I repeated.

"Self-existence?" said Mr. Brill. "Immortality? Omnipresence? Immensity? Eternity? Holiness? Righteousness? Truth? Omnipotence?" He spoke each word with a measured tone. He closed his mouth, breathed deeply through his nose, then reopened his mouth, the tip of the tongue in the middle of one of its laggardly trips across the teeth. "Love," he said quietly. He stood up and held his hand out to me. My hand still retained the moist imprints of my teeth, but I extended it. My spit came into contact with the dry skin of Mr. Brill's hand as we shook. The expression on his face, superficially unchanged, was touched by disgust. At the door he turned back to me. "What sports do you like?" he asked briskly.

I knew what the question meant. It was part of a test, a code, like the codes of devotion but, I had thought, distinct from them. I was being given the chance to make up for my failures as a worshiper. I liked no sports but I could not say that. I thought of Kevin. "Football," I said. Mr. Brill nodded and went out, assured that I was lying, that my conviction was inadequate, that I would never be a Baptist, that—even if some of my prayers were for the poor and the sick and the dead—most of them were for the love of Kevin or Ronny or Craig.

On the way home, Craig clambered into the back seat beside me, leaving his mother alone in front. She regarded us nervously in the rearview mirror. "How was the service?" she asked. Craig placed his hand on my thigh and squeezed it tenderly. Then he rested his hand there. I was afraid that his mother could see this, but I also knew Craig would see no shame in the gesture. "Jim was saved," he told her.

Secretly relieved that I had not really been saved, that my life could go on as before, I avoided Craig for several days. I attended mass at St. René with my mother and sisters, and took communion. If the masses lacked the inflamed theatricality that had previously so inspired me, I decided, that too should be taken as a source of relief. The masses did not lack the spirit of God, after all, and their tractability was safer, more amenable to teaching myself, if I could not become a Baptist, how to be the right kind of Catholic. It had begun to seem to me that, in any case, the closer I came to exaltation, the further I was from God. Shooting the breeze with Kevin or Ronny, I felt I had come back to them after a long time away. There was something reassuring about their commitment to the known world, about the way they sought transport only in what was comprehensible—drugs, say, or football. Kevin told me he noticed I had been hanging around a lot with that Craig guy, whom Kevin had thought was pretty weird, and I agreed that he was. But then one afternoon Craig appeared at my door and suggested that we go swimming because he thought it would be among the last of the warm days. He had not brought his bathing suit with him, so I lent him a pair of my cutoffs.

It was already mid-fall, and cool, so the lake was deserted. After a quick swim we sat on the shore, arms hugging knees. Craig's chin rested on his knees, and he was shivering. He asked me how it felt, being saved.

"Okay," I said. Then, seeing him shiver, I added sharply, "What's your deal anyway? It isn't *that* cold."

He looked at me. Seemingly by force of will, he immediately stopped shivering.

"I'm not like you," I went on. "I don't think it happens that way, being saved. Like, you walk into a church and then all of a sudden you're just suddenly saved. I'm sure, man! I'm really just so sure! Going to heaven depends on what you *do*. It depends on how you *act*."

"It's not about going to heaven," said Craig.

"Then what's it about? I've listened to you talk, and some of it makes sense, like that stuff about a personal God and all. But not everybody believes all that stuff, you know? Not everybody even *thinks* that way. I mean, there's Baptists, yes, but there's Catholics too. And that's not all there is. What about Jewish people? I mean, alls I'm saying is not everybody believes the same way and you shouldn't act like your way is best all the time."

"I didn't know I did," said Craig. "I didn't know you thought I did."

I remembered the night we had slept in the tent. I had listened to him speak of God that night. I had been in a state of sustained rapture. It had been his words that brought about that state, his words that sustained it, but it had also been, I realized, his voice, his body. And later, after his voice subsided, he had asked me in a low whisper if I too were not hot. Had he wanted me to take off my shirt as he had his? Would it have produced in him something of the inarticulate bliss his nakedness caused in me? Was it possible to reconcile that unspoken ecstasy with the spiritual transport he was able to describe so fully? "No," I had told him. "I'm not hot." I had refused; I had not wanted to get too close to the source of my feeling, because I feared it. But now on the cold shore of this empty lake, I was telling him that I was not like him, because I wanted him to consider forms of our kinship other than the spiritual.

"That's not what I mean either," I said. "This isn't coming out right." In frustration I lay back, facing the sky, stretched out on the rocky shore.

Suddenly he clambered on top of me, straddling me. He was holding a ridged, variegated rock, the size of a hockey puck. "This all comes down to something basic," he said urgently, his weight on my thighs. "Do you see this rock? Do you believe God made it?" With his free hand he gently clasped my wrist. Gently he lifted my hand to the rock he held, and I closed my fingers around it. He held one side of the rock and I the other. "Do you believe that God made this rock with His own hands?"

I did not answer. Then the rock was pulled away and the pressure lifted from my thighs. I looked at my hand, at the traces of dust there from the rock. When I sat up, I saw the rock hurtling through the air. I saw Craig standing on the shore, his back to me, his arms at his sides. The posture of his body suggested repose. I had not seen him throw the rock, yet I did not doubt that it was he who had done so. Why, then, merely because I had not seen God fashion the rock, should I doubt that He had done so? I watched the rock soar through the sky. I looked, nearer me, at Craig's back, its visible proportion, the clear, precise column of his spine, at the cleft in the seat of the shorts I had lent him. In a second the rock would hit the surface of the lake. It would make a splash that would perhaps be lost amid the rising din of the wind. It would create outward-moving circles as in liquid glass that has not yet found its final, solid form, and these would, before disappearing, interlock mercurially with the many other ripples on the top, already quivering, of the lake. But for another second the rock was still in midair, and it was *that* second when I knew, whatever else, that I thought Craig's *body* was beautiful; that I would have to find a place for such knowledge among whatever other knowledge I could forge; that my future life, which I could not before imagine, would depend on it; that in this way the lack I had perceived within me might yet be overcome. The rock reached the crest of its arc, buoyed up and suspended aloft but falling still, as if from an immeasurable height.

2

EYES OF WOOD

The desks in fourth grade, enclaves massed in neat rows, were distinguished by the novel fact of their having hidden insides. They were contraptions of taupy steel, the plastic seat connected to the desk itself by a tube of winding metal, with big, blotchy welds, the texture of old, hard scabs, suturing metal to metal at the joints. The tabletops were mock-wood slates, faint grain coated with a thick plastic sheen, hinged to swing upward, opening like a frog's mouth to show a narrow trough, meant to hold pencils, edging the outer end of a bigger cast-iron corrugated basin for books and rulers and folders. In first and second and third grades, the desks had no such recesses, making no allowance for privacy. It was in the fourth grade that secrecy, privacy's dark other, was at last given social reign.

I was reading *Pinocchio,* by Carlo Collodi. How this book, a cheaply bound paperback with a silly illustration of the titular rosy-cheeked long-nosed puppet on the cover, made its way into my desk I cannot say, for the fact that I was reading the book—a kid's book, a *fairy* tale—was a secret. It occurs to me that I stowed it in my desk to propagate this secrecy. If I had read the book only at home, it would have been not a secret, just a fact. Inside the crowded desk, the book, over time, had been pushed to the back, and it became wedged in the niche (created—like all forms of decay, also over time—by the gradual loosening of hinges) between desktop and tun, so that when one afternoon I swung the desk open, jerking it fiercely up and down to punish its resistance, the book fell out onto the floor, its binding giving way, its pages scattering broadly, a prolix cascade, across the gray tiles, the secret made public.

I was as instinctively right, after this inadvertent apocalypse, to foresee doom as I had been, before, to keep the book a secret. People otherwise bereft of imagination frequently discover that very quality in ridicule, and in the months following, my class-mates proved themselves to be artisans of scorn, inspired masters of mockery, improvising endless, unmerciful taunts, poems of de-rision, brilliant flights of contempt. Had the book been any other book—*Johnny Tremaine*, a volume of Encyclopedia Brown, a *Classic Comics* version of *Dr. Jekyll and Mr. Hyde* (all of which I hap-pened also to be reading at the time)—I would not then have fallen victim so helplessly to the malicious fertility of their un-stoppable invention. But it was *Pinocchio*—and so I was a baby, a mewling weakling, a tad, a squirt, a lambykins who could never hope to be a real boy. I was a puss, a pussens, a wussy, a fairy with a shameful yen for tales, a crinkling Jiminy whose own nose—pug, not long—became thenceforth the object of tireless, hateful scrutiny. It is not wholly inaccurate to suggest that my reputation, after this fall, never really recovered. Those who thereafter assented to let me befriend them did so in spite of my ignominy.

Pinocchio wants to be a real boy. Fulfilling the aspiration is, as one might imagine, an uphill battle. Its first requirement, before the quest is even fully betokened, is to learn violence. At the beginning of the book, in a terrible, unexpected fit of rage, Pin-occhio kills Jiminy Cricket, smashes him into pus-like pulp with a hammer. I'd seen squashed crickets in real life: the split abdomen, the oozing lymph and spouting chyle, the broken, tangled legs. In fact, like Pinocchio, but thoughtlessly, without anger, I had killed crickets myself.

The final stage in Pinocchio's apotheosis is to enter the belly of a whale to bring back his maker, Geppetto, who has been swallowed by the whale (called in the book, inexplicably, a "dog-fish"). This task, too, needs a certain violence: penetration, invasion. Pinocchio has not been born, but made, fashioned from wood like a piece of furniture, nailed together and hammered into shape; the weapon he uses to kill the cricket may be the same tool Geppetto used to construct him. His journey into the whale is thus his first visit to a womb. It is necessary that he become a father, that he enter the demonic mother, to reclaim his maker *as* his father, and so become a real boy. The tale is an Oedipal story in reverse: innocence follows the metaphoric sexual initiation. To accept the maker as a father—and to acquiesce to the equation of the father's physical act in reproduction with the father's symbolic authority in the world—is to become a real boy. But first the mother's body must be quashed, like a cricket's belly. More traditional Oedipal narratives, with that ribald crudity that is typical of them, take women as their objects: you become a real man, they assure you, by nailing a woman. *Pinocchio* presents a very schematic Oedipal drama to the extent that it is about a male developmental crisis successfully overcome, but it disturbingly circumvents the feminine, in a riot of violent directness: foregoing the route of marriage, the father nails his boy together from scratch, without need of a mother, builds an uncanny son, both double and other. Like many such stories, with its aggressive drive to legitimate masculinity, and with all its attendant misogyny, *Pinocchio* is a fantasy of procreation without women.

My classmates knew the story of *Pinocchio*, as I did, from its Disney version. The Disney *Pinocchio* differed from the other cartoon movies that I had seen, *Snow White, Cinderella, Sleeping*

Beauty, Dumbo, and *Bambi.* The others were about mothers, but there were no mothers in *Pinocchio,* and that may be why, though it was among the most superficially cheery of these movies, it struck me as one of the scariest. The peculiar horror of the other cartoons came from a disquieting loss of security that was connected directly to the loss of mothers. In *Snow White, Sleeping Beauty,* and *Cinderella,* a substitute mother torments the innocent heroine, while in *Dumbo* and *Bambi,* the mother is separated from her child, or killed. What troubled me the first time I saw *Bambi* was that the death of Bambi's mother comes halfway through the film. If it had come at the beginning, I would perhaps not have grown so attached to Bambi's mother. If it had come at the end, I could perhaps have come to accept it as an inevitable climax, like Charlotte's death at the end of *Charlotte's Web,* which I could cope with only by starting the book over again right away, to see Charlotte reborn. (The second time I saw *Bambi,* the mother was reborn, too, but she became for me then a figure of unbearable pathos: you know she is to die.) But, in fact, it came in the middle, and the end of the movie, for all practical purposes, and against all odds, is nonetheless a happy ending. With its delicate lyricism and its strangely exuberant emphasis on seasonal cycles, *Bambi* is really a story about recovery and growth after loss. The messages of these movies, in any case, were clear. Girls should be wary of how they trust, and boys must prepare to live without mothers. But Pinocchio does not have to learn this lesson, because he never had a mother to begin with, a fact that imparted an inexplicable quality of desolation to the whole film, despite its theatrical high spirits.

What would it mean, if you were an animated puppet who could already walk and talk and sing and dance, and exert all the forms of volition boys boast, to want to be a real boy? The ending of Disney's *Pinocchio* disappoints because there seems to be so little difference, practically speaking, between Pinocchio as a lively puppet and Pinocchio as a real boy. To be flesh and blood, instead of wood, might have inherent value, but if one already possesses the properties that flesh and blood ordinarily confer—sensation, animation, will—might there not also be advantage to be had in remaining wooden? The notion that it was better to be a real boy than a puppet who could do everything a real boy could do any-way was, in its way, a perfectly logical proposition, especially since it was self-evident that even a live puppet would likely be per-ceived socially as a second-class citizen, while a real boy could hope one day to attain superior status. But the theoretical simi-larity between animated-puppetness and real-boyhood, together with the unconvincing triumph of the final metamorphosis, made it apparent that there was an element about Pinocchio's desired improvement in condition that could not, for some reason, be spoken. Too committed to the pleasure principle, Pinocchio is also afflicted with an organ, his nose, that swells uncontrollably in states of excitation. It is, of course, not at all unusual for boys to be in possession of such an organ. The trouble is that the locale of Pinocchio's, displaced, gives away his deceptions.

I owned a plastic Ken doll and a pint-size reproduction of the ventriloquist dummy Charlie McCarthy. Both, demonstrably, were boys, though not real ones. The Ken doll's nakedness thrilled and troubled me. The doll's body was lithely proportional, with what I already recognized, despite its absence of nipples, as a beautiful chest: twin smooth shapely plates of plastic pectoral. But there was nothing between the rigid yet pivotable legs but the faintest swell of peach-colored plastic. The evidently more inhibited Charlie McCarthy sported formal attire that was sewn onto the dummy's body, and for a long time my curiosity had to be sated by merely tactile exploration. But one day the need for visual proof got the better of me, and I ripped off the dummy's clothes to see, with a certain sense of relief, the featureless expanse of pale flesh-tone plastic that stood in place of the unimaginable, unpresentable penis. Once ripped off, and tattered irreparably, the sewn-on garments would no longer clothe the dummy, and so that I would not have to explain why I had torn them off, I hid the dummy away in a closet. I comforted myself that the satisfaction of my curiosity was, in the end, worth the loss of the dummy.

There was a TV production around that time of *Pinocchio,* with Peter Noone from the rock group Herman's Hermits in the title role. I was going through a phase then of being drawn to mop-headed British lads, like Jack Wild, who had played the Artful Dodger in the movie *Oliver!* With shaggy-cropped hair, doleful eyes, and a disposition that moved between chipper cockiness and bouts of pensiveness that suggested a greater depth, Peter Noone, albeit flirting with coy manhood, was such a lad. In this version of *Pinocchio*, the puppet was clad in a hunter's shirt made of green felt, and in sheer olive-drab tights, rather like the clothing of another storybook boy, Peter Pan. In the TV version of that tale, Pan, cavorting in a spirit of airy, brazen enmity with that irascible old queen Captain Hook, swung back and forth from an unapologetically visible string attached to unseen rafters. The condition of suspension enabled—and the atmosphere of exuberance propelled—this Peter Pan to pendulate his dangling, tightly clad legs, especially in spasms of glee after he had gotten the better of the earthbound Hook, who with barely concealed longing would in answer brandish the potent prosthetic that gave him his fancifully evocative name. Hanging from the rafters this way, Peter Pan should have looked helpless and silly, and by any practical standard he surely did, but the measured yet spasmodic oscillation of the fine-muscled legs, the rotation of the hairless arms reasserted that very physical cockiness I took to be the gauge of a boy's power. Peter Noone's Pinocchio transformed himself from a puppet into a real boy by throwing off the puppet's girlish makeup, revealing in a flash unblemished cheeks and irresistibly cute nose beneath the greasepaint, rouge, and plastic, and by loosening the collar of the hunter's shirt to show at the neck a trim synecdoche of newly suggestive musculature. As an indication of actual change, the metamorphosis was no more convincing than it had ever been, but it proved ineluctably that to be a real boy had something to do with bodies and secrets—the secrecy that clothing borrows or necessitates, the body such secrecy hides and yields.

Melvin Airbets was one of four special-ed students in the school. He was a tall boy with a narrow face and curly hair short enough to show big lobeless ears that were pointed at the top. Although there was little in his appearance to certify his special-ed status, he was fully subject to the relentless mockery such status guaranteed. He was one of the tallest boys in the school, and the noticeable elongation of his torso and the concomitant foreshortening of his sturdy legs gave him the look of a centaur. This, together with the ears, and an equine aspect of his face, earned him the nickname, applied without affection, of "Mister Ed." Our gym teacher, Mr. Grimm, spoke of boys as specimens: a "good specimen" was an athlete; someone who was bad in gym was a "poor specimen"; and those who fell between the poles were "so-so specimens." Every system of classification must be judged by how it deals with its anomalies, and although ostensibly rooted in achievement, the grounding of this system in immutable essence was still dimly perceptible. For instance, Eric Lang was the best quarterback in the school, but he was also universally recognized (though never publicly identified) as a fat slob, so he was considered only a so-so specimen. I, on the other hand, couldn't throw or kick a ball more than a few feet, yet I had naturally developed biceps (the year before I'd been arm wrestling champ in the lunchroom), so by a slim but thankful margin I too achieved some moderate upward mobility into the so-so category. Melvin Air-

bets, no athlete, was still a very good specimen, and perhaps because of this, Mr. Grimm cut him slack that was not forthcoming
for others of his stripe.

In the Darwinian atmosphere of gym class, survival may depend on resource and tactic, and so reside in action, but superiority demands only its own proofs, and so resides in being. It was
not until seventh grade that we were segregated into locker rooms,
boys' and girls', but the first time I entered one, I thought it was
the most terrible place I had ever seen. With its cold concrete
floors; dim light; hissing showerheads; mazy, dank-walled hallways;
and suffocating, sweat-suffused air, the locker room in every detail
answered my conception of what a concentration camp might be
like. The locker room was a site that mimicked privacy—in the
little padlocked cubicles we were assigned—and mocked it at the
same time, demanding public, collective nakedness that was to be
unhampered by any idiosyncratic displays of untoward anxiety or
sissy bashfulness. It was the collective nature of the enterprise that
was meant to render the question of modesty irrelevant. "What
are you scared of?" Mr. Grimm would demand of anyone even
vaguely hesitant to undress. "You ain't got nothing we ain't seen
before!" That element of collectivity was also, however, what introduced relativity, since the collective so often gives up its cele-
brated political efficacy in becoming akin to the comparative, or
the competitive. Massed together as so many naked bodies, ordered to overcome shame not because nakedness was not shameful
(it decidedly was) but because such troubling inner urgings had
to be defeated for the greater good, we were nothing but specimens, good or bad.

It could escape no one's attention that, as a specimen, and even
in the limited terms the system embraced, Melvin Airbets was
more than admirable—not boyish, but manly, proportional, a Ken
doll made flesh, and finely curved, even beautiful. Although I
might not have thought of it that way at the time, I was certainly

aware of the paradox that a boy whom we all knew to be a "retard," shorn of the concealment we had all secretly learned to covet, denied the privacy for which a retard could have no use anyway, proved to be, in body, so far superior to the rest of us. Indeed, the collective awareness of this paradox, shared as our nakedness, was what made Melvin Airbets's body so remarked upon a spectacle of open ridicule. These remarks took the crudest possible turns, including the amplification of Melvin Airbets's nickname into "Mister Horse Dick Ed." A gentle boy, with big, moist, puzzled eyes, and unaligned lips that often suggested a crooked smile, Melvin would only turn away from such taunts. Once, though, Eric Lang would not let him turn away. Eric Lang cajoled, and prodded, and punched, and we all watched the fat, cruel body move with ever greater aggression upon the lean, gentle, withdrawing body. Eventually, Eric Lang shouted, reverting to Melvin's real name as a sign of surpassing contempt, "You know what, Airbets? You're such a fucking retard, I bet you don't even know what to *do* with that big schlong you got." With that, Eric Lang snatched Melvin's jockstrap, rubbed his own face in it, and then with a primitive, lusty yell, threw it to another boy, who threw it to another. It came to me, and I knew I could have ended the game, but grateful to be a meter rather than a bearer of scorn, I threw it, a bundle of dirty cloth forged to protect, to yet another boy. If allowed, Melvin Airbets might have felt gratitude too, but its cost would have been the wrath of the others. Finally Melvin cried, "Give it back," and the cry was a wail, helpless, broken, tearful, and desperate. Any human creature, hearing it, would have to have been moved, but we only laughed. Melvin Airbets's voice gave him away as a retard, in a manner that his body—which for that reason could never be forgiven—failed to reveal. That was why, perhaps, he spoke so seldom.

In the book *Bambi,* there is a scene that does not occur in the movie. It is a brief, poetic chapter in which two leaves, clinging still to their branch in the onset of fall, talk between themselves about the changing seasons and the ravages of time. They reflect on age, and fear, and on the many others who have gone before them. They know they too will soon be gone, and one leaf tries to comfort the other leaf. They talk in tones of regretful, elegiac melancholy, remembering happier days, before they are finally torn from the tree by a merciless gust of wind and borne away, separate casualties of autumn. The scene is an audacious digression from the plot, but in its inconsolable tenor, with its vivid, lyric awareness of mortality, it imparts a sense of loss that lingers as an undercurrent in the book. In fact, coming a few chapters before the death of Bambi's mother, this interlude serves to prepare the reader emotionally for that more palpable shock. Like the book, the movie asks us to look death in the face—Bambi's mother dies in both versions—and it was this imperative, somehow gentle, even loving, as if it were for our own good, that made me revere the story for its gravity and its courageous, unstinting honesty. This honesty was itself tinged with regret, and that was what gave it its limpid wisdom. But the movie, without the sad conversation between the leaves about to fall, lacked the larger honesty of the book. The movie made us realize that our mothers might die. Then, having refused to evade this harsh truth, it went on to try to comfort us. The book, in the guise of whimsy, with its conceit of talking leaves, makes us see that we ourselves are mortal, and from that knowledge there is no recovery.

Two names appeared on the title page of *Bambi*. One of them, "Felix Salten," had a quality of severity, of sternness and rigor, even as it carried an undertone of the faintly absurd: "Felix" was a funny name. Because the book used the trappings of children's stories—talking animals, enchanted woods—to present its verities, that mixture of strictness and folly made a certain sense. The other name, "Whittaker Chambers," a dactylic lilt and a brusque trochee, both names with initial stresses trailing off, conjured images of delicious aristocracy. A third name with similar connotations, "John Galsworthy," appeared at the end of a short note printed at the start of the book, but it was clear from the note that John Galsworthy was only someone who liked the book, and he did not know either Felix Salten or Whittaker Chambers. I imagined the latter two collaborators, united in comradely spirit, spinning their covertly wise tales over tea and crumpets by the genteel candlelight of a faraway manse—maybe a hall, like Toad's, of Toad Hall. (I did not know then anything of the transactions between author Salten and translator Chambers; in fact, the two never met.) They were, I imagined, men working closely, intimately, on a project that must surely, if they were respectable grown-ups, have been private; in the world I lived in, telling stories about the doings of woodland creatures would have been thought no fit work for men, and when I tried my own hand at the genre in imitation of them, I certainly knew enough to keep it a secret. I tried to imagine their high-flown colloquies, and in the breathtaking dialogue between the leaves I thought I must be hearing, somehow, echoes of their own innermost conversations.

But why should leaves, sexless, be thought men? Chambers's translation is notably coy in the way it conceals or reveals the leaves' sex. In truth, that is revealed only quite late in the scene, in passing pronouns tucked away in crannies of sentences that are so tortuous that, in one case, the referent of the pronoun never really becomes clear. In the moment it is thus revealed that the second leaf is female, the second leaf worries that her looks have departed. The first leaf tenderly reassures the second leaf that this is not the case. The first leaf calls the second leaf "handsome," and in my experience, that was a word applied to men, not to women. The tenderness, the reassurance, and the very word itself all suggest that there exist, between the first leaf and the second leaf, sympathies of a scarcely intelligible nature. They speak as lovers, and when the sex of the second leaf was obliquely revealed, after I'd read and reread, just to be sure, the tortuous sentence that proved it, it provoked in me the thrill of recognition any signs of same-sex love always caused. The disappointment that the leaves were not men was alleviated by the realization that they were both women. Years later, when I heard the chapter performed as a brief radio play, with both leaves given male voices, I concluded that it was the sameness that was all, female or male, first or second.

The name of Carlo Collodi had its own rhythmic allure, its own dark, Mediterranean exoticism, and after my disgraceful gilding by association with the book he had written, the more good-natured of my tormentors took to addressing me for many months afterward as "Carlo Collodi." It was in this way that I came to see how the sin defines the sinner. My defense, if one had been sought from me, would have consisted in nothing less than the fierce darkness of the book itself. They thought they knew *Pinocchio*—and it was, as it always is, their familiarity that enabled their scorn—but I knew what they did not—that this familiarity, as it always is, was incomplete, specious. I knew the secret of *Bambi,* that it is about the inevitability of our own deaths, and I knew the secret of *Pinocchio,* that Pinocchio murders Jiminy Cricket. These secrets were unknown to my accusers, and if they thought my sin was regression, I knew theirs was delusion. I had accepted truths they were yet too juvenile to acknowledge, even as they convicted me of childishness, but there was no way to tell them so. "You're wrong!" I could have shouted. "*Pinocchio* is *not* a book for kids, *not* a fairy-tale! It is dark, and brutal, and violent as the world itself. Look—see, here, in black-and-white: *He kills Jiminy Cricket!*" Thus might I have forestalled shame. It is perhaps for the better that the shout was never permitted. In the temperance of shame lurks the inherency of guilt, in the appearance of innocence, the darkest turn.

It was exactly the conflation of seeming innocence with hardened knowledge that drew me to books like *Bambi* and *Pinocchio*. I was surprised and compelled by their unswerving commitment to tell it like it was, with only passing regard for childish, tender feelings, and every time I saw a Disney cartoon, I made a point of reading the book so I could confront the truths or the horrors that had been left out of the movie—the heartbreaking scene, for instance, when Peter Pan comes back to visit Wendy, after she has grown-up and left him far behind. Perhaps I thought, in doing so, to master secrecy, to feel that I was a possessor of the secrets, not their dupe. But secrets breed, and there is always another one to be revealed. Whittaker Chambers (I learned, doing a book report in tenth grade) was a Communist, a spy, perhaps even at the very moment he was translating *Bambi,* and after renouncing Communism he betrayed those he knew who had also been Communists. The translator of *Bambi* may have been a comrade of other men (and quoted in his biography, he admits to early homosexual leanings), but he refused to keep their shared secrets, secrets he must once have cherished, and he thought to reveal them might redeem him. The television Peter Pan, so closely resembling the wiry, sexy, agile movie Peter Pan, was played, it turned out (as I should have been able to see very well for myself), by a woman—and not just any woman, but a woman who had once, allegedly, played the wayward nun in my beloved *Sound of Music* (though not, mysteriously, in the movie itself); and who, moreover, was a mother, the mother of a handsome man who played the hapless custodian of a sprightly genie on another television show. I had always wondered which part of Pinocchio's quest mattered to him more—to be *real*, or to be a *boy*? Would he have consented to become a girl, if that had been the price of being real? To refute one's own beliefs may be a form of wisdom, but to long for the secrecy thereby lost must constitute the only innocence still left to the wise.

When my copy of *Pinocchio* fell out of my desk onto the floor of the fourth-grade classroom, Eric Lang and Melvin Airbets were among those who gathered the scattered pages. "Hey, look," shouted Eric Lang, sweeping up a few incriminating pieces, "it's *Pinocchio*! This shot-wad's reading *Pinocchio*! Hey, shot-wad, can't you make that little pug nose of yours grow any?" Contempt requires reversal: Melvin Airbets's beauty becomes a target of derision; Eric Lang's rubbing his nose in a jockstrap, on the surface a form of *self*-abasement, becomes the means to humiliate another. Maybe that was why my own anger, my violence, was then so immediately undiscriminating. I saw a future of mockery open before me, and—a real boy—I reacted with a blow. I snatched the retrieved pages away from Eric Lang with such force that he was thrown backward. "Take it easy, shot-wad," he muttered, uneasily surprised. With equal violence, I grabbed the pages Melvin Airbets proffered, and he too fell back. If passive acceptance is the alternative, as I have learned too well in the years since, then aggressive counter to assault may be preferable. But Eric Lang picked up the strewn pages only to have more ammunition for his contempt, while Melvin Airbets gathered them gently, because they had fallen and he meant to help, yet I treated them both the same. The distinction between cruelty and kindness made no difference to me. I only knew I'd suddenly entered a world, remorseless, of strife.

3

PRACTICE

Why the violin?

The question lingered on the lips of those who asked it—and everyone, *everyone*, asked it—like grapes that have soured on the vine, and I, in my ten-year-old's feigned indifference, shrugged. "My grandfather used to play the fiddle" was an answer that dependably reassured my interrogators. "I want to be a comedian, like Jack Benny" was an apparent non sequitur that nonetheless worked nearly as well, although any subtle expressions of relief that might have followed that response were soon likely to be eclipsed by renewed concern, perhaps unspoken but still registered in a mild slant of the brow or purse of the lips, as wonder slowly awoke regarding Jack Benny himself. Did the fact of his too playing the violin absolve me or taint him?

In these encounters I knew well what reassurance was being sought. As a cultural object, the violin was so densely encrusted with ill-favored meanings that it would be less adequate to say that even a boy could understand them than to suggest that *especially* a boy would find himself most deliriously attuned to them. The instrument's pitch, at least as it was construed in the popular imagination I had access to, was a high whine, a piercing, banshee shriek, like the lament of a castrato. Despite this association with eunuchhood, the violin also connoted an unhealthily, unavoidably

phallic imagery. To play it, one gripped the neck of a long protu-
berance that jutted out frankly before one, ending in a scrolled,
studded head. The manipulations necessary to produce the music,
involving still another long thing, this one (an added bonus!) hairy
as well as long, could not but evoke the mechanisms, even among
those fully alive to the violin's elegance, of jerking off. According to
this conception, the violin's player was both feminized and phalli-
cally masturbatory, nancy and hoydenish, indulging unwholesomely in an obsessive display of pseudovirility that was unmanned
in its very exhibition.

My decision to choose the violin from among the available
instruments is hard to detach, in my memory, from the complex
dialectic of avowal and disavowal that, I think, always goes on
for a long time before, and does not stop with, the finally af-
firmed arrival at a ratified gay identity. I chose the violin in
spite of the stigma of sissyhood I knew I risked. I chose it,
knowing I would have to carry the case, in public, to and from
school, for all to see, twice a week. I chose it while others,
those who did not reject the choice altogether, picked more
neutral instruments: the sturdy drum, the robust tuba, the cool-
headed clarinet, the nicely idiosyncratic trombone (for in every
class, there is always one odd thing whose queerness pleases
rather than disturbs), or the high-flown flute (though the latter,
to be sure, presented an array of problems all its own). I *wanted*
people to see it, wanted them to have to think of me somehow
in relation to it; but I never hesitated to reassure them, at the
same time, that it did not really mean whatever they might be
inclined to think it meant about me. After all, my grandfather
had played the violin, even if he called it a fiddle, and I *did*
want to be a comedian, among the other things I wanted to be,
exactly like Jack Benny.

- - - - - - - -

I already knew what it meant to play an instrument because my best friend, Hardy, two houses down, played the accordion. I had actually seen him play it only once, but I knew of the hours he spent locked away in his room engaged with it in an activity called "practice." These were the hours when he was—inexplicably, stubbornly, even perversely—unavailable to play with me, and even after I should have been able to predict the occasions when these hours were in force, I would still show up from time to time at Hardy's door, to give him another chance to choose me over the accordion, only to be met there by his sister or his mother or his father with the curtly bisyllabic rebuff, "Practice." To play an instrument meant to choose something, the instrument, over something else—indeed, over *everything* else. It meant to give up afternoons of vast, amorphous freedom, to elect a species of play—for that was, however inaptly, what one was said to do with the instrument, to *play* it—that, mysteriously, banished fun and demanded laborious mastery. It meant to consent to rehearse for the condition of adulthood. When Hardy would eventually, after practice, rejoin me in the world of play I was still loath to relinquish in favor of that other world, he always seemed both exhausted and strangely rejuvenated, his voice pitched low, husky and weighted with superior knowledge, with gentle condescension toward my reversionary state, that poignantly atavistic innocence signified by the shrill squeak of my own child's voice, and his manner was languorous, worldly, world-weary. Depending on what games we played, and on the level of juvenile commitment or callow, rough-and-tumble participation they called for, this disposition might gradually become reabsorbed into more normal moods, but I knew it was always still there, and always would be, now, an undercurrent.

My wish to share in such latency, to acquire a set of richly teeming nuances of my own, may account for the decision to choose an instrument, but it does not account for the choice of the violin. Just as that choice had something to do with a desire to affirm provisionally and to negate equivocally, but in any case to produce or to explore, a kind of proto-queerness in myself, so it was related to a corollary wish to identify myself with Hardy, and to differentiate myself from him at the same time. The violin could not have been more different from the accordion. Daintily elongated where the accordion was heartily broad, the violin did not require the body's full attention as the accordion, burdening the lap like ballast and needing the power of two strong arms to enliven it, certainly did. I had once seen the great Jascha Heifetz play the violin on television (on Jack Benny's show, as I remember), and I had noticed that his virtuosity seemed almost casual, offhanded, his chin resting on the fiddle's prow, but his face turned away, despite the manic bravura of his playing, in an expression of workman's distraction, as if his thoughts were elsewhere, like a maidservant whose mad exertions working cloth against washboard with one hand still leave her plenty of leeway to milk a cow with the other hand. It is part of the violin's elegance to require only such partial allegiance, eschewing the vulgar demand of full compliance. It is part of the accordion's earthiness to use up all resources at hand, in a spirit of good nature, as if *not* to do so would constitute obligation or make up failure, a squandering, tantamount to waste, that the aristocrat can afford but common folk shun as sinful. The accordion moans, or wheezes, or toots, or honks. The violin squeaks or sings, soars.

The one time I remember seeing Hardy play his instrument was at a backyard gathering of his mother's family. Usually these gatherings, monthly cookouts, left me out as cruelly as the daily rounds of practice did. This one was special, though. Hardy's aunt, whom he called "Tante," was moving with her family into our neighborhood, and I was invited to the party because of the occasion, to meet the kids. Hardy's parents had moved to the United States only a year or two before 1960, the year he and I were both born, and they often reverted to speaking German, especially when they were with their many brothers and sisters. The songs Hardy played, as he sat in the middle of the driveway in a folding lawn chair of green and white stripes, were easy to recognize, even without words, as German folk songs. His aunts and uncles and cousins, listening as he played, clearly knew the songs, for they hummed along. They clapped in time and stomped their feet on mottled grass or solid concrete, depending on where they happened to find themselves. The accordion, I surmised, as I watched their artless, homely displays of pleasure, was the instrument of their people, like the trumpet of the alpinist or the tight-skinned drum of the savage, with uses that linked the instrument directly to the daily practices of their lives. Both that directness and their deep attunement to the accordion struck me in that moment as indescribably coarse, and I understood Hardy's relation to the instrument in a new way. It was a thing he practiced for *them,* his people, without even the dimmest aspiration to art that might have redeemed it. When he shut himself away to practice, he was not preparing to scale to the heights of the concert hall. He was only cobbling together a few modest ditties, only to perform them, like a poodle doing tricks, at backyard barbecues, to elicit the frivolous pleasures of his doting *tantes.*

Not being a foreigner myself, I did not have a people, and so my choice of instrument (I was relieved to conclude) would not be constrained by the false claims of a tribe. Rather, my choice would grant me access to a celestial domain, rife with the Old World mystique of high art, but not debased with the folkways of the common, or the silly, dispiriting rigors of daily life. Never would I lower myself to play at family functions. As it happened, in the few months that I took violin lessons, I was sometimes called on to do so, and in fact I subtly encouraged the pleas but disdained the request. As I watched my best friend hunched over his accordion in the green-and-white-striped lawn chair, fingering the mock-piano keys or the grid of little buttons arranged in neat rows, like the small black marbles on a Chinese checkers board, I saw his demeanor—never mind that he seemed to share in the happiness of his uncles and aunts and cousins—as a riot of servility, and I felt sorry, embarrassed, for him.

But I still felt jealous, too, jealous of the accordion. It was in his lap, his arms held it, encircled it, and he was playing with it, not with me. Is the embarrassment one feels for others always connected to the shame one feels, oneself?

The music store was in a business district along one of the city's most heavily traveled thoroughfares, a string of open motor-malls, roofed only with rows of wildly billowing pennants, and indoor shops under bright blue awnings. The store was only a few doors down from the place where, recently, we had bought our swimming-pool, an eighteen-foot-round aluminum-sided above-grounder, and it was more than a little troubling that acquiring my violin should involve such unseemly trafficking with commerce. The inside of the store reminded me of a pet store in its pre-packaging of goods that did not readily lend themselves to such display. It was set up like a grocery store, with successive aisles lined not with the cans and boxes that would have looked perfectly at home there, but with canted drums, pitifully bereft of players; carelessly propped-up cellos; and gleaming horns, upended or lying on their sides, that looked, despite their shine, like chromium husks, lifeless, left behind after the organic matter of their insides had been evacuated and hoarded away elsewhere.

At least a pet store, in its conversion of vitality into commodity, had the persuasion of pathos going for it: I could never look upon those tiers of stacked cages (the mournful eyes of puppies; the languid, prideful grace of kittens who hid their sorrow; the poignant exuberance of the hamsters on their spinning wheels, who were too dumb to know they were entrapped; even the cocksure spirit of the parakeets, who really seemed to like it there) without wanting to buy up the whole stock, to save the animals from their fate as merchandise. But the instruments in their places on the shelves looked completely inert, terminally inanimate. If any life were to come from them, it would take some superhuman force of will to produce it, and maybe that was, after all, the appeal.

By the time I got it home, though, I found that my violin was vibrant precisely in its inanimation. Its beauty was visual and tactile. Certainly its beauty was not, in my hands, auditory, for the first few tentative sounds I made with it (horsehair on catgut) were cringe-making squeals. These noises, in their awfulness, went beyond the proverbial screech of fingernail on chalkboard. They approximated a sound that lay in my psyche much more deeply within the region of disgust. The sound in question was that of a fork's tines coming into contact with the textures of crumpled tinfoil. This sound—more a full-blown *sensation,* really, than a mere sound—had the power to induce a revulsion so pure that it shot to the parts of me that were themselves ordinarily not notably sentient, the outer surfaces of my bones and the insides of my teeth, even the tips of my fingernails, which I would willingly have scraped across a thousand chalkboards if only it meant I would never once have to experience the sound, the sensation, of forks' tines against crumpled tinfoil. The specificity of this aversion is worthy of emphasis. The effect could not be produced randomly, by just any old utensil that happened to come to hand. A single-pronged knife or bowl-headed spoon, only by virtue of being fashioned of the very same stuff, still would not do the trick. It had to be a fork, because the feeling of disgust had something to do with the nature of tines, a trio or a quartet of spikes with space between them, like bad teeth. What's more, for optimum effect, the tinfoil most definitely had to be crumpled; if a fork somehow collided with a smooth sheet of tinfoil, it would produce an unpleasant quiver, make no mistake, but not the frenzy of disgust that would be the result if the tinfoil were ridged, wrinkled, crumpled. It was fortunate, to be sure, that the sensation was so specialized, for its intricate variables ensured that its actual occurrence would be relatively rare. Yet I lived in fear of its un- likely imminence, and had regular dreams about warring fac- tions—one, aggressors, who used forks as weapons; the other, defenders, who used wads of crumpled tinfoil as shields. The blunt, violent encounter of weapon and shield woke me in the night, again and again, in a terrible, wordless sweat. I assumed everyone in the world shared my aversion, and the only reason it was never spoken of was that it was, like all the other things that were never spoken of, so fundamentally horrifying.

The violin rested in a case the color of white skin that has been tanned over many summers, and the case had the hard smoothness of such skin. I ran my palm along its curvy surface, delighting in the contrast between supple hide and cool metal where, hinged and girded, the tan gave way to ridged strips or smooth buckles of bright silver. Green velvet, soft velour, lined the inside of the case, and a coxscombed strap held the instrument in place in the lower panel, while the upper panel held the bow, in its narrow green bed; the cake of resin, gelatinous but hard; and the jagged-edged yellow swath of velvety, all-purpose fabric, good for shining and padding, like the polishing cloth of a shoe- shine kit. The instrument itself combined fragility with sturdiness. The delicate neck called for tenderness of grip. The scraggy, card- boardlike bridge supported strings that seemed far more muscular than it did, so easy would it have been to snap in two, or to knock down, like the slivery card at the base of a tall house of cards. I fingered the smooth wood, hearty because it was wood, yet re- fined because of the diaphanous shellac that coated and colored it. The slender, symmetrical inlets carved into the wood on either side of the strings, shaped like antiquarian notes of music stretched and lengthened, not distorted but transformed, and the hole in its belly showed the violin to be empty, but because the emptiness was hidden, it was not the same as the hollowness, revealed, of the horns.

On days when it had rained, and the grass of the playground was soaked and puddled, the teachers would move their cars out of the school's parking lot so that recess could take place there on the solid blacktop, drier than the grass. I looked forward to these days because the lot was too small, too reined in, to permit ball games, so the boys would, as a grudging fallback, sometimes join in on the girls' games of jump rope. I, who hated the ball games, always joined in avidly, delirious with this new air of passing permission. The swish of the long rope's smooth, quiet arc called forth an effortless agility in me, a limberness, that I could never duplicate in the kick of a ball or the swing of a bat. Skipping nimbly just at the very second the thick rope slapped the rubbery tar of the ground, and running clear as it repeated its fast ascent, and cutting sprightly figure eights around the girls who held and twirled the rope's ends, I discovered a litheness in myself unique to jumping rope that imparted, because of this uniqueness, an irresistible aura to the activity. When the girls played alone, they formed a chain and leapt through the rope's momentous hoops in successive, democratic synchrony, and everyone took a turn holding an end. When the boys butted in, though, they made the game a chase, a competition meant to exclude, and the losers held the ends. I didn't mind, for once, the punitive nature of the sport because, dexterously eluding all pursuers and cunningly entrapping every prey, even turning the tables by racing ahead slyly to bring up the hapless chaser's rear, so you could no longer tell who was hunter and who hunted, I never suffered the penalties. To that date it was my only experience of athletic prowess, and if this exuberance let me understand, by extension, the excitement, the joyous rage, of other boys on the football field or the baseball diamond, it still did not bring me any closer to sharing it.

"Boxers jump rope," my father said on somehow learning of my skill as a jump-roper. "Boxers jump rope when they're in training." The tone of the remark, mildly uneasy musing, did not exactly express approval, but seemed in search of a way to avoid disapproval. He had not learned of my skill as a jump-roper, certainly, from me. I kept it secret for the same reason that I would not have dared to jump rope at recess unless it was a rain day with recess confined to the parking lot, and unless some other boys were doing it too. It was a thing girls did. To be good at it, and to be a boy, carried shame that could be lightened only by the fleet, immediate dazzle, in the irresistible act, of mastery's display, and a subsequent recourse to a silence both humbled and secretly exultant. "Gangsters carry things like that," commented my father, on seeing me with my new violin case. "They keep their guns in there."

My violin lessons took place in a narrow room off an out-of-the-way corridor of the school's nether wing. Neighboring rooms housed the offices of the speech therapist and the school nurse. The room was used principally for storage, and each day's lesson began with the teacher, Mr. Rosenzweig, and me pushing aside masses of educational junk to clear a space for practice, as the girls looked on. High stacks of yoke-legged chairs lined the walls, and portable chalkboards on wheels, their broad tilted slates a dusty green, and spare opaque projectors, long periscopes rising from their steel bodies like the stiff necks of swans, cluttered the room. Two of the three girls who took lessons with me played the cello, and they carried their heavy instruments with robust pride, so I could not understand why Mr. Rosenzweig did not let them help us move the clutter away, but they were only allowed to watch.

The three girls were Wendy Siroki, Karen Kerwinsky, and Denise Bolas. Wendy Siroki was famous throughout the school for a noise she made several times every day, a sustained horking noise, a long, loud, nasal implosion that she produced seemingly without consciousness, and certainly without regard for timeliness, for she was as apt to make the noise in the middle of reading hour, when it pealed through silence, as she was in the more hospitable climate of the lunchroom, when its sound could be lost in the general clatter. Those who speculated, mixing awe with revulsion, on the nature of this noise marveled at its constancy, and those who took pride in their own ability to make repulsive noises stood in contemptuous admiration of Wendy Siroki, because they could never imitate her horking, even when they were in the clutches of the most bile-clotted, snot-scalded cold, when the amplitude of bile and snot should have conduced to such mimicry; while Wendy Siroki was able to produce her trademark hork, baroque and rumbly, effortlessly, many times a day. The secret, it was speculated, lay in her refrainment from expectoration. Others who horked were champion spitters. Wendy Siroki, the champion horker, followed her feats of sibilation—these snorking, fulminating snuffles that seemed to originate in a constantly replenished reservoir of mucous where the channels of the nose met the tunnels of the throat—with a prim, stringent swallow. Karen Kerwinsky was rumored to be a bed wetter, and reputed to smell like pee, though I had never managed to discern the odor myself, while Denise Bolas's handicap had less to do with gossip and more with visible evidence. She was fat.

Five of us, four students and a teacher, sat in random groupings in the narrow room, spindly music stands displaying spread music sheets, our instruments hoisted or held between cocked knees. Mr. Rosenzweig could also have been described, albeit uncharitably, as fat, but his quality of tranquil dignity, made strong—not, I was pleased to note, genteel—by its manly briskness, forestalled the description. He wore brown suits of a heavy, woolen fabric, even as the spring came on, and haphazardly knotted bow ties under a substantial second chin that defined a thick, rounded arc, like the hull of a boat. He possessed the most useful quality of the teacher who believes deeply that his pupils will learn only what they *can* learn, and no more—that of imperturbability. The first time Wendy Siroki horked during a lesson, he paused for only a placid moment—while Karen Kerwinsky tittered, Denise Bolas gasped, and I blushed—before resuming his instruction. When he played for us to demonstrate technique, he closed his eyes or aimed them upward, his second chin bobbling like the underside of a hammock stirred by a breeze, but even then his attitude suggested potent concentration, not transcendence, not escape.

Mr. Rosenzweig's masculinity could not be impugned. He was married, and had children, and these facts afforded me a certain provisional sense of relief. They meant that the choice of the violin did not always or only signify a wholehearted commitment to queerness. At the same time, my confederacy with the three girls caused me some worry. Their oddness was clear to me, and to everyone else, but what defined them was the unknowingness we others, who knew they were odd, and stood to them in a relation of superior and empowering knowledge, attributed to them regarding their own debilitating quirks. Surely Denise Bolas did not know she was fat, or else she would diet; Karen Kerwinsky did not know she smelled, or else she would bathe; Wendy Siroki did not know she horked, or else she would stop. I had chosen the violin knowing the potential for queerness the choice entailed, and I thought that, if I wanted to keep queerness at bay even after having elected to flirt with it so openly, it would only be such knowledge that would allow me to do so. But were there aspects of me, I wondered, that I did *not* know about, but that others did, that linked me in some deeper ways to these girls?

When we played together, the sound was a disquieting cacophony of grates and rasps and scratches and grinds. The cellists, Denise Bolas and Karen Kerwinsky, seemed to view their instruments as imposing objects, heavy obstacles they were determined not to let defeat them, and in practice they went at the instruments with muscular vigor, using their bows as a lumberjack uses a saw to attack a tree's trunk. Wendy Siroki's way with the violin had a provisional, experimental briskness to it, as if with every stroke of the bow, every thrust of the fingers, she was testing the outcome of the note, like a housewife sifting through a bin of plums and squeezing each one to gauge its ripeness. She would prop the violin on her shoulder, but could never quite get the hang of the chin rest, so her head always seemed too upright, her posture slightly off. As she played, her eyes filled with the intensity of listening, and even though the erect tilt of her head suggested the demeanor of an eavesdropper with an ear pressed to a wall, it was clear that she was listening to herself.

For my part, I hoped to counteract the uninspired playing of my peers with a series of virtuoso maneuvers, heartrending tremolos, emotionally charged mannerisms of fingering, bravura spasms of the bow. Without rebuke, Mr. Rosenzweig advised me that such bold artistry might be more appropriate to advanced concertos than to the simple beginners' melodies we were trying vainly to master. "Try to get in tune with the other girls," he gently admonished. His use of the word "other" in the sentence troubled me. It seemed to differentiate me from them in a manner that was welcome, but on second thought it implied that I was somehow one of them after all.

One afternoon, on a hot spring day, to create a cross-breeze, we opened the window at one end of the narrow room and propped open the door at the other. Across the hall, the horn players, all boys, were rehearsing, and because of the heat, they had the door propped open too. The tinny, boyish whine of their music clashed with the plaintive strains of ours, and threatened to overwhelm them. As practice went on, the horns grew louder and louder. Unseen by Mr. Rosenzweig, I exchanged knowing, slit-eyed glances with the other girls: if it was to be a duel, we could certainly hold up our end. We assaulted our instruments with renewed force, and as the music grew wilder, it grew louder. In the heat, we all began to sweat, but we were hearing ourselves play above the noise from across the hall. Mr. Rosenzweig, wiping his own high, beaded brow, counseled moderation, but still the music got louder, still wilder, the notes giving way to the mad pressure of the earnest game. We may have been linked in sweat and strangeness, but it was in our need to meet the challenge of the horns that we were truly united.

It is harder to hear yourself play when you are practicing alone. The discovery of this fact came as something of a surprise, for it had seemed the silence provided by solitude should better have allowed the inward contemplation needed for outward concentration. In our first public performance, it was decided, each of us would play a brief solo in addition to the two longer pieces we would play together. Mr. Rosenzweig instructed us to practice on our own for at least an hour every day. These hours passed with the poky lag of a snail traveling uphill. I would begin in earnest, resining the bow's hair with the vigor of a barber playing a razor against a leather strop before shaving a good paying customer. The first few notes would sound, sure and forceful, with the ring of my eagerness to prove, if only to myself, my determination, discipline, and commitment. But the notes would always soon trail off, overwhelmed by the creeping awareness of my growing, laudably self-imposed but duly resisted sense of oppression. I would lapse then into daydreams, the violin resting in my lap, or swish the bow through the air like a fearless swashbuckler warding off imaginary combatants. Sometimes I would lose track of time in my reverie, counting the blue strands of the shag carpeting that covered my bedroom floor, and when the hour had passed, I would congratulate myself on my hearty diligence even when I had not practiced a lick.

The connection between practice and performance should have seemed quite direct. Practice was what you did in a spirit of strict self-mastery in order to perform better in a subsequent state of still-resisted exhibitionism. It rehearsed in solitude what would later be fulfilled in public, and the self-denial it demanded apotheosized in a final moment of triumphant self-display. Maybe it was because performance was a goal so far off that I could never see the connection very directly. For me, the fact of practice harbored an equivocal relation to self-disgust. The concept of performance always proposes the conquest of shame: the performer *risks* shame—such risk is precisely what a performance *is*—to defeat it, but even if the defeat is so total as apparently to render the idea of shame nugatory, its possibility still hovers over every performance. The aerialist takes to the high wire because she has mastered balance; the breathlessness of the spectator is as much a tribute to that mastery as it is an acknowledgment that something might go wrong. A performance that eliminates the variable of spontaneity, thus the threat of mischance or ruin, differs not only in degree but also in kind from one that courts disaster as a condition of its enterprise. A bad performance ends in the embarrassment that, itself, counteracts the deeper thrust of shame—a minor chagrin, the heckler's irk against the ham's indifference, the hack's obliviousness, the vaudevillian's corn, to ward off mortification. A great performance still traffics with shame, inversely to the degree it seems so victoriously to have ousted it.

Practice is, or should be, the arena where the performer learns to overcome shame—so completely, in the best-case scenario, that the performance shows no trace of the struggle. What this means is that, in practicing, the performer comes face to face with shame. Alone in my room, coaxing shrill, roupy notes from the instrument I had chosen with an awareness of its shameful associations, the ache I felt—a furtive, yearning restlessness with no object, clammy and arid at the same time—was the pang of a shame resisted. I played badly, so badly I could not imagine a time when I might play well. More to the point, as long as I remained aware of how hopeless, how bad, my playing was, I thought I would be able to spare myself the headiest agonies of embarrassment. The shame of a bad performance lies, in large part, in nothing so much as the failure of self-consciousness. The bad performer is bad because he does not know he is bad, because he can't see what others know about him, while the performer who knows he is bad is saved by the knowledge. Or so I thought. As long as I played badly, I could, Jack Benny–like, ward off shame by avowing to share my hearer's disdain. I could enact, in performance, something akin to what I had elected in affinity, when I had chosen the violin: to be queer, without being gay; or to inhabit the space of gayness, to perform its manifestations, to stand where I might be known, without the need to intimate that I did not know what was, in turn, known *about* me, without assuming the whole panoply of belief or being—the epistemology, or the ethic—that surrounded that space, where I knew I wanted to be.

The last musical performance of my life came a few years later, after I had put the violin aside forever. I was in the eighth grade then, and had taken a semester of music, also my last. Because of budget cuts, the regular music teacher had been laid off, and the class was being taught by the typing teacher. She was a skinny, wild-haired woman with gangly, multidirectional limbs, and she wore glasses with big, round, shocking-pink frames that perched on the very tip of her nose. With cold, strangely accusatory eyes, she gazed out over the frames at the classroom like a prison guard peering through the narrow chink of a cell's steel door. In class, where we hunched at desks behind bulky typewriters veiled in dustcovers, she encouraged us, for want of anything better to do, to perform. At a garage sale in the neighborhood I had acquired a cheap recorder. In its simplicity, the instrument fascinated me. It was nothing but a plastic cylinder with a few holes down its spine, but within minutes I was able to produce with it something more closely resembling music than anything I had been able to render in all my months of violin playing.

Performing for the class on the recorder, I played the themes from two movies, *Ben* and *Valley of the Dolls*. I had not seen *Ben,* because my parents would not let me, but the song, one of Michael Jackson's first without the Jackson Five, was at the time my favorite radio song. The song had a sweet, plangent lyricism. Ostensibly, it was about a boy and his rat—*Ben,* a quasi horror movie with sentimental overtones, was the sequel to *Willard,* about a put-upon geek who trains rats to kill his enemies—with the boy assuring the rat, in the sweet-voiced hum of a pop lullaby, that they would be together always. It could not have been lost on me that the song, whatever its apparent subject, was about one boy professing undying love for another. As for *Valley of the Dolls,* the paperback was one of the few books in our house, along with *Between Parent and Child* and a few Mazo de la Roche novels, and the movie had been a special presentation on *The CBS Friday Night Movie.* Under ordinary circumstances, its adult nature would have placed it off-limits to me, but because of its cautionary antidrug message, my parents gave me a special dispensation. (The week before, I had been forbidden to watch the television premiere of *Rosemary's Baby*—in which, I learned later when I caught the rerun on the sly, a minor character in the witches' coven, Dr. Shand, plays the recorder.) Impressed by the unflinching quality of the movie's gritty realism, and by the high seriousness of its moral attitudes, I was nonetheless most taken with the Dionne Warwick song that accompanied images of a pensive Barbara Parkins, clad in a fashionable fur coat, wandering among banks of snow. The song, a grievous yet matter-of-fact plaint, was about yearning, and the notes followed one another with a frank, straightforward inevitability that gave the lie to the stammering indecision of the words ("Gotta get out, hafta get, wanna get, gonna get out. . . ."). The song did not merely *express* longing, then, it *understood* it; and when I had learned the music by ear and could play the songs by heart—each note pure and clean and simple in the ingenuous strains of the recorder—I almost felt that I too, by understanding, mastering, these songs, might understand, might appease it.

By ear, by heart—the phrases reveal the bodily dimension of musical performance, as well as its strain to connect body to spirit, where the visible ear stands in for brute cognition, the hidden heart for ardent memory. As I played, assured in my mastery of these songs that I played for myself over and over in enthrallment (for the songs were already a part of me, and did not require practice), I imagined the intense responses of my listeners. My classmates were not ordinarily receptive to subtle forms of beauty, but I did not see how they could fail to be moved by my performance. Even they could not but see, surely, in the subdued but fervent rigor of my playing, the depth of my attachment and the passion of my understanding. The simple, clean, pure notes rang out in the quiet classroom, with the somber dignity of restraint, expressing the poignancy of their emotions without benefit or obstruction of words. To emphasize its pathos, I held the final note of the theme from *Ben,* and wiggled a finger on a notch of the recorder—a dying fall, lingering in the air, the note like the last orange ember in a bed of autumnal ash. As I plunged into the singsong melancholy of the theme from *Valley of the Dolls,* I failed to notice that a glob of my spit, having made its way through the vertical tube of the recorder's body, was now oozing out the other end, pulsating with the music like a slowly mutating pustule of lava in a lamp as it dangled from the recorder's airhole.

Such were the hazards of a cheap recorder. When I felt the first blob of saliva drop with a muted splash onto my shoe—blazing a trail, no doubt, for a subsequent avalanche of spit—I hastily dispatched the song's desolating crescendo and wiped another strand of bile from the recorder's underside. The typing teacher rearranged her limbs convulsively, like an impatient contortionist demonstrating a new pose, and sighed with profound contempt. "Who's next?" she barked, gazing over the shocking-pink glasses as the class smirked. The furtive goober clutched in my fist, I returned to my seat, red-faced, knowing all at once how little performance has to do with its vehicle, how very little my playing had had to do with music.

The violin recital was not, in fact, my first musical performance. We had all been forced to participate in choral programs—one at Christmas, one at Easter—throughout grade school, and so I knew something of what to expect. My solo piece for violin was a song called "In the Gloaming." The song was familiar to me by a different name as the theme of a TV show called *The Friendly Giant*. The show came on late on weekday mornings over a Canadian station we were able to pick up in Detroit. It was sandwiched between two similar shows, *Mr. Dress-up* and *Chez Helene*. The shows shared a format and a rhythm: relatively bland humans engaged in leisurely, pointless colloquy with puppets, digressing at an unnaturally listless pace. On days when I was home from school sick I watched these programs in a state of disbelieving, hypnotized fascination, marveling that the usually lively airwaves could sustain shows so completely indifferent to the need to be interesting. Their contrast with the energetic cartoons or frenetic game shows on other stations at that time of day was striking, and I sought them out as pacific alternatives to the noisy, coarse-grained norm. Watching them, I would lapse pleasurably into a drugged, trancelike stupor, and the unhurried, tunefully inert theme song of *The Friendly Giant* always markedly intensified this effect. Through such connections, I had come to associate the song with harmless infirmity (via the sick days), comfortable strangeness (the Canadian station), comparative high-mindedness, and anodyne allurement, so it seemed a suitable showpiece for my debut.

For concerts the gym was turned into an auditorium, folding chairs lined up in rows, stage curtain dramatically drawn. A veteran of years of choral concerts, I knew the atmosphere that prevailed there in the wake of this conversion—the high energies of the performers and the subdued restlessness of the parents and siblings who made up the audience, the smoggy dark of the room and the garish light of the stage. The hierarchy of player and spectator was a complicated one. During the holiday pageants I'd felt the Olympian rush of being above the crowd, looking down from the heights of the stage, but I knew that the performer's superiority always remained a purely theoretical one, even if its fragile cast was all that enabled the performance in the first place. The audience retained its control by virtue of its position, passive watchers enjoining the performer to act but reserving the watcher's customary power over the spectacle. Being above the audience did not ward off the specter of humiliation, but fed the headiness that specter too called up. The air of permission there, on the stage, was not liberating in itself, as in the parking lot on rain days. It was not the consent that set one free, but the allowance that gave one leave to risk a greater freedom.

One by one each ensemble, grouped by instruments, would perform, with their teacher conducting. We, the strings, would go last, in honor, we assumed, of our superior status. As we waited backstage, our solemn patience in composing ourselves and quietly tuning up matched the pedigree of our instruments with the dignity of our dispositions. In the course of those weeks, our competition with the rambunctious horns had escalated into a running feud. The fact that our greater solemnity enabled us to look askance at the horn players' raucousness certified both the fact and the solemnity itself. Before a teacher finally told him to stop, Bobby Adams, a horn player, kept blowing his horn as if it were a reveille trumpet assigned to wake the dead. "We're going to be loud, loud, loud," he boasted. "Wait till you hear how loud we'll be! We'll knock them all off their keesters, that's how loud we're going to be!" Wendy Siroki fixed him in a look of pitying disdain. "Being loud is not the point," she said. "Instead of being loud, why not just try being *good* for a change, nerdmeister extraordinaire?" "Loud, loud, loud," Bobby Adams went on shouting between blasts of the horn, "loud, loud, loud!" Wendy Siroki turned to me. "He wants loud," she whispered, "I'll show him loud."

From the wings, Wendy Siroki horked three times while the horns played. The horks were timed perfectly, and pitch-perfect, roaring through an interval's rest during a slow song, and sending a stir of rippling bemusement through the crowd. They were loud, and pure, and graceful, these horks, answering the coarseness of conviction, a boy's cocky coarseness, with the coarseness of necessity, a girl's, that because it was an answer, and because it was the feature of an imperative, was really no coarseness at all. They were perfectly timed, as well, to hold off the anxiety about my solo that I had been successfully postponing until then. They were, these boldly utilitarian if still palliative horks, a revelation. They meant that Wendy Siroki herself knew, and did not care, what others believed they only knew *about* her. This revelation came to me at such a moment that I stood for my solo with the pride that is the performer's salve. If the audience had clapped for us after the two songs we'd all played together, I had not heard it, so dazed was I with revelation and impending virtuosity. But if they clapped after my solo, it would mean I was received. I stood in a circle of light. I did not know where my parents were sitting in the audience, and because I did not know, I felt they were absent, but strangely ubiquitous, as I began to play. They were everyone in the audience, in the crowded darkness, and yet they were nowhere. I played, and found myself adding an improvised note at the end of a bar. I had experimented with this note—a quick riff—in practice, but decided to leave it out. Now, in performance, I restored it spontaneously, and—a mere instant, passing—it felt exhilaratingly right. It was what made the song my own, and anyone who knew the song, and gleaned the history of the evanescent note, would surely be moved by the evidence of my signature, this fleeting imprint. For my part, though, it was not my business to be moved, but to move others, to command them without force, and to know the difference. I'd been on the hearing end of the delicate, anodyne song myself, so I knew its mesmerizing possibilities. In the circle of light I was charged to make those possibilities known to others. The heads of all the members of the audience tilted, myriad dim domes in the dark room, lulled. I came to the end of the song with a sense, not of power, but of stirring mutuality. They all knew what a violin was, and what it meant, and I had shown that I knew they knew; now it was theirs to show they knew that I knew. After the music died, a second's brimming silence filled the hall, and it was heartstopping, resounding, not because it was silence, but because it was filled, already, with the lush portent of what followed, like a fast gust that passes when your footing is sure, embracing you in a fierce moment of stern acceptance—applause.

4

CHECKS AND BALANCES

Summer's end came late that year, 1971. Under ordinary circumstances the delay would have been welcomed avidly, but what held
it off, as it happened, was not a natural occurrence—a constancy
of weather, or a mellowing of estival spirit—but a profoundly
*un*natural one: a walkout, the "blue flu"—a *strike*. In Detroit, even
in its suburbs, labor was still labor, and so our teachers took to
the picket lines, hoisting rabble-rousing union placards, and sham-
bling in slow circles, the edgy, weary, endless rounds of warranted
and openly declared discontent. The newspaper ran a picture of
Mrs. Bridges, who had been my teacher in the second grade, and
who was to be my teacher again in the sixth, if it ever started. In
the picture, Mrs. Bridges glared into the camera with clenched
teeth as she held up her sign in one hand and a blazing cigarette
in the other. She looked mad. The governor, a burly man with
sideburns and three chins, appeared on television and hectored
the teachers, enjoining them that the strike was illegal, that they
were letting down (the three chins shook with the indignity of
it) the children of the nation. A week went by, a week of long,
hot days of unprompted freedom, freedom that could not, however, be savored, because the measure of these days could not be
predicted. The strike could end any day, or it might last months.
But then, just after the governor intimated that he was considering

firing and replacing every last teacher in the district, the strike unceremoniously ended, and the next day we were back at our desks.

Had Mrs. Bridges herself changed, or was it only my attitude toward her that had somehow altered? In second grade, she'd been kind, patient, understanding; now she was brisk, stern, truculent, and quick to anger, and she always smelled of harsh smoke. She addressed us as "People," in a tone of simmery foreboding: "Use your noggins, People!" "*People,* eyes front—about face!" Or, most ominously, "*Heads will* roll, *People.*" I kept thinking of that picture in the paper—the clenched teeth, the proud, rodentlike anger. The fact that she had married in the years intervening since the second grade—sacrificing thereby an unforgettable, cherished maiden name, Miss Purefoy—could not, in itself, account for the transformation in her character. The strike had shattered a certain widespread innocence, and classroom routines now were anxiously infused with the underlying possibility that the teacher would lash out, that she did not really want to be there, that she was fundamentally unhappy, and it was somehow our fault. If something out of the ordinary happened apart from the regular routine, it was even worse. "Attention, People," Mrs. Bridges said in the middle of a morning some weeks into the term, and her tone made it clear right away that the news she was obliged to announce was an unwanted disruption of the day's work. A new pupil would be joining us, she said, and she expected us to welcome him with open arms. The hint of a scowl that underscored her words suggested that the expectation might not be rigorously enforced.

His skin was the color of a half-ripened plum, burnished tan, his eyes the color of an overripe one—dark yet kindled. His jet-black hair was delicately kinked, but looked soft to the touch, woolen, like the unshorn coat of a young lamb. I watched Charlie Chan movies on Saturday afternoon TV, and greatly admired the cocky energy of Chan's Number One Son, but I had never met

anyone like him in real life. The new kid's name was many syllables long, but he said we could call him Luke. Mrs. Bridges could
not pronounce his last name. Luke instructed her gently; his voice
was low, boyishly assured, a more dignified version of Charlie
Chan's Number One Son. "Whatever," Mrs. Bridges croaked, after
Luke had told her how to say his name. There was an intensity
to his look; he looked at only one thing at a time, with an unusual
degree of concentration—not to overtake the thing, I thought,
but merely to see it truly—as if an invisible ray beamed from his
eyes, connecting him to what he looked at. When he turned this
look on Mrs. Bridges, she stepped backward involuntarily, flustered, as if from the force of the invisible ray, and she mumbled
that he had better take his seat. His desk was near mine. I stared
at the back of his neck while the day's lesson continued. Then,
with a slow turn of his head, as if he'd sensed that I'd been staring
at him, he fixed me with his look. I could see how it could make
others uneasy, this look, how it might startle them, in the directness and the intensity of its concentration, but it did not make
me uneasy. It warmed me, bathed me—caused, at once, a pleasing
tingle to begin in the small of my back—and I smiled at him.
He did not smile back, but something in his expression, not his
gaze, relaxed, and I could see before he turned away that he acknowledged my welcome. As I was to learn, he almost never
smiled.

A meatless Friday: lunch was grease-crusted fish sticks, dinner a
casserole made out of canned tuna, canned peas, and canned
mushroom soup, with a blackened layer of potato-chip crumbs
covering the surface. This was a meal I was able to consume only
if I thought of it holistically, and gobbled it in thoughtless mouthfuls, without breaking it down mentally into its constituent parts.
My sister, though, would eat only one ingredient at a time, and

she carefully segregated the soggy lumps of tuna from the clustered flakes of potato chip and the slimy peas, arranged on her
plate in a bed of gray-brown ooze that should, by my lights, have
rendered the whole exercise useless, if a tidy insularity was its
goal. "Who's the new boy?" asked my mother, doling out unre-
quested seconds in sludgy spoonfuls. Our neighborhood, right
next to the fifth-biggest city in the country, which was, for all
intents and purposes, the whole world, still enjoyed the advantage
of the small town: everyone knew everything.

"His name's Luke," I answered, and felt an unexpected thrill:
to speak his name.

"An Oriental," my mother said tonelessly.

My father ate with his chair pushed back from the table, sitting
on the very edge of the chair, both feet planted before him, like
a runner crouched at a starting line, and leaning forward over his
plate, surrounding it with his arms as if it were trapped quarry.
After each spoonful he immediately gathered the next, and held
it up near his face as he intently chewed the last one, jostling the
spoon a little as if to shake off unwanted excess, and then bolting
it into his mouth as soon as he'd swallowed the previous portion.
On *Mutual of Omaha's Wild Kingdom,* I had seen a big lizard
stalking bugs—the hunched, predatory stance, the sudden tongue
lunging out—and the combination of stillness, concentration, and
ruthless impatience, as if quickness in quenching an appetite
might alleviate the shame of it, reminded me of how my father
ate his meals. It was not between mouthfuls, but rather during the
interval while he opened his mouth to take in another mouthful,
that he asked, without wasted motion, "A Jap?" My answer was
not immediate, so he turned to look at me. "A gook," he asked,
digging up the next spoonful from his plate, particles of food
dropping from his brimful mouth as he spoke, "or a Chink?"

"He's American," I answered.

It was the right answer, but the only reason I happened to know it was because of an incident I had witnessed on the playground that day. Bobby Adams had confronted Luke beside the monkey bars and asked, "Where you from?"

"New York," Luke answered.

"No, I *mean*, where you *from*?"

"I know what you mean," Luke said calmly.

Bobby Adams pointed a finger in Luke's face. "We're at *war* with you people!"

"You don't *look* like you're at war. Where's your helmet? Where's your combat boots? And I don't know what good you think that finger's going to do you, but if you're at war you'd be a heck of a lot better off with a gun. You know what? I think you might lose that war."

Uneasy giggles rose from the crowd of kids that had started to gather, and Bobby Adams clenched his fists. "*No*," said Bobby Adams, shaking his head in flat rejection of Luke's sophistry. "I mean, *we're* at war. *America*."

"I know we are," said Luke. "Except it's not a real war because nobody ever agreed to it."

"In Viet*nam*," said Bobby Adams, irreclaimable. "We're at *war*— with the Viet*cong*!" He took a menacing step toward Luke.

Luke sighed. "You're at war with North Vietnam. So what if I'm *South* Vietnam? Huh? What then, Crazy-Fists? You're fighting *with* them, not against them, right? So would that make us on the same side?" Suddenly he patted Bobby Adams on the shoulder. "I'm not a bad fighter myself, Crazy-Fists, but I don't like to fight. Truth is, I can't stand it, so why not just get used to the idea that I'm American as you are, and let's just forget the whole thing, okay?"

Bobby Adams blinked at him. "You know karate?"

Luke laughed out loud and shook his head. "Sure, Crazy-Fists, that's right. I know karate."

"Can you teach me stuff?"

"Sheesh—I *don't* know karate! For Pete's sake, does everything always have to be only the way you think it is, in your own head?" Luke cuffed Bobby Adams lightly on the arm. Then he stepped back. "But who knows? Maybe I *can* teach you a thing or two. Who knows?" And with that he turned away, leaving Bobby Adams to slump against the monkey bars in the dim, uncertain haze of his own bafflement.

The following week, the atmosphere in the classroom seemed transformed, charged with the novelty of Luke's presence. The room's climate was invigorated and jittery, even as the undercurrent of anxiety that was constant rose ever more clearly to the surface. Any minute now, I was certain, one of my classmates would rattle off a jingle or let slip an epithet that would fully reveal to Luke, if he did not know already, exactly what sort of society it was that he had entered.

One such jingle, usually recited several times a week at lunch hour, found the speaker pulling back the corners of his eyes into a mock-Asian slant, and then chanting, "Me Chinese; me play joke; me go pee-pee in your Coke!" Among the most satisfying objects of any lunch hour was to deprive one's fellows of their appetite, and the jingle was a dependable instrument to that end, but for all I knew it might also have illuminated the actual propensity of Chinese people to relieve themselves in the soft drinks of others. Because I'd been brought up, not to doubt or to disbelieve social stereotypes, but to recognize them at once yet politely refrain from speaking of them, or otherwise drawing attention to them, I pursued alternative methods to incite lunchroom disgust, and on the whole eschewed the recitation of the jingle. Another schoolyard rhyme showed its purposes less clearly, but was more sweeping in its scope: "Chinese, Japanese, Siamese— *look at these!*" Again the speaker simulated slanty eyes with busy fingers, pulling the corners of the eyes up on the first word and down on the second. With the third word, the finger leapt to an unexpected position, underneath the nose, aping a mandarin mustache that was evidently as characteristic of the Siamese as upward-slanted eyes were of the Chinese and downward-slanted eyes of the Japanese. Ultimately, though, these nuances gave way to the anarchic glee of that surprising last line, on which the speaker suddenly improvised a quick pair of makeshift titties— the jubilant referent of the "these"—by pulling his shirt outward with clenched thumbs and fingers into twin, pointed protuberances. Typically, this jingle was addressed by taunting boys to indignant girls who were just beginning to develop breasts themselves. Its invocation of Eastern peoples, then, turned out to be something of a red herring, since the real target of derision in the end was not Asian physiognomy but female maturation. Indeed, for me, the hilarity of the jingle lay in its audacious leaps of logic. What did being Chinese, Japanese, Siamese, after all, have to do with titties? But it is, of course, bigotry's most common ploy to install its complacencies by seeming to conceal them, slipping them by unnoticed, and that is why children, who have yet to refine their hatred, are so prone to them—because our lives as children are clouded, and led in the dark.

Or at least mine was. That was why, all unknowing, I felt Luke's presence, one desk over and one desk up, as bright enlightenment and revealed obscurity, much like the blades of sunlight that suddenly shimmered through the classroom's venetian blinds midway through an overcast morning. It had never even occurred to me before to consider how an actual Asian person—say, even Charlie Chan's cocky and all-American-seeming Number One Son, the only prototype I had—would greet the rhymes that were so familiar to me, so acceptable in their familiarity. It had not occurred to me, because it had seemed so unlikely that such a person would ever come within their range to hear them. But maybe if he did,

I now considered, he would not think they were so funny. I was well aware, after all, of my own loathing for any rhyme that seemed even vaguely to implicate me—like the infamous "Jimmy crack corn, and I don't care"—even if ridicule was not its apparent intention.

All that week, then, I tried to hear the lessons as I thought Luke might hear them, so that even the lessons, usually so neutral, so remote—the least interesting thing, by far, about school—were changed by his coming. For weeks we had been talking about genes, and all the bluster of fact and fiction that went along with them. We'd learned about dominant and recessive genes (causing me worry about the implications of my grandfather's baldness—according to family legend his hair fell out all in one night!—for my own thatch of fine red hair), and we'd done group demonstrations of a range of personal characteristics—eye color, hitch-hiker's thumb, tongue-rolling ability—in order to learn the concept of traits. It was no wonder, then, that when we moved from genetics to politics, I assumed the trajectory was a wholly natural one, and I could only think of the structures of governance themselves as wholly natural—as natural as baldness, or a hitchhiker's thumb, or the color, or, for that matter, the shape, of one's eyes.

This impression would not very likely have been discouraged by the teacher, since there were aspects of her presentation that even seemed to foster it. On the chalkboard, she drew an elaborate diagram outlining the branches of government: a rectangle to represent the Legislative branch, a triangle to represent the Judicial, and a circle to represent the Executive, with complicated lines, like the latitudes and longitudes of a globe, winding circuitously among the forms to interconnect them. In its compendious, cross-referenced arrangement, the diagram reminded me of the map of the solar system that hung on a wall of the classroom, sun, moons, and stars suspended in starry black surround, illuminated in comfortingly explicable correlation; or of a similar diagram Mrs. Bridges had concocted on the same chalkboard the week before, to illustrate the numinous cycles of rainfall.

Mrs. Bridges stepped back from the chalkboard and wiped her hands together. "Now, People, eyes front!" she said. "Who can tell us what all these different branches of the government *do,* and why we have them all?"

A silence fell, broken finally by Bobby Adams, who was the only one of us who never shrank from a proud display of ignorance, and whose only discernible inner disposition—for all his other quirks were public, familiar, and ordinary, and generally shared, to boot—was a loathing of silence. "I know *this: my* Dad voted for Nixon!" he crowed.

"Good, Bobby," Mrs. Bridges said mildly, though through slightly clenched teeth. The sally was apparently not so wide of the mark that it could not be guided back into the jurisdiction of relevance, a hidden diamond yet to be mined. Mrs. Bridges took up her pointer, as if it were delicate weaponry, and she waved it at the chalkboard. "And in which one of all these branches do we find the President of the United States?"

"*All* of them," said Bobby. "He's the boss, the main guy, the Big Kahuna—and he makes *two hundred thousand bucks* a year!"

"That's fine, Bobby," said the teacher, "but it doesn't quite answer the question." She put down the pointer and folded her hands, the fingers clenched in crabby, conditional expectation.

From my desk, near the back of the room, I was able to observe much of the hidden life of the classroom. I could see Alan McWhirter's furtive but meticulous nose-picking, and witness the covert stowing of the newly excavated boogers on the underside of his desk. I could see the twins, Midge and Melanie Ellis, passing their incessant secret notes across the aisle and constantly exchanging meaningful, conspiratorial looks. I could see Gillian Hack polishing or filing her long fingernails, slowly and methodically, her pampered hands resting in her lap under cover of the desk, in the folds of the big, fur-lined coat she always wore because she was always cold, and I could see Larry Gohlke sorting through baseball cards across the room. Bobby Adams, forced by the entrenched notoriety of his reputation to sit up front where the teacher could keep an eye on him, was in point of fact the only member of the class *not* busily engaged in some covert activity or private pursuit as the lesson ran its tedious course. My own distraction was the observation of all the others, and I wondered vaguely if their penchant for these preoccupations, largely unseen in the lower grades, were not evidence of growth that it would ultimately be incumbent on me, too, to follow. In the lower grades the teachers had always been granted our unquestioned, adoring attention; perhaps the discovery of intrinsic purposes of one's own, indulged even in a public forum ostensibly intent on other goals, was a sign of maturation.

Luke's distraction, a slow, ornate doodling in the margins of his looseleaf, was among the least of the class's offenses against courtesy, and so it was with some surprise that we heard Mrs. Bridges sharply and suddenly calling him to account. "This isn't art class, young man," she said, "so if you can just tear yourself away from your masterpiece, maybe *you* can answer the question for us."

Luke set his pen down on the desk in front of him and drew himself up. "The President's in the Executive branch of the government," he said. "He's the Chief Executive."

"That's correct." The teacher unfolded her hands and reclasped them, grudgingly, behind her back. She turned away from Luke. "And *why* are there all these branches of the government, People? Why not only one?"

For my part, I had not thought of three as any particular abundance, and although I was certain that the cause was as natural, and as arbitrary, as the number of my own genes, knowledge of which had done nothing to alter the state of my body, I searched my mind. The twins, across the aisle, put their hands up in unison. Midge was recognized. "Because then we wouldn't be as *free*," she blurted. "You know what I mean? Then it would be just like back in Hitler times, where everything is just like what only one single solitary person says, and whatever he says goes, and only like one person gets to have a say, and nobody's, like, *free*." Frantic motion of the hands conveyed the zealotry of her high regard for the freedom common to us all. In the grip of this zeal, however, Midge apparently had forgotten herself: what made this apparent was the fact that Midge, usually so proficient in concealing the wads of chewing gum she always harbored in her mouth, now chomped the gum loudly between her teeth, amid the fervent syllables of her speech, punctuating that disquisition with the ill-seasoned pops and smacks of teeth on gum. Gum, as everyone knew, was a particular bête noire of Mrs. Bridges, and on those occasions when it was discovered, it was forcibly removed from the felonious mouth and punitively affixed to the offender's face—cheeks, nose, forehead, depending on the teacher's mood—where it adhered as repulsively as the boogers stuck to the underside of Alan McWhirter's desk, but even more publicly. Waiting for the teacher's approval, Midge sat in an attitude of anticipation, her eyes quizzical and one of the previously flitting hands held out still and flat with the palm turned up, as if she were offering an invisible, plentiful platter. Mrs. Bridges's eyes narrowed sourly, suggesting that she was as aware of the gum as everyone else was, but a speech about freedom hovered in the air, in need of ratification, so the time perhaps seemed inopportune to levy the usual authority. "That is correct," Mrs. Bridges said.

No question was pending, but Luke's hand went up. "What *I* don't get," he said, "is why *three*. Lots of countries have more. Like in Taiwan. In Taiwan they have *five*, and they call them *yuan*, and each one does its own thing but each one watches over all the others too."

"Taiwan," said Mrs. Bridges distantly. "What grade did you learn about Taiwan?"

"No grade," said Luke. "I read about it. At home."

"At home," Mrs. Bridges repeated. She looked around the room with an air of mild vexation. "Well. That's very interesting, Luke, but we're not learning about Taiwan just now. We're learning about the United States." She glanced absently down at the piece of chalk she held, and it seemed to remind her that it was time to turn back to the board. CHECKS AND BALANCES, she wrote there, in big yellow block letters. "How nice," she said to the chalkboard as she wrote, her back to the classroom. "How nice, that some people read at home."

Everyone liked Luke, and over time I was forced to face the fact that any worry of mine over how others would receive him perhaps told more about the shape of my cognizance than it did about the forms of their ignorance. He was good in sports, and that in itself went a long way toward ensuring his acceptance. He could kick a ball higher and farther than anyone else in the schoolyard, and this difference approximated the desired sameness closely enough to redeem him. He was funny—his strutting, preening, husky-voiced imitation of Flip Wilson as Geraldine whooping "The Devil made me do it!" wowed them in the lunchroom—yet he was also earnest, given to timely humor but not prone to needless frivolities, and this was a quality much to be admired, as we were just then starting to realize exactly how serious a business life really was.

Still I kept my distance from him, until the time when the class was grouped in work teams commissioned to produce replicas of government bureaus, when I found myself assigned to a group with Larry Gohlke, Midge Ellis, and Luke. Groups were assigned different tasks—ours was to make a map of the Pentagon—and accorded separate work spaces, no doubt to teach us the twin values of collective endeavor and private enterprise; and this splintering into scattered clans seemed very much to evidence a new freedom, as if we were being, at last, trusted. Some groups were allowed for the prosecution of their labors the liberty of betaking themselves away to the library; others repaired to crannies of the corridor, still others to sequestered corners of the classroom itself. Our group got the coatroom. An epidemic of chicken pox was sweeping through the school at the time, and Luke had been out sick the week before. Now Larry Gohlke and Midge Ellis were stricken, but I, by virtue of past suffering, was immune, and so it was one afternoon that I found myself alone in the coatroom with Luke.

"That lady sure hates me," Luke said. Mrs. Bridges had just poked her head into the coatroom and, seeing how little progress we had made on our map of the Pentagon, yipped, "Get the lead out, People!" before curtly withdrawing in a cloud of cigarette smoke.

"She's like that with everyone," I answered. "They were on strike, you know—the teachers. Before you got here." I thought if he knew about the strike, he would be inclined to observe a greater obedience in class, and refrain from further testing Mrs. Bridges's already strained patience.

"Good for them!" He held up his fist in a spontaneous show of solidarity. My hidden agenda appeared to have been lost on him. We were sitting on the floor among scattered drafts and unfinished sketches. "She's right, though. It's not going very well. Personally, I think the whole thing's dumb anyway. You know what the Pentagon is? It's where they plan the wars." He drew his legs up to his chest and hugged them. He gazed at me, resting his chin on his knees. "I'm antiwar," he said.

I nodded. I admired the conviction, but doubted that such an ideal could ever be sustained in a world as brutal and as unforgiving as the real one. "I don't ever want to *go* to one," I said. "I know *that* much."

He cocked his head slightly, continuing to look at me with an expression of great seriousness, as if I had put forth an axiom worthy of consideration. Then, suddenly, he thrust his legs out in front of him and, sitting back, asked, "Want to see my scars?" He lifted his shirt, without waiting for an answer, and looked down past the rolled-up cloth of the shirt bunched under his chin, gazing at his own chest. "Chicken pawx," he crooned, making the word sound like the clucking of a chicken. "Chicken pawx pawx pawx pawx pawx!"

I too gazed upon the exposed chest. Around the belly button clustered blemished flecks, white against the smooth, nut-colored skin. The belly button was an outie, its complicated folds coming to a skewed little point in the middle. A band of underpants showed below the belly button, but my gaze followed his finger as it traced a slow line upward to a scar, higher, that inscribed his skin apart from the others. This scar was shaped like a white star, not the five-pointed star of a kid's drawing, but an actual, sky-bound star, circular, with little flows and flares around its sketchy circumference, and with a tiny red dot at the very center. The scar itself was centered between his nipples, which were small, brown, and scabby, yet soft-looking, and he rubbed the scar softly with the tip of his finger. My breath stopped. The closeness, the suddenness—it was as if it were my own body that he touched. Then he poked the scar, with its nippled shape and its pale aureole. "My third tit," he said.

"Don't worry," I said. "They'll go away. I had the chicken pox, and the scars went away."

Giving me that same serious look, he said, "I'm not worried." He dropped his shirt down and leaned backward, arms propped behind him, looking at me. "You're a smart one, Mister Freckles," he said. "I can tell. How come you never talk?"

I shrugged. I could not speak. I was thinking of the chest, now covered again, his chest—as much of the forthright suddenness of its display as of the color and the texture, and even the smell, of the chest itself—and of the jingle, that jingle, that kept running through my head: *Chinese, Japanese, Siamese—look at these!*

In class, far from restraining himself, Luke became ever more persistent, constantly asking questions, always talking about how they did things in Taiwan, or raising some other extraneous issue, so that Mrs. Bridges then had to explain to him, with increasingly strained patience, that however interesting these matters might be in and of themselves, they had no bearing whatsoever on the object of our study. Knowledge of the strike had done nothing to stay Luke from an eager pertinacity that seemed, if anything, only fueled by the teacher's growing impatience and fatigued resentment. Especially after the tribulation of the strike, it was clear that Mrs. Bridges's breaking point was well in sight, and we all waited anxiously for the axe to fall. All but Luke, who seemed entirely unaware of what was looming so visibly to the rest of us. I gazed at the back of his neck now with a new combination of chagrin and proprietary pride. The tufts of hair at the nape of his neck were of like texture to the sparse strands of hair that lightly brindled his chest. I knew this because I had seen it. He had shown it to me. He had shown me something of himself, and I was grateful, but still I marveled at his incorrigibility. It was from the midst of such a reverie, one afternoon, that I was abruptly stirred by his latest outrageousness. "If you think that the people of the United States of America *really* elect the President of the United States," I heard him say, "then you're just living in a dream world!"

A numbed silence followed, until Bobby Adams, tried-and-true silence-breaker, sneering deliriously, piped up. "What the heck are you *talking* about?"

"You say your Dad voted for Nixon, Crazy-Fists? Well, maybe he did, but the fact is he didn't *elect* him. None of the people did. The President of the United States is elected by the Electoral College, not the people."

Bobby Adams aimed his contorted face at the teacher. "Is that true?" he asked.

Mrs. Bridges turned her eyes from the ceiling to cast a doubt-fully corroborative glance at the thick teacher's manual opened on the desk in front of her. "We don't get to that unit until *seventh* grade," she murmured.

"Sometimes the guy that gets elected even has *less* votes than anyone else, and he gets elected anyway just because the Electoral College says so! They can do anything they want. They don't have to pick the guy people vote for. And three times in history, they picked a guy that got less votes than the other guy. Three times: John Quincy Adams, Rutherford B. Hayes, and Benjamin Henry Harrison!" He counted them off on his fingers.

"Is that *true*?" Bobby Adams repeated.

Mrs. Bridges's limp hands, with their nicotine-stained fingers, hung at the ends of helplessly dangling arms. As if to fortify herself, she wrung them briefly. "Not everything is as simple as pie," she said after a long, tubercular sigh. "There's two sides to every story."

From this debate arose, at length, the idea of the classroom election. There would be two candidates, it was decreed, and five groups of voters that would simulate an electoral college. Any candidate to win the majority of the votes in a group would, in keeping with the laws of the country, earn all the votes of that group. In this way we would come to see the obscure wisdom of even so seemingly undemocratic a process as this one. The candidates would canvass and campaign, just as in a real election, and post posters, and make speeches, and the winner, like any governor, would be responsible for the civic well-being of the class for the whole rest of the year. It was, in its way, a true inspiration on the teacher's part, and the wicked gleam in her eye when the idea struck her told me she knew it. Not only did it let her off the immediate hook, but it dictated weeks' worth of eminently justifiable busywork that would also have the advantage of multiplying opportunities for cigarette breaks. Best of all, it substituted practical action for ivory-tower ratiocination, with a wholesome, prudent pragmatism that might well be the best re-venge against the anemic solipsism of mere hairsplitting intellect, and that was certainly the very bedrock of our education. And this revenge was hardly incidental: the winner's victory, in the long run, as anyone suspected who had seen that gleam in the teacher's eye, would likely prove to be a pyrrhic one, and nomination to the office of class president a decidedly punitive honor. Nobody was surprised, or at least I wasn't, when Luke was picked as one of the candidates.

His opponent was Annette Kern, with whom I had a long and tortured history. Several grades before, in an experimental con-versation among a group of boys regarding which girls we, who had so recently spurned all female company, had crushes on, I had produced, under duress, the name of Annette Kern. The same afternoon she had stationed herself before me on the playground. She had a disquieting habit of always standing too close to one, and the smell she gave off was that of a medicine cabinet, with Listerine, orange-flavored chewable children's aspirin, and hydro-gen peroxide especially prominent among the olfactory elements. On that occasion she stood even closer than usual, so I knew right away that word of my extorted confession had reached her, and my heart sank. She told me she'd heard I had a crush on her, and she wanted me to know that she did not mind. Then she turned on her heel and strode away. Not minding struck me as being so very much the opposite of welcoming, that all of our interactions from then on, a constant roundelay of arrested development, followed the same pattern: the placing of herself too close, the issuance of a blunt revelation or a stern but vaguely fond demand, the turning on her heel and the striding away—all while I stood by, stock still, and let her run the predictable course of the routine. It did not promise to provide a real basis for the cultivation of genuine sentiment. Yet it was not an arrangement I sought to deepen or to alter, thinking it better to endure such brief and intermittent transactions than to relinquish a theoretical girlfriend. At the Halloween party the year before, she had placed herself in front of me and said, "Kiss me." She was dressed as a fairy princess, and I was dressed as a glow-in-the-dark skeleton. My skull-mask was pushed up on top of my head to give my hot face air, but as I leaned in obediently, missing the target and only grazing her neck with my lips, the edge of the mask poked her in the eye, just as the tip of her wand scratched my ear. Then she turned on her heel and strode away. Pain seemed to be the only thing we could exchange. After she became a candidate in the election, and I was chosen as an elector, responsible for tallying and reporting the votes of my group, I noticed her giving me long looks across the classroom. Her bluntness was a symptom of her honesty, and I knew that the significance of these looks was that she would be at great, scrupulous pains to avoid even the appearance of favoritism or impropriety. These wistful, weighted looks brought the red into my cheeks right away; maybe the interval between embarrassment and desire is a distance one never really learns. Annette Kern placed herself before me one day soon after these looks commenced, and said with matter-of-fact intonations, "We better cool it for a while." Before she turned on her heel and strode away, she looked into my eyes, sadly. That brimming pause, unprecedented and unrepeated, was the truest and most beautiful thing to pass between us. I would remember it, for it would always be in the moment they were leaving me, from then on, that those who said they loved me seemed to love me the most.

Two members of my group, Alan McWhirter and Melanie Ellis, declared their allegiances early, with the affiliations dividing along gender lines too predictably for comfort: Alan for Luke, Melanie for Annette. At lunch I sought out the remaining members of my group to accomplish some hasty solicitation of my own, hoping to forestall an unpropitious outcome that I was already starting to dread. Mary Zaremba looked at me, dramatically unimpressed, through the severe screen of her black horn-rim glasses, her lip curled in an attitude of outrage mild enough to demonstrate that my repulsiveness was fully equaled by my insignificance. I had the advantage of knowing that there was no love lost between Annette Kern and Mary Zaremba, but when I pointed this out to Mary Zaremba herself, her eyes only narrowed further. Voting was a very private matter, she informed me, and she was not in the habit of discussing her private affairs with dorkbrains. "It's only because she's a girl," I said, aghast with an accusatory outrage of my own. "You're voting for her *just because she's a girl!*"

"That's right, dorkbrain," Mary Zaremba answered coolly. "I'm voting for her just because she's a girl."

The last member of my group, Perry Trubell, was a small boy with a squeaky voice and an extremely round head, with plates of greasy, wispy hair draped down either side of it. His head was always turned oddly to one side, the round face pointing upward at a funny angle, as if the head was on wrong and might roll off at any minute; and his big pop eyes were very round, as round as his head, whose shape they repeated exactly, with furry arcs of eyebrow half-circling them. "You don't have to tell!" he answered my query in the strangely urgent, squeaky voice. "You're allowed to keep it secret!"

I heaved a sigh. As usual, these yahoos were learning all the wrong lessons. "You're *allowed* to keep it a secret," I said. "That doesn't mean you *have* to. Now come on. Just tell me who you're voting for."

"I'll trade you," he said, bidding to change the subject. "I'll trade you my urine sample for your pus-drink." These were commonly accepted terms in the lunchroom for orange juice and milk. I looked down at the little carton I held, suddenly valuable, striped with its colorful bands of red and white. "How much do you want it?" I asked.

Annette Kern promised to prolong recess and lessen homework. Brazen, she promised movies once a week and parties once a month; shameless, she promised the relaxation of the dress code, so we could wear shorts in spring and blue jeans in fall. And she promised to increase exponentially the number of field trips, and make them to better places—the zoo, not the auto-factory; the amusement park, not the museum. It was not at all like her. Where had gone, so quickly, the honesty, the reliable conscientiousness? If absolute power corrupts absolutely, then perhaps potential power corrupts potentially. When Luke took the podium, he looked out at the class with the same direct, unflinching gaze he had always brought to the act of looking. He made Mrs. Bridges admit, then and there, before every known constituency, the un-likelihood of the institution of any such measures as those that Annette Kern had dangled so brashly before us. In the event of his election, Luke proclaimed in even tones, he would promise only to provide the staunchest advocacy of all students' rights. That was all. He stood before the class, with upright dignity,

clutching the sides of the lectern, and thick, reverent silence de-
scended, like a cloud of peace after conflict. It was a triumph. In
that moment his victory seemed assured. Annette Kern blanched,
the teacher flushed, and I realized fully, looking up at Luke with
a wash of warm pride, what I'd already suspected vaguely. I
wanted him to lose.

If there was one thing our education was bound to teach us, it
was that any perpetual lack of skill or resource could always be
compensated for by a determined show of temporary industry.
The map of the Pentagon was not going well, so in a last-ditch
sprint of vainglory meant to save our grade, we contrived to sup-
plement it with a papier-mâché model of the whole Pentagon,
cooked up to impress, if only with its intricate sedulousness. It
was better in the long run, we knew, to overshoot the mark wildly
than to miss it altogether, especially if one's calculated excesses
could also claim the showy virtue of being unsolicited. One afternoon I went to Luke's to work on the model. He lived in an
apartment, not a house, and not only did that fact alone deny a
certain homeliness, but it was immediately evident even to one
so oblivious as I of the ins and outs of domestic décor how ill
appointed the place was. A dirty carpet-remnant covered the floor
of the front room, strands of jute tasseling out randomly around
its unbound, messy edges, and a few folding chairs, folded, leaned
against a wall. Pizza boxes stained with ribbons of grease were
stacked in a corner, and a folding table was heaped with unwashed
dishes.

"I live here with my dad," Luke said, with a shrug and a
chuckle. "He's an intern, and he works a lot, and me—well, I
guess I'm just not too neat. My mom's still in New York."

"How can they be married, if she's there and he's here?"

The question was innocent, but I had cause right away to regret it. "They can't," Luke answered. "They're not." He shrugged again. "I'll probably go there for the summer."

To judge by his room, you would never have known that he was not neat. It looked so much more like a kid's room than the rest of the place looked like a family's home that the difference reassured me. The bed was fastidiously made, with books neatly shelved on a ledge of the headboard. There was a poster hanging on the wall—it depicted a riderless motorcycle—and papers were piled evenly on the desk. The unfinished model of the Pentagon, looking bereft and hopelessly lopsided, was the only blight on the landscape. Popsicle sticks that would simulate spokes around the roof of the Pentagon were scattered across the floor. We sat together among them, and poked around halfheartedly at our project for a while. Whatever ambition or inspiration might have given rise to it had long since flagged, the only real obstacle to human endeavor being time itself.

"Do you *want* to go there?" I asked. I had never been out of Michigan, myself, aside from exotic but brief jaunts across the river to Windsor, Ontario, or across the state border to Ohio, and the question reflected both the obstinate spirit of the provincial and the timid hankering of the curious.

"Sure," he answered. "I want to see my mom."

"Do you like it better here or there?"

"I haven't been *here* very long. But you know what, Mister Freckles? I don't think it matters so much *where* you are. It matters *who* you are."

I had no idea what this claim could possibly mean, and the onset—familiar but vexing all the same—of a mild dizziness that came on whenever I was confronted by the incomprehensible was promptly, breathtakingly heightened when Luke suddenly grabbed my arm and pulled it to his arm. He wore short sleeves, but my sleeves were long, and with the same brisk expedience with which he had lifted his own shirt in the coatroom, he rolled up my sleeve all the way to my shoulder, and held my arm firmly against his arm. "Look at all them *freckles,*" he said. "*Look* at them."

I could feel his skin, smooth and soft and cool, but because of the firmness of his grasp, I could also feel, as I usually could not, my own, hot, blemished. He ran his finger along my arm, in just the way he had touched his own scars, and I felt for a minute that he did not see the marks on my skin as imperfection. He only wanted to touch them, to see what they felt like. But I pulled my arm away.

He looked surprised. "What's wrong?" he asked.

"You think you're better than me just because you don't have freckles?"

He fell back, and let out a shocked little laugh. He had the ability to laugh without smiling. "No!" he said, and I could tell from the force of the exclamation that the idea had never even occurred to him.

"Then don't be such a jerk."

"Don't be such a jerk," he repeated at once, a deranged falsetto.

"Now you're *really* being a moron."

"Now you're *really* being a moron."

"If you don't stop it . . ." The sentence trailed off, and I couldn't help laughing. I was always a sucker for this shtick—it seemed to convey so eloquently the repetitious indignity of being human.

"If you don't stop it . . ." The falsetto escalated into a mocking screed. "What's the little baby going to do? What's the little baby going to do? Is the little baby going to run away? Is the little baby going to run on home to Mommy-Wommy?"

"Cut it out!"

He was on his knees, leaning toward me. He wasn't smiling, but there was also something in his face, a tranquil intensity, a recognition, that made me feel charged, excited, not scared. "Make me," he said, in the quiet, seething tenor of his ordinary voice, and then he was upon me.

We wrestled fiercely, wildly, passionately, arms gripping and legs flailing and clenching, and he laughed as we strove, but the laughter did nothing to lessen the intensity of what was too close, too intense, to be a contest. The laughter only heightened it, emboldening me, in the knowledge that its goal was play, not conquest. His body was so close that I could feel the laughter starting in it, and rising through it, like sounding light through a prism. I worried that in the abandon of our wrestling we would roll upon the model of the Pentagon—but then I thought: *Let us; let us crush it!* Then it would be gone, it would be out of the way for good, and the grappling could go on, even more freely, without any restraints. I could come even closer to him; that last inhibition removed. "Who's got who?" Luke finally gasped. His head was locked under my arm, but he was on top, his arms clenching my trunk. He maneuvered himself sideward, so that we rolled over, and he tightened his grip.

"Give?" he grunted.

"Why should I?" I tightened my own grip, and struggled to wrap my legs around his legs, and we stayed locked together for a long time, until he said, "Okay—*draw.*"

We lay panting on our backs, side by side. "You're pretty strong," he said. He lifted himself wearily, turned toward me, propped on an elbow, and looked down at me. "We're pretty equal."

I caught my breath, and smiled up at him as he leaned over me. "I thought you didn't like to fight."

He did not smile back. He almost never smiled. "That wasn't fighting," he said.

That dizziness was familiar that had come upon me just before the wrestling, and gone so quickly; but if what was strange eluded all comfort, then what was familiar could bring a disquiet all its own. I wanted him to lose the election, because he was different. The knowledge that his parents were divorced only hardened my resolve: this was what such difference came to. It mattered who you were, to be sure, but where you came from was hardly an incidental factor in the judgment of character. If Luke lived among us for the rest of our lives, even if he did not return to New York in summertime, he would still never achieve the purely endemic citizenry of Annette Kern, because it was not a thing to be achieved, only one to be possessed or not, as the case warranted. Would nativity *always* outweigh gravity? That I could not say. I was different too. I knew the community I lived in deeply valued the whiteness of skin, and made it a condition of acceptance, but my own skin was *too* white, and dappled with spotty pigmentation that, if perfected, could easily have rendered me colored. It was only the miscarriage of divine handiwork, leaving me somehow unfinished, that spared me the ire of prejudice but let me taste its bittersweet flavor. I too was different, but he was, perhaps, or therefore, like me—he'd said we were equal, and he had compared our arms and then denied that he saw the difference between them—and I wanted him to lose because he was like me. If I was unfit, then so were those like me, and if he won, then he would belong to them, and less to me. Yet however deceitful I might be among others, I vowed always to be honest with myself, even if the honesty was brutal. Cruelty to others was sin, cruelty to oneself the dimension of a higher good; and when I was completely honest with myself, I knew that it was because he was different, most of all, that I wanted him to lose. The votes were counted, and they were split exactly as I'd predicted. Ideology aside, after all was said and done, boys still pledged allegiance to boys, and girls to girls. Our group was the last to report, and would determine the outcome. We too were tied. Mine was the deciding vote.

The sixteenth day of a new year, 1999—a gray Saturday—and on the radio, in tones of sonorous, droning hysteria, a member of the United States Congress, flavorfully named Henry Hyde (as if combining Jekyll with his alter ego in one chubby, unctuous persona), urgently hectors the Senate. For the first time in many years the president of the United States has been impeached in the House of Representatives, and now, according to Hyde, in order to preserve a sacred covenant, to uphold the rule of law above the power of state—so he grandly puts it—the Senate must vote to remove that president from office. Hyde's voice is husky with outrage, until he begins to read a letter from a third-grader in his district. Then Hyde's voice takes on a tender, sentimental quaver. "The President is *a* important man," Hyde reads, punctuating the cuteness of the boy's mistake, unashamed to exploit the sweet naïveté of his Rockwellian constituent; and if the President is not held responsible for *his* actions, the boy's letter goes on, then how will the rest of us ever learn right from wrong? To judge from a thickening of the Congressman's tones, he is moved immensely by the simple purity of the boy's reason. But those on the other side of the aisle of course know better. In their view Hyde's oratory is mere performance, the whole process deeply and irreparably "political."

How could it be otherwise? What was at stake was a legislation of sexuality, and its evocative reconstruction in public, and as any gay person knows, that is always political. In a very real sense, it reaches the essential condition of the political: the negotiation of private desire with public constraint. The President had had sex with a female White House intern, it appeared, and then equivocated to conceal this evidently ignoble act. The concealment could hardly have been less successful. In the course of the investigation of the events surrounding it, an endless series of unappetizing tableaus involving the President and the intern were compulsively conjured, generated, and then transmitted into the fantasy lives, thereby enhanced, of the nation's citizens. Pornographic in their intricacy, these tableaus may have been soft core in their conception, but they were decidedly hard core in the unstoppable obsessiveness of their dissemination, and the tumid repugnance with which they were pumped up was met head on with the bashful eagerness with which they were swallowed. A society terrified of sex will, my own experience attests, multiply unthought images of it, just as a child scared of monsters will keep jabbering about them, in the hope of allaying the fear. The culmination of the whole enterprise was the production of a thick book, a tome with the emotional primitivism of a novel by Samuel Richardson, the encyclopedic ardor of a tract by the Marquis de Sade, and the adolescent prurience of the letters to the editor in *Penthouse* magazine. This book remains readily available, under the fanciful title *The Starr Report*. If you have the stomach for it, and the will to face intimations of a culture's vacancy, you can read it for yourself. The numbing complacency of this work represents what was, for me, the defining feature of the entire grotesque charade, as of American politics itself: the utter inability of any of its participants to step aside, even for a second, from the provincial positions in which, despite the vacancy of these positions, they remained entrenched. Had they been able to do so, they might have glimpsed, if only for that second, the whole sorry business for what it must have seemed to anyone not mired in it: the pitifully familiar spectacle of a horde of silly, class-privileged people, up to their usual tricks.

As a citizen of the country in which this paltry pageant ran its depressing, inevitable course, I felt called on by civic obligation to refine a set of opinions about it. This obligation was accompanied by a prideful sense of my own political sophistication, an awareness that let me formulate conclusions about such circumstances somewhat, I fancied, apart from the given patterns. For me, what made the whole affair so representative was how pungently it reeked of what I'd come to understand as heterosexual privilege. If this intern had been male, and the very same acts performed, not just the outcome, but every conceivable feature of the phenomenon would have been wholly otherwise—not legislated, but banished. In moments of frivolous perversity, I lobbied among acquaintances to have the President brought up on charges of sodomy (like Mr. Hardwick, of *Bowers v. Hardwick,* in 1986), just to make that very point. But of course the real point was the unimaginability of such a circumstance within this fervent context. The whole episode testified to nothing so much as a society's shameful inability—however much I'd prefer to avoid the vocabulary of shame—to imagine *other kinds of people* inhabiting the roles in question. If we could imagine differently, *then* might we be able to conceive of presidents, at last, who do not claim sexual domination as a routine prerogative; or failing that, we might teach ourselves to conceive of "monogamy" itself in entirely different terms—perhaps not those of prohibition, but those of celebration, or maybe even according to some completely different set of imperatives altogether.

A conventional wisdom among the President's detractors and defenders alike was the notion that presidential libidos have historically been notably unfettered, if previously better protected in their outlets. But the next logical step in the argument was rarely taken: to conclude that these time-honored dalliances, whether castigated or countenanced, were themselves direct by-products, not of the relatively insignificant individual whims of these silly men—who were *they,* after all?—but of the much larger forces of the culture and its limitations. Collectively we had been able to imagine only one very specific kind of being as the president:

precisely, a white, heterosexual, class-privileged man, with a whole history of old-boy associations and fat-cat networks behind him, a whole set of explicitly patriarchal assumptions and values that enabled the complacency of entitlement. And this was what we had even in that neo–flower child of counterculture and feminism, the first president to be impeached since Johnson, whose vilification required the tireless invocation of those eternal bogeys, Our Founding Fathers, by prosecutors who as social types were in nearly every respect the exact likeness of both those Fathers and their errant son. For all I knew or cared, "Henry Hyde" might just as well have been "Rutherford B. Hayes," or "Hubert Humphrey," or, for that matter, "Richard M. Nixon." The fat ruddy face was all too familiar a mode, as were the affected, orotund diction, the lofty manner of invoking ideas only to vacate them, the practiced statesman's stance giving way to the waddling poodle-walk. As far as I could tell, the template had not changed one whit in hundreds of years, and I scorned the hypocrisy of all those who, without acknowledging this crucial determinant, still expressed disgust over the most recent scandal.

Such obstinate dispositions smacked of my earliest forays into political thought, and I sensed that for all the complexity of what I took to be my very gradual awakening—an evolution still, I hope, in progress—basic aspects of my political identity would always remain unchanged. One afternoon, as a boy, turning on the TV in avid anticipation of catching Liza Minnelli on the Mike Douglas show, I was faced instead by a large gallery of sullen, seemingly interchangeable men arrayed thickly around a gloomy, official-looking chamber. The proceeding the men were so dourly engaged in exuded an air of great moment, but its profound triviality was evident almost instantly. The men posed questions in tones of high seriousness, and nearly every question prompted a reported lapse in the respondent's memory, followed by much shuffling of papers, or dire whispering among white-maned cronies, before the next question was mounted. It was all a performance, as anyone who truly looked could see, as much a performance as Liza Minnelli's unjustly preempted one would have been, but free of the joyous exhibitionism of performance—for, as anyone could equally see, if anything were ever to come of this proceeding, it would be covertly wrought, maneuvered behind the scenes, for all the high-minded public display. It went on and on, afternoon by afternoon, preempting a whole season's worth of sorely missed pleasures, and something *did* come of it, if little more in the long run than that all-purpose suffix *-gate,* tacked thereafter onto any noun that it might prove expedient to convert into scandal by those in love with cliché as the most efficient antidote to thought.

Politics as such is frequently defined theoretically, even among its enthusiasts, as the rationalization of self-interest, and it is that definition that typically earns the word its quotation marks, and its users' contempt. Perhaps it was just such contempt, or the realization that one would always have to choose between Liza Minnelli and the Watergate hearings, between aesthetics and politics, that caused me to renounce politics altogether during so much of the long apprenticeship of my adolescence. But it was something like the knowledge that it was Liza Minnelli that I wanted, and not the Watergate hearings—the knowledge that it was *someone else's* desire, and not my own, reflected in the suppression of the former, and the supersession of the latter—that brought me back to it. Fourteen, fifteen, sixteen, seventeen—all through those ages I elected to make myself into an aesthete, above politics, outside the fray. I read Oscar Wilde, whose politics were lost on me then, and I pronounced eternal, art-for-art's-sake verities unsullied by worldly considerations. The political was the opposite of the individual, and it was the individual I sought to valorize, especially my own glorified selfhood. The more undeniable my sexual identity became, the more aestheticized I willed my intellectual or emotional or cultural identity to be. It was, like so much in my boyhood, a way of asserting and disavowing a gay self, at one and the same time. The posture of the aesthete was itself gay-identified, of course, though one would never speak of it that way, even if its whole purpose was to bring body back to spirit, or to experience body as if it *were* spirit; but it was still well removed from the crude militancy of the sissy-boys who were starting to show up from time to time on the news, in their tight denims and elephant-bells, prancing openly through city streets, *flaunting it,* in a show of prissy solidarity, meant for no other purpose than the vulgar, selfish one of getting their own piece of the pie.

It was, I think, precisely the issue of deniability that brought me back to politics, in a way, and made me confront the need to forge a political identity to complement the other identities I was trying to construct. Watergate had been about nothing if not the Decay of Lying. All those men, defined just like the rest of us by history, made what they were by what they wanted—and each one engaged in highly public, theatrical, remarkably tedious bouts of denial: *I didn't do it. I don't remember. I am not a crook.* Those denials were not contrary to what the men were—powerful leaders of a big, powerful country—but rather a *part* of what they were, maybe the decisive part. Political disillusionment set me against denial. To refuse *their* forms of power—sham power whose only function that I could see was to let them get their rocks off, that contemptible power, fake but all too real, that had done so much to damage us all—I would have to stop denying what I was (*I am not a crook*) and start affirming it (*I am—yes, yes, I am . . .*). In search of political identity I subscribed to a series of what I took to be political magazines—*Commentary, Harper's, Partisan Review*—canceling each subscription successively as each magazine in turn published articles calling implicitly or explicitly for the eradication of gay people from the population. It was a long, long apprenticeship. By the time I was nineteen, attending a gay rights rally in Ypsilanti, the aesthetic was still at war with the political. "The personal is political. Everything is political!" chanted the keynote speaker at the rally. I'd never heard the slogan before, and I doubted it, on instinct. But when the cheer went up, our voices raised in a proclamation of our worth, mine was joined with those of the others—a larger crowd of gay men and women than I'd ever thought I would live to see all in one place—a call in the midst of that exuberant crowd, but indistinguishable from the collective, proud and beautiful as it was.

The myth of the collective is the real danger of politics. The collective inability I've alleged of our culture to alter political frameworks for the better is inevitable, because the collective is a false entity. This is a fact—so many voices still unheard, so many differences yet to be realized—that politics as such has no way to acknowledge without undermining its own bases, but must find a way to assimilate. As much as I long to repeat experiences of collective transcendence such as those I associate with the time of my coming out, I'm suspicious of them, still and always, as the denial of genuine otherness. When you learn that I am gay, you still know nothing of my self, even of my sexuality, except what you think you know about gay people; and when I was in that life-sustaining crowd at the rally in Ypsilanti, I was not among people any more "like" me, necessarily, than I was in my sixth-grade classroom. No one of us is identical with another, or even with ourselves, because we live in time, and difference is everywhere. Political justice can arise only where social conditions enable the necessary identification with otherness, but if it is when you accept the inevitability of self-interest that you stop fearing politics, it is when you recognize the limits of such identification that political justice becomes truly possible. Until then, one has no way of knowing—maybe one *never* does—that one is not simply remaking what has been projected as different, as other, into another version of oneself. When the foreigner enters the native's terrain, the lesson *should* be that whatever difference we think has thus intruded was really already there all along, in some other form, but unseen, effaced, or denied. It is a lesson nobody knows as subtly, perhaps, or as powerfully, as the gay child: the child who longs, so deeply, to be like the others, who is taken so readily to be like the others, since the crucial difference is not "visible," but who sees reflected in the difference of others a difference that has already been gleaned, or discovered more fully, with terror, or with wonder, in the self.

"Everything is political!" chanted the keynote speaker, with her short-cropped hair and her primitivist earrings. I thought she looked unwholesomely *manly*—a militant lesbian!—and it seemed, at the time, like an instinct for me to feel this way. If I met her now, I know I would think that she was beautiful, and that too would feel like an instinct, but perhaps I would have the wherewithal, now, to remind myself that it was not one, really. "If *everything* is political," I declared, stridently approaching her after her speech, "then *nothing* is political." She stepped back and looked me up and down with a sly smile. Then she tousled my hair, playfully. "Hey—Carrot-Top," she said, somehow without condescension, as if she knew something I didn't, *"get over it!"*

I think, I hope (*Hey Marie, wherever you are, listen up!—and thanks . . .*) I have.

What had we learned, the teacher wanted to know, from the election?

Her fingers drummed the desk, expressing impatience yet discouraging response. Melanie Ellis had learned that you should never give up hope because it is always darkest before the dawn and you can always pull it out in the end if only you just stick to it, and the best girl always wins. Alan McWhirter stood mute.

Bobby Adams repeated that his father had voted for Nixon. Larry Gohlke had learned that some people just never listen and never learn what's good for them, and they pay no mind to the difference between right and wrong; they just make up their own minds right away and only do what *they* want to do, with no thought for the welfare of others, or the greater good. Gillian Hack had learned that girls vote for girls and boys vote for boys, and that is exactly the way it should be. I kept to myself the lesson that the appearance of collective desire comes in handy to hide individual whim. If anyone else had learned anything about the Electoral College, it was not reported.

Luke offered no comment, and possibly out of deference to his loss, he was not called on to make one. The next day I went to his house one last time, to finish the model of the Pentagon. The front room had been neatened—dishes and pizza boxes gone, chairs unfolded and placed squarely around the folding table—so that it now looked like a parody of an actual home, performed by an ungifted parodist.

We were sitting again on the floor of his bedroom, and the model of the Pentagon looked shabbier and more hopeless than ever. "I don't mind losing," he said, "long as I know all the people I *really* like voted for me."

I said nothing. There was a silence. Then Luke carefully pushed the model across the floor, against the wall, and I realized he was clearing a space for us in the middle of the floor. Then he knelt beside me, and cuffed me on the arm. "Come on," he whispered.

"What?"

He reached out again, and nudged my shoulder. "Come on," he repeated. He moved closer to me.

"No," I said.

Still kneeling, he leaned against me. He clasped my shoulder in one hand, and draped his other arm loosely around my neck. "Let's wrestle," he said.

"No."

"Why not?"

"Because."

He disentangled himself from me and leaned back on his haunches. "Because why?"

"Just because."

"Just because why?"

"I don't want to," I told him.

5

QUESTIONS OF TRAVEL

"Should we have stayed at home and thought of here?"

—Elizabeth Bishop, "Questions of Travel"

Some words spring up like flowers, hardy perennials that occasion no surprise when they reblossom year after year. *Mama, down, no, doggy, want*—the first learned, when words are neither proper objects nor narrow subjects, and neologism is the rule. The student of human languages, coming to any one of them for the very first time, typically gets wise to nomenclature in a state of giddy receptivity and relaxed inquisition. It is not so much that all seems new as that everything seems possible—unless, or until, recognition dawns that once things are named, possibility ends. The addition of *bye* to the burgeoning lexicon (especially if its common variant, "bye-bye," like *Mama,* has taught the advantages of reiteration and homonym) disrupts the infantile fantasy, cherished less by infants than by their hopeful mentors, that words mean simply. Universally taught in tandem with a supple wave, that word proves finally the impoverishment of what had seemed for a time so plentiful, so ample in the capacity to accomplish. But no: words, after all, only seem to extend what the body has already limited, and they mean nothing without the intervention of gesture. Soon the child acquires the all-purpose "Why?" with the upward lilt of the voice and the veridical widening of the gaze usually taught to accompany it, and after that nothing is ever the same.

Other words never yield even that brief appearance of unitary integrity. They enter the mind already in a state of doubleness. These are the ones we learn later, without feeling we've been taught them: the growth of a vocabulary finds its metaphoric analogue not in the cultivation of a garden but in the spread of an untended, overrun field. The difference between these two classes of words marks the widely unmarked passage from infancy to childhood and measures the distance between the given and the examined, the received and the accepted. "Bye" is a correspondence: *Someone is leaving.* "Bye-bye" names an act: *You yourself are leaving*—or, more properly, since the mixed blessings of volition have yet to be conferred on you, *being taken somewhere*. Because, whether by cultural dictation or natural decree, nonsense remains the most accessible and direct mode of communication between children and adults, it is no surprise that "home," as a place or a name or a thing, although it shares monosyllabism with most of the other first learned words, comes only later, through a process of negation. We know we have a home only after we've gone away, and the only cure for the familiar grief of departure, the trauma of travel, is a return home.

Vacation was one of the words whose meaning I took for granted—we'd always gone on vacation—but whose value eluded and thereby fascinated me. There was a whole category of such words. They were the ones I always tripped over in speech. In fact *category* was one of them, because of the way it teasingly evoked and then veered away from *catechism*, and because *gory*—

a funny word, learned from my mother's incessant, uneasy query regarding my love of horror movies, "How can you *stand* to watch all those gory shows?"—was embedded in it. Usually the words contained in this class were characterized by length, complexity, and a combination of strict familiarity and unassimilability: *homily* (of or relating to a home?) or *liturgy; orthodontist* or *pediatrician; multiplication* or *smorgasbord.* This last was at issue only because we regularly ate Sunday dinner at a restaurant whose fare was served up in that style, the exotically named Sveden Haus. The blandness of the food (boiled meats, canned peas, watered-down mashed potatoes) was made up for by the invitation to linguistic experiment that the fanciful and comfortingly familiar foreignness of the place seemed to issue. On these occasions, I got to say the word—rendered in my idiosyncratic pronunciation as "shmork-ishburd"—over and over, and I seized the opportunity to do so. My best friend, Hardy, offspring of German-speaking parents, said "buther" for *butter* and "sweather" for *sweater,* linguistic aberrations I privately ridiculed; but I was still well aware that the class of words I fetishized lured me into irresistible solecism myself. I'd once referred to the overseer of my braces as an "orthodontasaur," and was so pleased with the mistake that I repeated it proudly. But I was less pleased with my inability, rehearsed every year, to say "vacation," which I mangled most often, rather inexplicably, into something on the order of "VAKE-a-shin," or "vuh-CAME-shun."

Every summer our destination was the same: Up North. This designation, at once mysterious and exact, referred to Traverse City, a town on a bay at what would have been, had the metaphor of the mitten the state resembled been made literal, the tip of one of the leftside rightward backhand fingers. There my father had grown up, and while two of his brothers, like him, had migrated south to ply the trades of the city, the rest of the family had stayed. We went back each year, obstinate and slightly baffled pilgrims. Sometimes we were bidden by a family occasion like a wedding, other times drawn by an annual attraction such as the Festival of Cherries that recurred every summer to celebrate the season's crop, but always we were held at the mitigated behest of Vacation, that aspirant ritual, wishful escape, and collective horror.

The journeys were as predictable as the sojourns themselves were divinable. Usually before we'd cleared the driveway of our house the first bout of parental rage would erupt, a pleasureless orgy of blame, denial, and recrimination (my sisters and I mute with recognition and a shared rage of our own in the back seat): an assigned task forsaken, a needed item left unpacked, a common courtesy slighted. The first leg of the trip was converted by anger's well-known alchemy into an aftermath, a simmering and a brooding, and only a gradual, if temporary, exoneration: After all, we were on *Vacation*! Past the depressive rubble of Flint, beyond the smoky decay of Saginaw, the road would little by little open into the green hills of Grayling, the high skies of Gaylord (*Gaylord!* I repeated inwardly. *Gaylord.*). The wares of roadside stands, my father warned, would only instill a sure case of the trots, and in a car on a long trip there just happened to be no place to trot to; but the exhortation, usually voiced for its own comic sake, not for its cautionary utility, never stopped our indulgence. The sweet, stemmed cherries, ripened between purple and red, came in little cartons woven from frazzled strips of wood, fastened with rusty staples to a rounded stave at the top. The meager flesh was rich beyond belief with tangy juice, mellifluous, somewhere between the delicacy of the berry and the vigor of the more robust fruits, and the slimy, hirsute pits were good for spitting. My sisters and I played Slugbug (the first one to spot a Volkswagen Beetle gets to punch the others—ten times for a blackie) or made up Rorshach-naming games with fleecy, mutating clouds; or else we watched mercurial, silvery mirages writhe and puddle in the dip of the road at the shifting horizon, or passed the time listening to the portable eight-track resting in a lap that bounced in rhythm with the music (Herman's Hermits, the Carpenters, and above all the Partridge Family). A high crest in the road would finally announce our arrival, and it was always the same, and that was good: a sudden downward sweep before us, a valley, in the summer bloom of lushness, green and purple and red and blue, a new land, even if it was the same one every year, with a great and endless distance where there was no horizon because the sea and the sky were one—and every year I caught my breath.

In the 1968 *World Book Encyclopedia,* under "Frog," there was an intricate anatomy of the creature named, consisting of many thin, plastic, membranous, transparent sheets laid one over another, and with every sheet you lifted, you stripped away another layer of the frog's guts, the veins and the vessels and the unexpected organs and the complicated arteries, until sheet by sheet you came all the way down to the unadorned skeleton printed on a page as diaphanously solid as all the hundreds and hundreds of other slender, gilded, paper pages of the thick, heavy book. The frog's anatomy was one of the selling points of *The World Book Encyclopedia,* or so the door-to-door salesman who'd palmed the set off on us had presented it; and certainly, as he'd demonstrated it, I'd been held in a quavering state of grossed-out fascination, poised between epiphany and puking. Through the medium of these gelatinous pages, I thought, I might somehow learn the workings of bodies, but then I would have to live with the knowledge forever. (I remember that as the salesman thumbed through the wildly colored cellophane pages, he'd debated the spiritual value of *Jesus Christ Superstar* with my sternly dissenting mother.) For years, whenever I laid eyes on a map, I thought of that frog's anatomy. Maps typically boast the substantiality of ordinary paper rather than the repugnant viscosity of filmy plastic, but they also reveal the complexities of geography—the ribboned highways, veiny rivers, blotchy lakes, and tissued borders—to resemble more than passingly the frog's dense innards. So close was the resemblance that the dry touch of the map's surface often gave way to a remembered sensation of gross liquidity, producing at once a nearly Sartrean reaction of nausea and disgust. I could never look at a map, especially not in a moving car, where my sense of equilibrium was already compromised, without risking an instant headache or a plunging vertigo. I knew vacations were outward treks, not inward journeys. But this feeling of nauseous confusion, of sick-making imbalance, of unwanted confrontation with an interior landscape that one had rather not on the whole acknowledge, could not be put aside, and you cannot, of course, go on vacation without a map.

At the Foothills Motor Court, our room was a boxlike cell of proliferating squares: beds, bureaus, mirrors, the obligatory TV—even the chairs, tight leather studded at the seams with rows of little gold bumps, like the exposed teats of an upended pig, ran to squarishness. Journeys heighten awareness of the horizon's status—in ordinary life its place can remain unthought of for months at a time—and the Foothills Motor Court was like nothing so much as a little reachable horizon, right there before one, a squat, lengthwise row of accumbent rooms, embowered in a nest of green with hills of sand, the dunes of Northern Michigan, rising beyond it. The rooms there, each like the other, with the minute variations among them only emphasizing their neglect of the aesthetic, were still endowed with an unshakable aura by virtue of their being the only familiar places away from home where I had ever slept routinely—stopgaps, accidents, emergencies didn't count, and were rare in any case. As my sisters and I, bedecked in thongs and terry cloth, scampered to the pool, we made a point of passing the rooms that were being tended by the maid. There, in front of open doors, were parked big carts bearing piled towels and stacked sheets, and vacuum cleaners with long, convoluted hoses that made the stationary vehicles look like humpbacked, hibernating creatures with long trunks. We strained as we hurried past these doors to glimpse, without being seen, the obscure interiors, for it was only in covertly inspecting the rooms of others this way that we could heed the laws of compliance while confirming the unbending rule of likeness.

Vacation tests, either as a goal or a side effect, the sway of sameness. As a matter of course, the trip diverges from everyday life, if only to lighten the return, and accord is its most elusive aim. Bound together ineluctably for three or four days—we knew enough to keep vacations short—the five of us, a quintet of variably contesting wills temporarily migrating north, turned into a hydra-headed monster seeking ruthless pleasure at intervals whose speed, drift, and peregrinations were all at once urgently unsynchronous, irregular, and hopelessly reliable. Even if the provisional routines that became more familiar year by year made it conveniently axiomatic that we should all want the same things—a swim, a nap, a soda from the pop machine, ice cream, a visit to Grandma's, or a jaunt to a tourist trap—there was no decree in force to command that we all want them at the same time. Through such means Vacation weds strangeness to familiarity. Deeply familiar to one another, we might become stranger, even to ourselves, the farther from home we traveled. If there exists such a thing as collective desire, it is not on the family vacation, it seems safe to say, that it will ever be found.

Consider the case of my father. For him, these trips were a homecoming. As we neared the place of his birth, his voice took on a timbre that was otherwise altogether unknown, tender and rapt and husky with feeling. We had all seen him cry in front of the TV, watching Johnny Cash or Billy Graham, and so we knew that he was not free of tender emotions, in spite of his gruff manner. But this was different. The stories he told, as we headed northward, of his childhood and life on the farm were, like the vacations themselves, much the same year after year, but the shock always seemed new: the realization that he'd had a childhood at all—a full life, *before us,* dim and sunny at the same time, like those pictures in the family albums, photos of the world taken before I had come into it, where people I knew and loved, too young yet to mourn the future, flashed indomitable smiles that horrified me because they failed to acknowledge my absence. My father's stories, too, annulled the pertinent fact of my own birth, yet they seemed intended to delight their listeners, and he certainly loved to tell them. They ranged from the comic to the tragic, from lighthearted tales of farmyard doings to grim accounts of 'the death of a boyhood friend or the murder of the family dog by hillbilly ruffians. His favorite (and mine) involved a manure fight with all his brothers in the barn. These fights—I could *see* them, pungent missiles of dung sailing through the exuberant air!—were forbidden, so when the barn door swung open and their own father stood seething and unflinching on the sudden threshold, they all shouted their denials at once. As they did so, though, they saw that one of the telltale slugs of manure, hurled against the wall, had stuck there, a big glob of muck, right above the spot where their father stood in the open doorway. They all watched helplessly as the manure oozed slowly downward, and the story ended, amid the equally helpless gasps of the narrator's hilarity, with the evidence making further denial useless, plopping unceremoniously right down on top of Grandpa's bare, bald head.

The point of these stories was simply to commemorate, but their real purpose was to usher us all back into that Traverse City of the mind that my father reentered every time we went on vacation. The fact remained that we were leaving home as he was coming home, and even as the voyage joined us, the difference separated us. *We are going back to where I come from,* these stories said, and the glad assertion doubled as a bold exclusion. These oral memoirs (for that is what they were) were so vital a part of the trip that I came to feel, year by year, as if, on Vacation, we were traveling backward in time. At times I wondered if the reason for our trips was to oust oblivion, to go back to the place where these stories could be verified. To leave the city where we lived was to return to the country of the past, a time made simple by a chastening that did not even have to be accounted for as loss, where my father had been (or so it seemed) a happy little boy. The "brown cows" our grandmother made for us every time we came—vanilla scoops of ice cream in milky soda, abundantly afloat in big glasses, ornately imbricated fountain-goblets funneled on tiny, sturdy stems—charmed most powerfully in their ritual relation to the brown cows of days gone by, and though past excursions of shopping had made clear that our grandmother bought her clothes at Grant's or Milliken's, they still resembled the garments of olden times, if only because it was she who wore them. Visits ratified, over time, the tug of memory ("Did Uncle Willy *really* fall out that window when he was only two—and he wasn't even a *little* hurt?") even as memory proved the temper of time ("Remember when Boogie fainted at Jerry's wedding—only last year, wasn't it?"). The family homestead was cluttered with furnishings burnished with everyday use in the eyes of those who lived there, but tarnished as so many antiques from the vantage point of the vivacious future we had traveled from. If travel truly bespeaks failure of imagination, and memory the victory of mind, the journey ends with only fallow proof, and forgetfulness worries time, which needs no evidence.

One summer, right before a planned vacation, my little sister Jenny, then an infant, got sick—a florid burst of rubella blemishing her soft, sallow skin. She was not even a year old (I was eleven), and I couldn't believe her tiny body could sustain so virulent a rash. But it was the threat to the trip that spurred the more immediate distress, even though the equivocal value of vacation was already clear to me, and because our mother worried constantly that we, the older kids, might feel deprived by attentions to the baby, she insisted that the three of us, my older sister and father and I, go on vacation without them.

Jenny, newborn, had never come on vacation before, and so was not yet so vitally established as to be truly missed. But my mother's absence from the trip, a novel and vexing disturbance that might change everything, promised at the same time an unprecedented liberty, the caretaker's bothersomely vigilant hand in the enforced repose of separation. Our father's placid indifference at times resembled solidarity, the furtive permissiveness and default understandings of the grown-up who still, theoretically, recalls what it's like to be a kid, and entrusted to his capricious watch we might gain reach, we thought, of freedoms usually denied. No need to guard against the sun, no calls to curb consumption of candy, no reminders of dangers whose probable occurrence it was our mother's office alone to predict. Maybe we'd even discover what happened when the needs of food and sleep and care were left to fend for themselves, and we could only imagine the exuberance of such an outcome, never before given leave to explore it. Our father encouraged these thrilling speculations. At a roadside stop we bought rock candy, thick ribbons of crystallized sugar linked in coarse lumps by frayed-ended lengths of braided twine, and Dad urged us to eat up all the sweets at one go. "Don't be such a tight-mouth," he said. "Your mother's not here—we can do whatever the heck we want!" By the second day of vacation I was sunburnt and stomach-sick, and badly bruised and scraped by the dreamy carelessness that made me trip and fall and skin my knees and wound my bang-prone elbows whenever, I'd now learned, there was nobody there to counteract it.

Uncle Willy and Aunt Sally lived in a house on a bluff across

QUESTIONS OF TRAVEL | 115

the street from Suttons Bay. The house gave the appearance of having been built upside down. It was wedged into the hill so that, in front, a glass door-wall led into what should have been the basement and, behind, a sharp incline of the ground rose to what became thereby a provisional drive, accessible by a driveway of blindingly white pavement that wound up from the road. My cousin Billy's room could not, I suppose, have been right underneath the garage, but when cars pulled in or out above they sounded like airplanes growling and whirring and coasting directly overhead. An unfinished spiral staircase led from one level to another, and year after year the thin partitions between rooms, marbled with the gray swirls of dry-wall, went unpainted, and the house itself remained unfurnished, except for frameless beds, a few random barstools, and a pool table. The house seemed forever under construction, eternally in progress, and if our journeys to Traverse City were meant to enforce leisure, forestall progress, and so fend off duration, that may be why this house, especially with a vista of lake spread before the front windows, seemed such an ideal haven for Vacation. It was hard to imagine anyone living there every day—and for the most part, I did not try to imagine it—but the house was the perfect refuge from the claims of the diurnal.

A trio of Billy's friends, Nelly, Petey, and Turk, hung around every year and eventually lured Billy away every time to a basketball court across the way, next to a marina, just out of view of the lush panoramas the house's windows disclosed. In past years, I'd never been allowed to go with them because my mother forbade me to cross streets without her. Nelly, Petey, and Turk were older boys, too, and there was an aura of danger and mischief about them that she probably wanted to protect me from. Petey wore bell-bottoms and long-sleeved paisley shirts and sandals, but Nelly and Turk wore only tattered, soiled cutoffs with zippered flies slackened and made saggy and prominent by long summers of wear, and the dirt on their chests and backs and arms and legs mottled their deep tans. Their grime-streaked feet were always bare, toenails caked with what looked like wet gray sand, but they trod, fearless and dauntless, along gravelly ground as if their soles had toughened over time. (My own bare feet were tortured by the slightest pebble.) Before they coaxed Billy away, there was always much ritual hesitation on his part, the already familiar bout between familial and affectional bonds, about whether he should leave the cousin he saw only once a year for a game he could play in a company that was boisterously available any and every day. I always encouraged him to go, and watched every year, with longing and relief, as the four of them strode across the yard, toward the great lake, without me, and disappeared beyond a bait store at a bend in the road. My encouragement showed the advantage of a selfless sacrifice that also acknowledged the terrible mollycoddling, for which, of course, I was secretly grateful, but of which I hoped it was clear I was only the victim. My mother thought our country relatives unmindful and reckless, and they thought she was highly strung. But this was the year I'd cross the gap, find some route between these usually incommensurable dispositions.

It started with the crossing of that street—a swell of transgression, bringing me nearer the wide, open sea. The basketball court that taboo had forced me, over the years, to fancy was bigger, grander, more imposing, with higher, statelier backboards, than the one reality presented, with cracked, weed-choked cement and ragged, stringy nets drooping from asymmetrical hoops. We played Shirts and Skins, Nelly and Turk taking Skins because it was their glad and thoughtless destiny, Petey and Billy and I, already clad, Shirts, because it was our fate. The game was fast and rough, Turk crouched so close to me that I got whiff after whiff of his grimily sweet, close smell, and he flailed his arms, guarding me, with an athlete's thrashing grace. The second time he knocked me down,

I offered to even out the sides by sitting out, on an improvised doctor's sudden, makeshift orders. After the game, Turk and Nelly hurled themselves in a billow of sweat off a nearby pier into the bay, and their whoops and hollers as they leapt and splashed were so loud they riffled the sails and tilted the keels of the boats docked in the marina.

"So you got asthma?" Turk sat on the pier after his swim, cut-offs soaked from dusty blue to navy. Droplets of water trickled and dried on his chest—one drop beaded at the nub of a nipple—and he dangled his legs in the water, swinging his feet back and forth in a way I was sure would look sissy if I were doing it. I hoped I had imagined the extra weight he'd given to the first syllable of my condition—like Jack calling Piggy's affliction "ass-mar" in *Lord of the Flies.*

Officially, I thought, I did have asthma, or at least a doctor had once speculated that I might, though I hadn't had an attack since infancy. "Yeah," I answered, looking down at an angry, furrowed knot in a board of the pier. "I'm not supposed to run too much anyways."

Nelly stayed in the water, floating effortlessly on his back. He reached out suddenly to grab Turk's foot, a lazy incitement. Turk pulled away and kicked up with the assaulted foot an easy, fierce slash of water at Nelly, who spit and twisted and dove away. "Cut it out, pussy-wipe," Turk said coolly, "unless you're ready for a smart licken."

"I'm real scared," said Nelly, peacefully afloat again, folding his arms behind his head and languidly paddling his feet.

"You better be, pussy-lick." With no nod of the head, but only a bend of the voice, Turk turned attention back to me. "Why can't you run too much?"

Maladies, I reasoned, might lessen any pansy-assedness to be attributed to me, if it were adjudged beyond my control. Besides, since the nuances of so sophisticated a disease as asthma could easily elude country folk, I thought it might take more than a little shortness of breath to exculpate my early withdrawal from the game. "I got crooked toe-bones, too," I said, adopting the sheepish modesty of the gravely handicapped.

"Crooked toe-bones?" I caught him glancing down at his feet, curling his own dirty, wet toes. "Shit, I never heard of that."

"It's rare," I said.

The curled toes straightened again, the fine hair of the un-clenched knuckles glistening. "How do you get it?" he asked.

A congenital deformity was always preferable to an acquired one. "Born that way," I answered.

A brief silence allowed them to absorb this intelligence. Then Turk said, "Where's your Ma, anyways?" In the city, we said "Mom," curtly genteel; the open-ended drawl of his syllable, com-mon to the locale, implied some accusation.

Before I could answer, a big splash rose from the bay, the sudden expression of Nelly's boredom. "Do you live by Tiger Stadium?" he asked.

"Not too far," I answered. It was not technically a lie, though I'd never been there, only driven past. "I'm going this summer," I added.

"Team's crap this summer," Nelly said.

"When are you going?" Billy asked, surprised. If the brag were true, he would have expected to have heard it sooner. He and Petey leaned against big poles along the dock, and Billy had been choosing studied silence as the best safety against gilding by as-sociation with his enfeebled city cousin, while Petey had been staring distractedly out to sea.

"When David comes for a visit." The casualness of this was meant to provoke further interrogation, and I glimpsed a grati-fying rift right away in Petey's distraction. Something about the paisley and the bell-bottoms told me he would be the most impressed by what I was going to reveal, though it was Turk's interest I really courted. "He's coming this summer," I said.

"Who's David?" Petey asked.

"My pen pal," I said. "Out in California." I chuckled in a riot of self-effacement and exhibitionist modesty. "He's on TV."

"What's he on?" Billy asked guardedly.

"*The Partridge Family,*" I answered.

"David Cassidy?" Petey bolted forward, hot surprise sudden as a fist. *"You mean David Cassidy?"*

"So what," said Turk, with serene contempt. "What do we give two hoots and a half for about that fag anyways?" With that, he threw himself out toward the water, landing right on top of Nelly, set to him with clenching arms and legs, and the two of them fell together, shimmering forms, beneath the quickly recalmed but still foam-veined surface of the lake.

Far from stanching desire, rebuff can usually be counted on to aggravate it, and after the encounter on the dock, I demanded thenceforth that my own whims be attended unequivocally, pushing aside the meek inhibition I usually observed to persuade my kin I really was of their stock. I wanted to go to a drive-in, not to the family cookout, and I wanted to see a play, not go to the beach. I wanted to seek more cosmopolitan pursuits, not the usual backward rites, and in the aftermath of an unforeseen humiliation I would not be put off. The Cherry County Playhouse was performing a comedy called *Wake Up, Darling!* starring Robert Reed of *The Brady Bunch* fame, and the Grand Traverse Drive-in was featuring a movie called *Showdown,* starring Dean Martin and Rock Hudson. Though neither of these exhibits particularly appealed to me in its own right—Robert Reed was just a stuffy TV dad, and I hated Westerns—they both filled the general bill well enough, and I required the gratuity of packaged spectacle to compensate for the caprice of skittish consort, a predictably controlled environment in favor of an unmet chance.

If I could recruit my sister to the cause, I knew it could be won without recourse to tantrum, though the latter tactic could certainly not be ruled out prematurely. In any case, it was clear that Patty's compliance would be hard-won. "You're nothing but an ooky little fuss," she hissed. "I am not," I cried. "And you always have to get your own way." "I do not!" "I want to go to Aunt Sally's." "I want to go to the drive-in." "I want to go to the beach." "*I* want to go to the *theater!*" "You are just a snotty little brat." "*I am not!*" "And David Cassidy is *not* your pen pal, either." "I did *too* write him!" "And he never *ever* wrote back." She folded her arms emphatically, to signify the irreversible completion of a fully rested case. I tugged fiercely at the stubborn, knotted arms, as if merely to undo them would be to gain reprieve. *"Maybe not yet!"* I screamed. "Oh, like he's really going to write back to some mangy little fartfaced snot anyways." "He is, he is, he is!"

In truth he never did. I'd been moved to write to him by a feature in *Tiger Beat* called "Your First Date with David!" The layout of this feature depicted the presaged date in a series of overlapping photos with the camera occupying the enviable position of the eponymous "You." In that vicarious vantage point the reader was led breathlessly through the tastefully provocative date's many exciting phases, from first blush ("David's right on time, 'cuz he's always punctual and never late!") to last hurrah— the chaste front-stoop kiss only a fond peck on the forehead, the preferred leave-taking measure since levelheaded David refrained from "lip-kissing" (as the magazine helpfully coined it) on a first date. Everything about this compelling spread was poised to stir admiration. In the shirtless pose that began it, the arms were thrust back and the chest forward, the pert nipples boyishly erect, but nakedness apart, all thought of carnality was primly banished by the steady expedient of a wholesome smile. In the accompanying profile of David's likes and dislikes, I discovered what appeared to be a number of striking affinities between us. For instance, David professed his love of reading—though he lamented the lack of available time in his busy schedule of taping and concert gigs to pursue that occupation—and he disliked conceited people. I too loved to read and felt aversion toward those who put on airs. Although brief, tactful mention had been made of these affinities in my letter, the primary purpose of that missive had been to offer a joke for use in the script of his show. It had seemed most circumspect to initiate our contact on a purely business level, with the understanding that a more personal relationship could be cultivated between us, on the basis of the already noted affinities, following my gainful employment on the staff of *The Partridge Family*. (The proffered joke had been swiped whole-hog from a joke book, and boasted not even the remotest connection to the show's characters, themes, or attitudes.) This ambition, I had resolved, would go discreetly unadvertised until its fulfillment was a done deal; Patty's knowledge of the communiqué was the result of a momentary and regrettable lapse in the pledged discretion. After the consummate realization of the objective, friends and family could only be stricken with admiring wonder about how I had ever managed to keep so grand an imminence hidden. At home, I did not even mention in company (though I dwelt on the prospect in solitude) that I had put forward the egregious overture, though I would certainly not have thought of it as risk, and even David Cassidy's mere name, aglow with a new nimbus when intoned by heedless others, remained assuasively, superstitiously unspoken by my own judicious lips. Those formerly trustworthy lips had been loosened by travel, I thought after the episode on the dock, unhinged by place and distance. Away from home, where familiarity checked invention, I had somehow thought to prevail by creating a truth, showing my real stripe, even if it had to be made up out of whole cloth first. It was the hunger for wisdom that sped me toward miscalculation—and probably jinxed the outcome, since David Cassidy never did reply—and afterward, only the purest contempt for the rubes who had mocked me could slake the worldliness I knew was not yet mine.

Vacation begins with election and volition. The traveler chooses a place to go, and exerts the happy will to make the trip. The appearance of contrarian spirit around the issue of the family vacation, in the maturity of a family's history, is a common egress. As we kids got older, we grew to resist the enforced pleasures and convivial obligations of the ritual vacation. If, as was devoutly claimed, it was meant for our own enjoyment, then some small voice in destination and chronology should surely have been ours to raise. After a summer when Hardy's family went to Germany for nearly a month—and on an *airplane,* no less—our own abbreviated, proximate stints Up North started to seem ever less enviable, ever more deficient. The motivating power of jealousy in the acquisitiveness that shapes suburban life must never be underestimated; Germany was out of the question, but our demands were remorseless, and minor variations were slowly introduced into the annual routine. One year we drove to Toronto, where I learned to love the call and clamor of cities. Another year we went to King's Island, a theme park in Cincinnati, and there, in the strange and lazy drawl of the townies, I heard the exacting fidelity of region: language was a feature of place, as I'd already begun to suspect, as well as a function of mind.

Robert Reed was a pale substitute for David Cassidy, and Rock Hudson and Dean Martin no substitutes at all. *Wake Up, Darling!* turned out to be an Uproarious Farce (so the program described it) involving boudoir slapstick, mistaken identities, imagined cuckoldries, hilarious concealments, and hairbreadth escapes. Aside from Robert Reed's unrestrained mugging, the play's most striking felicities appeared in the design of the sets, with many real doors that snapped neatly shut in tight, unsteady frames, but with no walls around them. The plot required characters to run with mad abandon from room to room, in and out of these doors (frames wobbling every time), and necessitated, in one memorable scene, Robert Reed's ensconcement inside a closet, to prevent discovery by a jealous husband. The closet was a door without walls. Standing behind the door, inside the invisible closet, but in full view of the audience, Robert Reed continued his incontinent mugging without interruption, and the crowd howled with laughter. At the end of *Showdown,* after a tender but manly farewell, Rock Hudson rode off into a sunset that was painted gaudily on a sheet of muslin. To earn its persuasion, what was real needed what was false to buttress it; that need blurred the difference between what was false and what was real. I had gotten what I wanted, because my mother, in a phone call from home, had intervened on my behalf. The desires had arisen in her absence, but could only be rewarded through her mediation. The reward made the pain of her absence keener, but I'd still welcomed her absence at first, even desired it, and so authored my own woe. One day I would have to leave them all. The thought silenced me. My father and sister had roared with laughter during *Wake Up, Darling!* I'd sat beside them, watching the man on the stage hidden in bright light inside the imaginary closet, listening to the strangeness of the laughter, and only incidentally joining it. Afterward, they said I was still nothing but a little fuss, but they allowed as to how the play had not been such a bad idea after all, and on the trip back to the city, they teased me for my silence. The words I would have spoken would have been words they knew, because I had no others, but the meanings were different, and could not be conveyed. The hope of vacation is that we will come to know again those with whom we travel; the bane, that we can't. Maybe the past *is* a foreign country, but its quaint and onerous customs are still, for all that, only too familiar.

6

TENDER

All summer long my father listened to ball games on a little transistor radio that sputtered and squealed with static amid the persistent hums of the game. He'd lie stretched across the living-room couch, his hands folded behind his head, with the little radio balanced upright on his chest, as Ernie Harwell called the play-by-play, and the summer dusk shaded imperceptibly into darkness, while I'd lie on the floor reading comic books, aware dimly of the hoots and yawps and cheers ululating from the radio, or the lesser noises emanating from the street, until the light faded and I could no longer make out the colorful panels of the comic books or the sketchy word-balloons. Then I'd join my mother in the kitchen, where the television glimmered and murmured, and the ashen solemnity of *Peyton Place,* or the docile cheer of *My Three Sons,* would coax me to sleep.

Relaxation was rare in my father's life, even when he lay sprawled across the couch he'd still be wearing dress shirts and slacks, and the businessman's shoes whose resonant clomping woke me every morning when he put them on as he readied for work. That was what it meant to be a father: you wore heavy shoes and went off to earn Money. I might have had a less sharp sense of the oppression this arrangement entailed if I did not know where it was that he went. We had only one car, and on days when my mother needed the car, she would bundle us kids into the back seat to drive my father to work, in the sleepy dark just before dawn, so I knew that the place where he worked was a structure made out of somber brick, hulking in the antelucan light, with a big green door and a single slit of narrow, glazy windows along the top of each side, right where each wall angled into the flat concrete of the roof. Because the windows were so high, the point of them did not seem to be to permit views of the outdoors, and because they were glazed, they did not let anyone see in. Their function seemed to be like that of the slots I was always careful to carve into the top of a box in which I'd trapped a bug: though a heartening sign of the captor's humanity, these slots were meant only to prolong survival—and often they failed even in that stingy purpose—but they could never even pretend, and therefore did not aspire, to bring any greater happiness to the lives going on inside the confines of the box. The big green door opened with a heavy whoosh, and after my father disappeared behind it, it slammed shut with a blunt, metallic thud.

The only reason to go to such a place, day in and day out, was because there was, mysteriously, Money to be had there, and one needed Money to live on. While my father had never given any sense of taking particular pleasure in his job—it was just the thing he did, day in and day out, and the categories of like and dislike, so vital to my own life, seemed entirely irrelevant to his—it was clear that he was made uneasy by leisure. He called it "lollygagging," or "gilding the lily," or, inexplicably, "goosing the liver." After dinner, a meal he always consumed with hasty, businesslike efficiency, he read the paper with a similarly functionary briskness, holding the big pages aloft, scanning with a practiced appraiser's speed, especially the minute, impenetrable columns of the stock exchange, and turning the pages as a salesman might flip through stacks of samples in search of a pertinent one. There was no air of interest or curiosity in this enterprise, though industry and diligence were part of it, but some time later, when he put the papers aside and rubbed his tired eyes, a wistfulness would come into his eyes then, and he'd say, "Well, kid, maybe now we can take a little time out to goose the liver." Ritual atones for sloth: I knew the ritual, and so I'd jump up from where I was already encamped on the floor among comic books, and run off to fetch him the radio.

The radio was encased in a pouch of leather, porous in the front, with a weft of pinprick holes, like the ones in the wafers of an ice-cream sandwich. A tiny, delicately serrated knob at the side, in a niche of the pouch, when spun with a quick thumb, produced a wheezy rasp, like the whine of a Martian's sonar, and because I loved the feel of the radio leaping to life in my hand, I flipped my thumb up and down to turn it on and off over and over, before carrying it from its place on the bedroom bureau to the living room. This I did secretly, because my father would disapprove of such frivolity, as I knew he would disapprove of the immense pleasure I took in the smell of the leather pouch. Alone in my parents' bedroom, I stood beside the high bureau, held the radio to my nose, and sniffed my fill. That was when I noticed that my father's wallet, thickly folded, was also atop the bureau. This was an all-but-unprecedented circumstance, since the wallet usually left my father's pocket, as far as I knew, only when he was called on to pay for something. On an impulse, I reached for the wallet, also made of leather, and held it to my nose. Its pungency was muskier than that of the radio's pouch, more ripened, almost musty. The bills inside, all twenties, were all new, and so pristine they clung together, as an unused thing will to its mutual likes. I peeled one of the unfledged bills from the stack, which did not appear thereby to be noticeably diminished. Whenever I was alone in my parents' room, even if it was on a mission they themselves had assigned me, the room seemed guised in shadow, and I felt covered by a veil of secrecy. Maybe it was that feeling that led me, when my father shouted from the living room, to pocket the money. "Snap it up, kid," he yelled, "else we'll miss out on all the Say-can-you-sees!" I refolded the wallet and put it back on the bureau. I skipped down the hall, light with thievery, and, forgetting myself, flicked the little knob to turn the radio on and off again and again as I went, all the way until I reached the living room, when my father told me to stop.

As a student many years later, I studied the work of the Soviet filmmaker Sergei Eisenstein, and the piece among his corpus that most fascinated me was not one of the ardently dogmatic films for which he was famous, but a simple pen-and-ink drawing made in 1931, when he was in Mexico to make a film that was, as it happened, never completed. The sketch depicts Christ on a diminutive, canted cross, flanked on one side by a looming, sketchy female figure and on the other by another figure, smaller and eerily distorted, trailing a ghostly, larval child-figure by its upraised, amorphous hand. The drawing is whimsically primitive, perhaps in imitation of strains in Mexican art, but it also resembles the antic scrawls of James Thurber. The figures are embryonic, featureless, incorporeal, but what is really striking about the piece— as about so many of the greatest of Eisenstein's films—is the complexity it realizes in spite of its dogged conceptual simplicity. Carved in Christ's abdomen is a little slot, into which the figure on the left feeds little disks that could be coins, or could be the wafers of the Eucharist, and the hunched, maternal figure on the right holds a coin, too, apparently next in line for a deposit. The drawing is obviously a Marxist commentary on religion-as-the-opiate-of-the-people: the crucifixion as piggy bank. But its dogmatism is undermined in its execution. An ambiguity of perspective, an interplay of line, causes the viewer initially to confuse Christ's arm with that of the figure feeding coins into his body, and at first it appears that the Christ figure plants its hand against the other figure's forehead to hold off the insertion, and so forestall desecration. On fuller view, however, one is startled to realize that the hand pressed against the figure's forehead is its own, the arm twisted unnaturally backward. The arm of the Christ figure is, in fact, extended in an ambiguous reach, beyond the other figure, not in the attitude of an embrace, but in the spirit of abetment, as if the Christ figure welcomed the money. The drawing presents a discomfiting image of usury, made all the more uneasy by the didactic obscurity of its sexual overtones: one of the figures appears to represent erotic, the other maternal, womanhood, while the money-giving and money-taking cohere as bodily penetration, and a few errant squiggles—the mother's buttocks, the Christ-figure's pelvis—suggest that sexuality is not to be contained by anything so temperate as mere shape.

My own first experiences of money, as of so many of the roles of symbol, occurred in church. At every mass I was given a quarter to drop into the wicker basket that was held out, pew by pew, at the end of a long wooden pole, like a holy broomstick, by a deacon who passed from row to row, or else to deposit into a more portable container that passed from hand to hand among the congregants. I much preferred the baskets at the ends of the poles, brandished humbly by the deacons themselves, since that procedure seemed so much more ritually endowed, so much less worldly, than the baskets passed awkwardly, discommodiously, among yawning, snuffling, mumbling churchmembers—as if the whole thing were nothing but a slightly tedious game of hot potato. When these baskets came to me, I could still feel the sacramental thrill of offering as I dropped my coin into its modest bower of other coins and random bills, but it was when the deacon held out the basket at the end of the wooden pole, and I piously relinquished my coin into that more exalted receptacle, that I truly felt the surge of devotion. Then, it seemed I was transacting directly with the divine, dropping the coin, as it were, right into the unbloodied wound of Christ's eternal body, by which he had saved me from sin. And the exchange was gloriously reciprocal, like the magical commutations of a gum machine, where the plunk of a coin and the crank of a knob produced the colorful, sugary bliss of the gumball. So, in church, I received the consecration of a brittle little slab of host, took Christ's body into my own body, and gave in return the wafer, bright or dull, of a coin.

But the offering was never really mine to give. The money belonged to my father, who did not go to church. Whenever I ventured to ask why not, my mother replied, in a tone that was unreadable to me, "He's Lutheran." Awaiting the circulation of the baskets, I would sit between my mother and my sisters in the high pews, clutching the warmed coin in a tight fist, palms moist with the worry that God, a Catholic, would frown upon the offer of the Lutheran's coin. The exultation I could still bring myself to feel on dropping the coin into the sacred plush of the basket came more and more to merge with the fear that followed the offering: if God did not accept my coin, would He refuse me? I could no more imagine the fate of that coin than I could really fathom the source of my father's money. I knew only that I, called on somehow to enter these networks, was still outside of them; my participation was strictly a matter of gesture, of ritual. I imagined one of God's minions hunched among vast heaps of coins, biting down on the surface of mine, like a Dickensian miser, to test its mettle, and finding it wanting, in spite of my pale wish that the clammy lamina of my touch might linger, anointing the coin's face with the fervor of my hope. Though I must have absorbed by then Biblical edicts regarding the falseness of money and the sinful pride of accumulating it, these coins felt real as I held them in my hand, and in my experience the basest matter was still more visible evidence than the highest manifestation of spirit. As so often in devotional experience, in Eisenstein's drawing shame and supplication are one—the cowed figure at once advancing and withdrawing, taking the risk of oblation, yet flagellating herself in the bow of her head, a gesture beyond humility—and the shape of the coins mimics that of the shape of Christ's wounds. I had no money of my own: my piggy bank was always empty, not just because of the feverishness with which I spent money as soon as I came into it, but because the piggy bank itself, actually a leering porcelain monkey (I was reputed to like monkeys) with a dark gash in its belly, frightened me with its uncanny aspect. Though I looked with terror on the prospect of spending my life inside buildings of somber brick with big green doors and high translucent windows, I knew that, in any case, I could never really be welcomed in such places. The world did not owe me a living, as my father took to instructing me from the age of nine onward, and as I grew, the sound of my offering falling to rest in its commissioned place faded from the resonant echoes of veneration into the dingy, meager chink of lucre clattering against geld.

This descent was already under way by the time I stole the twenty dollars from my father's wallet. Like sex, money adumbrates a category of experience so basic that its pervasiveness shields its meanings; especially from the vantage point of a child, those meanings remain out of reach, so oblique as to seem, not elusive, for that would imply the possibility of access, but utterly impervious. The child clutching the coin feels, perhaps, a moment's thrill of gain before recognizing the impalpable power of kind, the unspeakably disproportionate rift between the infinitesimal and the infinite, that seems so fully to designate a child's relation to the world. A blade of grass, however sifted, scrutinized, caressed, or held like a reed between erect, paralleled thumbs, and blown upon, to make a music that could render all earthen grass as auratic art, still cannot yield the fullness of a field of grass, nor even of a reined-in square of manageable lawn; and a handful of sand brings one no closer to holding the greatness of the beach, the vastness of the coast. A coin is not Money itself, a bill still less so; it was, in fact, because I had stolen a bill, and not a coin, that I was able, for a little while, to hold off the guilt that would finally overtake me. Coins were actual matter, and even if bills were assigned a higher worth, they were still only paper. Coins took up broader space. They were likelier to be missed, and a thief's guilt is best measured not in the heinousness of the crime, but in the likelihood of getting caught.

"This bill is legal tender for all debts, public and private." The words were inscribed on the surface of the bill amid other random jottings and drawings, exuding an air of whimsical dignity, though as primitive in their way as Eisenstein's self-conscious scrawl, that pictured the White House, a president, oak-leaf clusters, leafy scrolls of border. The word *tender* made me think, for some reason, of tickling; I had come to believe that tickling was fundamental to the mysteries of sex, mysteries still so enigmatic I had no words for them, and was going through a phase of asking people regularly, and quite out of the blue, if they wanted me to tickle them. The night of the theft, I slept with the purloined bill clutched in my hand, and fell asleep tickling myself with its delicate, vellicative edges, silently repeating, *tender tender tender tender*— and the next day I spent the money.

I rode my bike up to Cunningham's and spent the money on refills for my toy gumball machine, a deck of magic cards, a big bag of miniature candy bars, and three paperbacks: *The Haunting of Hill House, Kiss Kiss Bang Bang,* and *Polyunsaturated MAD.* These expenditures left nearly half the money still undisposed of, even if more than encumbered already by the promiscuousness of my desires. The boy who tended the cash register had a face as sweaty and lopsided as a melting snowman's, with round white cheeks and a nose as pointy as a carrot, and I saw his envy of my acquisitions in his little beady eyes. The tips of his fingers tickled my palm as he counted out my change, and I noticed little wisps of hair, thrillingly different in color—burnished copper, not hale brown—from the tresses heaped moplike atop his head, and I felt pass in an instant from his body to mine the electricity of exchange. The money he gave me from the till was not his, any more than the money I had stolen was mine, but maybe it was true that no money was really anyone's, and money's only salient purpose among us was to bring the contact needed to pass it from hand to hand. The boy at the cash register was funny-looking, but the charge of his touch pulsed through me with slow, heavy power, like thick sap moving through a tree's trunk.

Studies show—they always show some damn thing—that kids figure out their relation to money, and to economy more generally, by the age of ten. By then, such studies suggest, kids know if they are poor, or rich, or somewhere in between. Even more to the point, they have formed clear notions about their numismatic futures—that they will always be poor, or that they may become a little richer than their parents were, or that their pecuniary possibilities are limitless, or that their lives aren't worth a plug nickel. There is probably no way to gauge the accuracy of such predictions, especially since I would guess that these predictions are rarely articulated, but by the time I stole the twenty-dollar bill from my father's wallet, I knew with absolute certainty that I would spend my life in a state of fiscal impotence, unfit ever to earn my keep. I was haunted by the unforgettable last scene of an extraordinary movie I'd seen on TV, *I Am a Fugitive from a Chain Gang*: the fugitive's genteel girlfriend, long after she has reluctantly given up on him, happens upon him in an alleyway, and she sees all at once the depth of his degradation, the dissolution of the life he has been forced to by nothing but inexorable circumstance, by the sheer inability to make himself into a decent breadwinner, and moved to pity and revulsion she asks him, "But where will you go? What will you do?" And then: you see his face, hard, scraggly, haggard, scared-eyed, and in the second before his face is swallowed up by the shadows that surround it, before he runs off—the hollow, fading noise of the footfalls is the last sound you hear—he answers, *"I steal."* The desolation of it chilled me every time I thought of it. But if such was to be my fate, I sometimes reasoned with a bitter shrug, then there was little point in deferring it—though most of the time I hoped to hold it off for as long as possible. Still, I wholeheartedly stole a pack of gum, giving myself up, and felt something of the thrill of larceny that would have to compensate me for the charms of an ordinary life; and sometime later, as my final crime, and despite the guilt that had finally overwhelmed me after the first time, I stole yet another bill from my father's wallet. If shame was my métier, then let me come into the closest possible union with it: the alleyway of destiny awaited me, only there would be no girlfriend to pity me; and it was that very lack, of course, already well gleaned, that predetermined my profligacy.

What I had not yet learned well enough by then was the hardness and the fastness of the rule of class. The myth of upward mobility dictates hard work as its only requisite, but for all intents, there *is* no myth of downward mobility. The truth is, though, that it probably requires as much effort to move down in a class system as it does to move up, only nobody ever really aspires to the former course, and the hidebound nature of the system insures that it will all come to much the same thing in the end anyway. I grew up and I flunked out of college in my first year, and my parents despaired of what would become of me. My father's inquiries along these lines were less delicate than those of the genteel girlfriend to the fugitive from the chain gang, and at length they drew from me the following impassioned outburst. "I don't even *want* a *job!*" I cried. "I don't even *want* to earn a living, okay, so why can't you just leave me alone? *I hate money!*" My father gaped at me, stricken with flabbergasted disgust, and then he began to laugh, a harsh, helpless, retching laugh that shook him to the core, and between spasms he repeated with reflexive derision my fiery declaration—"He hates money! *He hates money!*"—until the bout of laughter devolved into a fit of coughing, and he sank into a chair, limp as a deflated balloon, dazed when the fit finally passed, and muttering over and over, as he tried to get his breath, the impossible, preposterous, incomprehensible words: "Hates money . . . hates money . . ."

The only explanation I can think of for why my father's wallet should have bulged with all those new bills, tempting me with their uniformity and plenitude, is that it was around that time that he risked the American Dream, and started his own business, and must have needed a lot of ready cash on hand. It worked: our family moved, at least for a while, from the marginal lower middle class to the authentically *middle* middle class. Hatred takes two forms: vanquishment and possession. It is hard not to hate the idea of money, but nearly impossible not to desire the ideal of money. Poor most of his life, my father thought about money constantly, and about little else; and he must have hated it, at least as much as I claimed to, but his hatred took the form of possessiveness: a hyperawareness, a compulsion to accumulate and to gamble, a desire to achieve invulnerability to what he hated by at once getting it and risking it. It is impossible to imagine that my father did not miss the money I stole from him, but it was never spoken of. My own efforts to rise above money, to strive for an uncorrupted romance of impoverished, bohemian purity, were finally in vain: I was born into the inevasible middle class of the United States of America, and—even though I still feel as if I've never really *earned* the money I live on—there I remain.

The guilt, when it came, hit like an oceanic wave that lifted

me mercilessly and pitched me against a hard floor of sea, unexpected and completely unavoidable—all the more so, perhaps,
because of how successfully I'd avoided it until then. After I spent
the money, I reasoned that the worst of my sin was past, since the
change I'd gotten from the twenty could be declared theoretically
free of taint, and so spent guiltlessly. True, the twenty had been
stolen, but now it was gone, and the money that remained had
been given to me freely, and was therefore neither product nor
evidence of any theft. Money was a force, not a thing; but if that
was so, then why should a commandment so sternly prohibit its
pilfering? It was not mine. Nothing was mine. Was the act venial
or mortal? The crime of wanting—how blackened was my soul?
Please, raise me up. Tender faith: It is only because of the desire
to be good, only that, that one should be so troubled. Surely if I
were really bad, then I would stand in nothing but cold indifference to all venery. I would not suffer so. Was there not good, then,
in this suffering? But the volition of evil, perhaps, outweighs the
longing, however real, for good. The truly good do not suffer
guilt, but welcome it. They know they will be freed. I do not. It
is as I am, always, it is what I am. A good can be undone, but a
crime cannot. It can only be mourned, or regretted. The guilt of
loss, the shame of gain, and the terrible aloneness of both: the
tain of worth, the mire of worthlessness. Absolution only others
could grant. Want otherwise, desire otherwise, desire not. Help
me, save me, I cannot save myself. I steal. Forgive me, Father.
Forgive me, for I have sinned.

7

THE ANIMAL'S GLANCE

*I could continue to think about the matter, but the
animal had sunk back out of the stammer of its glance
into the disquietude where there is no speech and almost no memory.*

—Martin Buber, *I and Thou*

Lack calls forth desire, but it is desire that conjures lack. Every
gift-giving occasion in our family was a spur to disappointment,
because however lavish the endowments, they could finally only
serve as cruel reminders of what we wanted most deeply, and
could not have: we wanted a dog, but our mother forbade it. By
her lights, dogs were filthy animals. Fearing the contagion of dirt
above all others, she wouldn't even allow live plants in the house,
preferring gaudily genteel displays of strawflowers or—a prized
possession—the artificial palm tree flowering in a hallowed corner
of the living room, its mock-wicker pot overflowing with plastic
moss. My sister's desire for a pet was especially single-minded, and
it was not unknown, even after the most unrestrained orgies of
present-opening, for her to burst into tears and rush from the
room. In these instances she must have come face to face with
the irrevocability, the grim specificity, of desire. She had gotten

everything else she'd asked for, but she had not gotten a dog, and even the most extravagant offerings can never appease, can only taunt, if they appear to deny the very condition of want.

The truth was, I was far less committed to the desire for a dog than Patty was. "If I don't get a dog," she would confide in conspiratorial interludes when we were alone, "I am just about going to *burst*. I swear, if I don't get a dog, I'll bust wide open and spew my insides out all over the floor. If I don't get a dog, if I don't get a dog, *I'm going to go stark-raving mad*, I'm just going to break down and die! *Aren't you?*" Somewhat halfheartedly, I would agree that I was. But in fact I wasn't so sure about dogs. My sister's obsession was delirious and free floating, and it seemed that she would have been willing to accept any old dog, however ugly, however mangy, just so it was a dog. Not so I, and perhaps because I recognized that the prohibition was so entrenched, I found myself more amenable to the substitutions my parents engineered than my sister could ever bring herself to be. For her twelfth birthday—I was nine—she got two books about dogs, a cosmetics kit, the soundtrack album of *The Sound of Music,* and a toy gumball machine. I coveted these gifts ardently, and my sister seemed mildly contented with them too, until her class at school gave her a birthday party the next day. Her beloved teacher, Mrs. Miller, owned a pony, and she brought it to school that day for the kids to ride during the party, in a lot adjacent to the school. It was only after this brief but ecstatic contact with real horseflesh that Patty realized the paltriness of the gifts she had received, and she promptly repudiated them, swept them aside with a fanatic's intractable, clear-eyed sedition as the ersatz they were. I inherited the record and the gumball machine, and if my ready acceptance of the bequest caused me any worry about the staunchness of my own convictions, I was able to console myself by accumulating huge mouthfuls of gum—wads the size of baseballs—while listening over and over to "Edelweiss," the most beautiful song I

had ever heard. Patty had learned the value of dogged perseverance and unswerving commitment; from then on, she would not
be put off, and the agonized, excruciating sessions of pleading
with our parents, escalated, now typically ended with a new sally:
"If I can't have a dog, then can I have a horse?" For my part, I'd
learned that beauty is the only dependable compensation.

In American suburbia, the acquisition of the family pet consoli-
dates the family itself by way of the very processes of acquisition.
One need pause for only a moment over consideration of the
rituals of bourgeois pet ownership to see how readily they are
defamiliarized, made strange, yet how completely they have been
familiarized, accepted as ordinary. To be sure, among the other
things they are, they are, these rituals, exercises in the containment
of otherness. The pet is a profoundly foreign being, an animal,
welcomed into the family and, whether one views such reception
as induction or abduction, made one of its members, given a
name, granted a status, anthropomorphized into kin. Yet the terms
of the kinship remain indefinable. Is the pet to be understood as,
or even as like, a sibling, a child, a lover? The only thing that is
clear is that the pet cannot be understood as, or even as like, a
parent, unless it be an enfeebled one, for the pet requires care,
which is what parents are meant to give, and in that sense the pet
enables all members of the family, in relation to the pet, to adopt
at least provisionally the role of parent. Still, the pet vivifies a
heady range of possible relations within the family—the teasing,
playful affections of the sibling, the dependency and mischief of
the child, the physical immediacy of the lover.

The romance of the family is typically sustained by enforcing
clear distinctions and rigid boundaries among the types of relation
the family as a social unit makes potential. Every family is supposed to contain a pair of lovers, for instance, but the physical

dimension of the love must be hidden, displaced to the offspring that are its putative products, and whatever love circulates among the rest of the family, even if it is understood to be somehow generated by that of the lovers, must not reproduce it. The love within the family must differ, not in degree but in kind, from that which generated it, even if that love remains its chief model. The family pet is nothing more or less than a cute, cuddly gauge of consent to the prohibition of incest, yet its secret function, the one that evokes the joy with which it is so promiscuously embraced, is to threaten the clarity of boundaries that determine the emotional lives of the family. The family dog, in particular, becomes the vehicle of desire's circulation in the family, as it interacts freely with each member, licks everyone with the same unbridled tongue, nuzzles every crotch with the same direct curiosity, accepts in a spirit both innocent and openly sexual the bodily pleasure, the petting and cooing and stroking, given with none of the restraint the father must bring (for instance) to contact with his son. A family whose members might never touch one another would at the very same time think nothing of engaging routinely, one and all, albeit separately, in wild bouts of face-licking, back-rubbing, breast-kneading, full-body action with the family dog. To grant the deep strangeness of this daily condition is only a modest step beyond acknowledging how rarely we allow ourselves to think of parents as lovers.

In most extended families of bourgeois suburbia, I'd be willing to bet, there is someone like my Uncle George, a tall, taciturn man with big, heavy-soled shoes, giant hands, Joe E. Brown bucket-mouth, thin lips fixed in the long smooth arc of a permanent frown, hawked nose and beetling brow, high forehead and flat top (add a steel bolt at either side of the neck and you'd get a stock-company Frankenstein), whose plainspoken gruffness could ever be penetrated only by the family dog. Like your typical American dog family, Uncle George's family consumed a mini-genealogy of dogs over the years, always replacing the last one after a suitably brief period of mourning, and while I could only guess at Uncle George's grief at the passing of each pet, for I was never witness to it, it was clear, in a way that nothing else about Uncle George's emotional life was clear, that his love for each of the dogs, from Sport to Schatzie to Tiger to Honeypie (the last one, to his regret, he'd allowed his wife to name), was equally expansive, identically pledged. The dogs were devoted to him, and they'd sit at his big feet, accepting the endless caresses of the big hands that, in my view, touched no other living creature, but opened themselves to the bodies of the dogs with a tranquil, undisguised love. If I ever saw Uncle George play with his sons, I don't remember it, but every visit to his house found him out in the yard, throwing sticks for the dogs to fetch, over and over, a show of pampering too indulgent to call patience, except by contrast to the impatience he exhibited in every other circumstance. Only then, throwing that stick, would the arc of the permanent frown, still retaining its blunt severity, slowly remold itself into the brief reprieve of a temporary grin.

Uncle George was only one of the many types of pet-lover— the intemperate wrangler, rolling across the carpet with dog in arms, the childless couple for whom the coddled pet serves as surrogate offspring, the genteel comrade whose love is soulful and whose pet must learn to content itself with the odd brisk pat— but a whole catalog of them would only go to show the link of displacement and desire that, if not a condition of every love, surely inflects the love of every pet. The most straightforward love of a pet typically subsumes a quality of giddiness, something nascent, that if allowed to ripen might turn to horror, for it is nothing but the undercurrent of recognition: a love as open, as direct, as nobly inarticulate, and as steeped in loyalty as it is free of commitment and fetter as the one the pet offers, which we can only strive to reciprocate, gives the lie to the restrictions on the kinds of love we might feel ourselves capable of. The pet's love is an ideal that shames us with the sense of how profoundly the kinds of relation we pursue, infinitely more complex than those of an animal, but impoverished for all that, would need to be changed, if such an ideal were ever to be realized. Uncle George's love of his dogs may have been only a vicariated version of a love for his sons too freighted to express. I have no doubt, though—because I saw it—that his sons' play with the dogs, too charged with want ever to be truly carefree, sought mysterious transmissions of the love they too saw that their father had given, but not to them.

For those who grow to queer desire, congress with a pet is often their earliest experience of it; for those who don't, sometimes their only one. The pet's love is deeply bisexual, the constraints of gender relaxed; we project our categories onto pets, of course—thinking of cats as feminine, for instance, or dogs as masculine—but the allure of the pet is to enable these projections while still standing in complete indifference to them, or to any of the categories determined by merely human language, and the question of whether a given pet is male or female is usually exhilaratingly moot. Girls can love equally the boy cat or the girl dog, without even really feeling bound to distinguish between them as truly gendered beings, and the only time a boy can lovingly enfold another boy in his arms without fear is when the other boy is a pet. The practice of neutering answers imperatives of domestication, to be sure—the hand of repression is never really asleep—but it derives from the many senses of the pet's ambisexuality, as both a tribute and a measure of control. Indiscriminacy may be the gay man's sin, but it is the pet's charm, and the undeniably sodomitic aspect of canine copulation inevitably provides an early inkling to those who witness it even furtively that there may, just may, be more than one way to skin a cat.

Melanie Klein says that every gift is meant to lift some burden of guilt. In our state of intolerable deprivation, my sister and I began to feel we could no longer even think of ourselves as a real family. At the end of yet another unfruitful conference of pleading, during which Patty had literally writhed on the floor in agonies of desire before our unyielding parents, she finally collapsed on the rug in defeat, then lifted her head a moment later to ask bitterly, "Was I adopted?"

Even the grotesque pets of so many of our coevals conferred a sanctity on their households that ours, petless, was denied. One cousin had an old dog with a dead leg and red, slime-coated eyes, an animal that dragged its failing, reeking body forward with its two front legs alone; a playmate down the block owned two gigantic alley cats with mangy coats, tattered ears, and spindly legs twice as long as their roly-poly bodies, so that when they arched their backs to hiss, a practice their foul tempers made regular and their thick bellies difficult, their forelegs would become intertwined with the ropy stalks of their hind legs. Coming into contact with such animals made me aware of the unthinkable oddness of pet ownership. It would have seemed no less strange to me if the houses that harbored these ungainly creatures had also given berth to assorted misfit monkeys, big-eyed lemurs, or tame armadillos padding from room to room. Yet even these freakish pets were better than the pale substitutes—stuffed toys, every book in the Lassie, Flicka, or Stormy series—that were all our parents would offer. Finally, though, the incessantly repeated claim that their refusal of a pet condemned us forever to be less than a real family got to be more than they could bear, and they gave in. But it was the submission, still, of the dominant. They got us a fish tank.

The aquarium stood alight in a paneled corner of our "finished" though still slightly gloomy basement. The little red rocks that lined the bottom of the tank resembled a lush array of a brand of novelty bubblegum I loved at the time—nuggets like forty-niners' gold that came in a sack with a drawstring—and the whole idea of the fish tank appealed to me because there was an aquarium in the waiting room of my pediatrician's office, a huge rectangular vessel of glass that ran the length of one wall, inside a big oaken cabinet, below the rainbowlike vault of a shark's body (*Is it real?* I wondered at every visit) mounted on the wall. Seated on the bench in front of the aquarium, peering at the vivid simulation of briny depths within, watching the calm, variegated collectives of placid fish gliding through the water in improvised schools or makeshift solitudes, I discovered the only comfort that was ever to be found in that place. Our aquarium was a fraction of the size of the one at the doctor's office, a simulation of a simulation, and the stool before it accommodated only one sitter at a time, but still I hoped to regain, seated in front of the fish tank, something of that familiar solace, even if only a fraction of it in proportion to the reduced scale, of gazing upon tranquil rounds of aquamarine life.

The trajectory from giddy novelty to well-versed privity is known to every lover, and is either sought or feared. As a rehearsal for the conditions of the domestic, the lessons of pet ownership in the disposition of the lover may, in theory, mean to teach the deepening of love in the onset of ken, after the bloom is gone. In practice, however, these lessons can provide one's earliest sad schooling in love's passing, from first passion to late affection, a deepening experienced, at times, as a slackening. One may still love the too-known pet—the crabbed cat, hardened in habit, or the flatulent old dog—but it is not the same love extended so fervently in the first blush to the adoring kitten, the devoted puppy. The fish began as fire-new wonder, the electric-colored tetras certifying the existence of neon in nature, the stately angelfish showing the prevalence of grace, the wild-whiskered algae-eaters the need of workers in even the most leisured societies, and the whole mass, in its diversity and tropical color, proving the universality of community's contracts. But it took only a week or two for them to move from that state of glory to a subsequent state of outworn obligation, when the most burning question they raised was who would have to clean the tank. The aquarium was an enclave of sterility, equipped with its own swimming-pool-like apparatus of cleanliness (filter, mini-vac) that made it safe for bourgeois consumption, but one afternoon, when one of the oldest of our mollies, whose swollen belly had escaped our attention, began spouting little white maggoty larvae and then, before my disbelieving eyes, without so much as a by-your-leave, blithely eating them, it was clear that all the instruments of the antiseptic, humming along in happy concert, could only *seem* to hold the dirty needs of living bodies at bay. It was hard to imagine the blunt, scary reality of sex taking place in that pristine environment, yet there the evidence was. We managed to save a few of the little white tadpoles from parental cannibalism, but this second generation of fish was an unbeloved one. We'd seen the true nature of fish, the irrefutable power of instinct, and we knew that even these fish, the ones we'd saved, would revert in a flash, belying the civilized gratitude of which they were really incapable, to the irresistible degeneracies of their kind. As they died off, one by one, the fish went unreplaced, and the fish tank's knell was a long, desolate period of flagging ruin, a deathwatch, ending with two final, desperate, confused, spooked-looking fish, drained of color but clinging to life—even though they were clearly, despairingly perplexed by the cruel fate that decreed they abide as the last of their kind—darting crazily to and fro amid now-untended murk. It was with some relief that the aquarium was finally unplugged, emptied, cleaned one last time, and stored in a closet.

The substitute's triumph is a gradual, hard-won process. You have to *learn* to accept the replacement for your true desire, and by the time you do—this is what our family's experience with pet ownership taught me—you're likely to find that the substitute is as close as you'll ever get to the real thing. It will perhaps come as no surprise that the fish tank did nothing to shut my sister up. Her reactions to the fish themselves were a complex mixture of contempt and a forlorn pity that could even, given time, have edged little by little toward a degree of affection. Patty looked upon the fish with mitigated scorn, because their status as substitute was so clear, yet she pitied them, because they were such helpless pawns in our parents' pathetically transparent stratagems to make her forget her real desire, which they persisted in denying. It was not the fishes' fault that they were fish, and not dogs. The pleas for a dog went on, unabated, given if anything an *extra* charge by the terrible lurking fear, made more real by the fish, that one might always have to accept a substitute, that all of life would wane, with never a dog to love.

Our next pet, a cat, was a somewhat better substitute, nearer a dog, suggesting at first that we might be rising gradually, hopefully, to the sought-after apotheosis. The kitten was the product of the litter of a neighbor's cat, and she was already some months old when we persuaded our mother to let us have her on a trial basis. Her coat was the color of butter gone slightly rancid, and so we named her Butterball. We'd made a few stabs at naming the fish, but we could never tell them apart consistently enough to make the names stick. The naming of the cat was therefore our fullest share of the proprietary thrill, the humane conditioning afforded by the fact of the family pet. It was to remain so, for it soon became clear that we were not gifted with the rudimentary solicitudes or the sophisticated indifferences inspired pet owners tend, without ever even thinking about it much, to cultivate. In no time at all, under our family's anxious tutelage, Butterball metamorphosed from a sweetly carefree kitten to a skittish, mean-tempered cat. Our mother had agreed to the trial run because she thought cats were cleaner than dogs, but she still wouldn't allow Butterball in the house, so the cat spent much of her time in a big box in the garage, a living arrangement that could only provoke bitterness and misery. When Butterball finally stopped eating, we spent hours trying to coax her, pushing the food into her resistant face or forcing her to watch as we shrilly mimicked our own mock-delighted consumption of it. She grew thin, and all night in her box she caterwauled, the whines weakening by the night as, day by day, we helplessly watched her feline vigor fade. She wasn't happy. We could not make her happy.

To me, this came as no surprise. After all, we were the family who couldn't do anything right, for whom the assembly of the simplest toy (how I dreaded those portentous words "Assembly Required"!) always devolved into a riot of exorbitant frustration, of mismatched parts and feverish quests for lost screws; the family for whom so common a task as the installation of a garage-door opener, which no other family in history, to my knowledge, had ever had any trouble with, became a sprawling spectacle of shamefully unconcealable ineptitude, entering neighborhood lore by requiring two excruciating weeks of hit-or-miss antics; the family that could never even get the hang of the operations of the swimming-pool filter. Our filter, though built with the most painstaking, nervously exacting adherence to the instructions, still reversed its proper functions in practice: it sullied, not cleansed, the pool's water, and after many months of failed efforts at correction of this inexplicable situation, we could only in the end resign ourselves to it. For years, until the day a windstorm made the pool's aluminum sides cave in, we plashed about like clumsy seals in water whose filter seemed to suck out cleanliness and spit back dirt. We lived in a world of unworkable gadgets, malfunctioning appliances, and ballywacked toys that it seemed wiser, on the whole, to leave broken than to subject to a course of repair both doomed to failure and likely to make things worse. When my mother, late in the day, finally got her long-wanted dishwasher, it made her so nervous that she went on thoroughly washing the dishes by hand before loading them into the spanking-new machine.

How could such a family ever hope to nurture a pet? I'd always secretly dreaded getting a pet, I realized, because I was afraid we wouldn't be able to take care of it, to figure out how it worked. It wasn't that we didn't follow the directions that accounted for our collective mechanical impotence, and it wasn't neglect but a hopelessly ineffectual vigilance that nourished Butterball's relentless decline. Either you've got it or you don't—that is the lesson of the family pet, and it's a lesson that partakes of the bluff wisdoms by which we come to learn sexualities as surely as the image of the tamed animal corresponds to the civilized hopes of our gnomic metaphors for our sexual selves. It soon became obvious that if we kept Butterball she would surely die. We comforted ourselves that giving her up would be the best expression of our love, but we must both have feared, my sister and I, the portent of later failure in this benevolent renunciation. This last lesson in the cult of the pet doubled as early instruction in the ways of heartbreak.

"An animal's eyes have the power to speak a great language," writes Martin Buber in his fiercely reserved but expansive meditation on the concept of relation, *I and Thou*. In quiescent moments of exchange, looking into the eyes of a cat, whose eyes register traces of consciousness at least in their consent to look back, Buber discovers the prototypical transactions of self with other. These entail curiosity, surprise, the flattery of acknowledgment, the sensation of another's awareness, experienced as if it were anything but oblivious consciousness of ourselves. The language Buber brings to his account of these moments is the language of transcendence, but if these moments make possible the hoped-for conversion of the *It* into the *Thou*—of the meeting with the world of objects not oneself into the intuition, the apperception, of divine presence—they still end in a reversion touched with Buber's lordly, earthy conviction of the hopeless poignancy of the human condition: "In no other speech have I known so profoundly the fleeting nature of actuality in all its relations with being, the exalted melancholy of our fate, the change, heavy with destiny, of every isolated *Thou* into an *It*." The common postulation of exchanged looks with animals as a gauge of relation, or as a model of otherness, may reveal only how steeped is relation in dominance. We look to the cat for the confirmations of the other because we think a cat lives somewhere between the human and the insensate, and we are continually reassured by the need of creatures whose dependencies we invent. Claude Lévi-Strauss ends *Tristes Tropiques* with an image strikingly similar to Buber's, whose book Lévi-Strauss may have known: "[A]n essence . . . may be vouchsafed to us in a mineral more beautiful than any work of Man; in the scent, more subtly evolved than our books, that lingers in the heart of a lily; or in the wink of an eye, heavy with patience, serenity, and mutual forgiveness, that sometimes, through an involuntary understanding, one can exchange with a cat."

Now: Flash-forward—I'm grown, and living on my own, far from the site of my childhood, pursuing desires easier to achieve but harder to understand than those of my childhood, and I'm saying good-bye to a man I have loved as deeply as any man I've ever loved. He is leaving me (that's how I understand it, even though we were never really "together") for another man. Gay men will have accomplished nothing, I believe, if we do not create new kinds of relation—to one another, and to others, and to ourselves—different from the ones we have been given. This man is leaving me because he wants kinds of relation more like the given ones than I want, and he knows he cannot have those with me, but thinks he might be able to have them with this other man. That is how I understand what is happening, and whether or not it is true, I know that I understood it this way at the time so I could go on loving the man, as I knew I wanted to, after he had left me. He is leaving me, but at the moment it is I who am leaving, departing, after having spent the afternoon at his house, saying good-bye to him. I've embraced him, folded in his warmth, the nearness and knownness of his smell, and now his cat, Cadmus, is rubbing against my leg, in a request for some share of the attention. Two memories, minor but powerful, converge at once. In the middle of the night he calls me and asks if he can come over to put his arms around me. That is just the way he puts it, and how characteristic it is (I think, in the swell of nostalgia), the immediacy, the middle-of-the-night off-centeredness, the physical directness, in love with the lure of synecdoche. How characteristic of him. Another time: We're playing with the cat, sprawled across the living-room floor, bathed in a pure afternoon light, endlessly teasing the cat with a ball of yarn, and playing our fingers together upon the hair of Cadmus's proffered belly, laughing, but not talking, for a long time—a mute, shared pleasure. Months later, about the man he has left me for, the man who is leaving me says, dryly, in passing, "Our best times together are when we don't talk," and I think right away, again, of the time we played with the cat, fighting off the crude rise of sentiment that rules me and would, unresisted, make me say, "Do you remember that time when . . . ?"

"Oh, Cadmus," I cry, "did you think I would forget you? How could I ever forget my own dear, sweet Cadmus?" I lift the cat in the air, hands under haunches, cat legs dangling with loving docility, and I look, deeply, into the cat's whiteless, glittery eyes. The man who is leaving me, but whom I'm leaving, has eyes I would think beautiful, I'm sure, even if I did not love him, placid and piercing at the same time. But though I later chastise myself for this prideful, frivolous refusal of a last pleasure, I don't let myself look into his eyes now, as I leave. Instead, I look into the cat's, and the cat, tail twitching in provisional pleasure, looks back. *Is it possible that you think of me? Do I exist in your sight? Do I really exist?* "Good-bye," I whisper. "Cadmus, good-bye." And Butterball, now many years dead; the cat we didn't know how to love, or for whom our helpless love could somehow provide no real sustenance: Looking into her eyes for the last time, I could not demand, *Don't forget me.* I could only ask, and only of myself, *Will she remember me?*

"Heavy with patience, serenity, and mutual forgiveness"—but what is it the animal forgives, and of what do we forgive it? Even though Lévi-Strauss does not answer the first question directly, the answer is to be found, I think, at the end of his book's penultimate chapter. The world was not ours to destroy, Lévi-Strauss says there, and yet we destroyed it, and did so knowing all the while that no other world would ever be given us. That is a thing that we did—it would never have occurred to animals, our enemies, compatriots, and cherished pets, to do it—and a thing much in need of forgiveness. But what is it, then, in these pregnant encounters, that *we* forgive? The pet looks back, inquisitive, but without judgment. It has no thought to characterize, or to make us believe we should be other than what we are. The animal's glance *reminds* us of what we are—that is its only wrong—or persuades us toward discovery, and for that we bestow forgiveness, so as not to have to acknowledge the reminder. It is a different kind of forgiveness from the one we imagine we find in the happy, yielding eyes of pets.

8

INITIATE

The two cultures, we're told, divide squarely along the line that separates art from science. For donnish, cultivated, well-fed and well-heeled, comfortably poised, Olympian types like C. P. Snow, purveyor of this famous hypothesis, that partition may well have held true. But in the here and now, many a seventh-grade boy will tell you, the split lies elsewhere. Art, at least in some rarefied form, may still occupy one side of the gulf, but on the other, rising forbiddingly like a Gothic manor of too many rooms, with a dark steeple housing a bodeful bell that tolls for us all, looms *gym*.

That year began as an extended experiment in leave-taking. It was in November that we were scheduled to move. My parents had hoped to cinch the deal on the new house before the school year started, so that my entry into the new world of junior high would not be sundered, but the negotiations dragged on and on, and by the time school began I found myself, in the company of my lifelong peers, whom I was bound to leave, ascending to the stern but familiar portals of MacArthur Junior High. The place had been my destiny forever, but if the satisfaction of a fate fulfilled was upset by the prospect of the move, it was offset by the aura of departure. The news of my impending move was widely public, and it wreathed me in a nimbus of farewell, while touching all around me, the people and places I'd spent my whole life among, with the light of elegy.

In this warm pure light, the terror of starting junior high was diffused. But in November, at my new school, it would be redoubled; and even in the valedictory atmosphere of these last days, I still tried to see it plain: new school, new teachers, new kids—and I the newest. There, in that new place, the glow cast by the approach of my departure would abruptly convert into the dark plunge of my arrival. Flint, the school I would be transferring to, held no place in my private mythology. It had never been foretokened as a goal, and its aspect was portentously modern, a one-storied sprawl of brick and steel, while MacArthur, with its high windows and homely wooden ceiling beams and lush courtyards, harkened back to the quaint schoolhouses of days of yore. Just as the house we were moving into, an L-shaped ranch with a built-in garage, a sliding doorwall, an oblong porch, white limestone brick, and black trim around the windows, told of a new era on the rise, so the school, built to accommodate the district's boom of births, was only another inexorable step on the automated walkway—like the roads in *The Jetsons*—to the space age. Not only was I being nudged upward, unwilling, toward the undesired pinnacle of junior high, but I was at the same time being hurried into a dropsical future that I dreaded and despised.

The strangeness and the newness of MacArthur were vitiated not just by its mythical dimensions in my inner life, but by the fact that my sister had already gone there for two years, and not only survived but flourished, and by the fact that everyone else I knew went there too. On the first day of seventh grade, in gym class, as I stood dripping and humiliated from my first public shower, the gym aide who was distributing the towels fixed me with a bold, inquisitive look. He was one of the Swann brothers, Keith and Kelly, twins, both ninth-graders and gym aides; and though I would learn in the months to come to distinguish them by the moles on their cheeks (Keith's on the right, Kelly's the left), by the curl of their hair (Kelly's downier, Keith's straighter), and by the tint of their skin (Keith's a shade lighter, Kelly's a shade darker), I couldn't tell them apart then. The Swann twin in question stood in the doorway of a low-lit bunker with two barred steel panels, like cell doors in prisons, the bottom one secured and the top one open to allow him to reach over it and issue the towels. He wore only gym shorts, and I noticed that a pattern of freckles on his chest resembled the configuration of the Little Dipper. He was about to give me my towel when a burst of recognition made him pull it back on instinct. "Hey— you're Morrison, aren't you?" he asked. I squinted at him through the haze of myopia and the mist from the showers, and acknowledged that I was. "Your sister's a real doll!" he hooted as he passed me my towel. "She's a living doll!" I covered myself with the chintzy warmth of the towel. In this gym, terrible as it was, I could still be clothed in familiarity. At Flint, where I knew no one, and where no one knew me, there I would be truly naked.

Junior high—this was its scariest claim—demanded growth. That demand was its whole point, its very reason for being, and the demand lurked everywhere. The demand was not satisfied simply to be met wherever it appeared, which was, to repeat, everywhere. It was not enough to show merely that one was capable of such growth. The refinements of theory were all very well, but it was the rigor of strict practice that junior high most pitilessly called forth. *You must change your life!* was the blunt admonition, unspoken but ubiquitous, of junior high. And even at that, it was not enough to thrust aside the childish pleasures and infantile beliefs that one had formerly cherished, or to renounce the mewly kid one had previously been content to be. No: the safest haven, the surest course, was to show, or at least to affect, that one had already attained the expected maturity, already learned and accepted the ultimate truths that junior high laid bare. Junior high was not a place where one would learn—and this was itself one of the countless lessons prerequisite to one's strenuous probation there. It was a place where one was called upon, routinely but without mercy, not to gain new knowledge but to exhibit knowledge, the prideful knowledge of a lifetime's progress, as a fundamental condition of one's survival.

Restriction and choice were the contradictory elements of this demand for growth. Everyone had to take gym, and everyone had to take a shower in gym, each and every day. The upright efficiency of showering as an activity, so much more expeditious than a child's dawdly baths, itself heralded and certified nascent adulthood, even if the brisk revelations the showers enforced showed the limits that still obtained upon maturation. Stripping away protections, these compulsory showers were seized on by those who got the point of junior high as forthright opportunity to demonstrate that they had no need of these protections. If comfort were needed—and if comfort *were* needed, it was best not spoken of—it could be taken in the idea that everyone else was in the same boat. The restriction of rule included the advantage of unanimous observance. Freedom of choice brought the detriment of ambiguity. One was granted new reign to choose what science to take, for instance, and thereby given handy occasion to profess yet again that what appeared to be a dizzying discovery—that there were differing sciences—was really a truth universally acknowledged, nothing but the affirmation of a long-recognized fact. But that freedom also entailed the facility of exploration. In seventh grade, for the very first time, one whole hour was reserved as an open elective. Most girls took Home Ec. Most boys took Shop. I took Drama.

For many years, whenever anyone had asked me what I wanted to be when I grew up, I replied that I wanted to be an ice-cream man. It was, in its way, the truth. I admired the spanking-white uniform of the ice-cream man, and liked the idea of spending my days cruising slowly through the quiet streets of neighbor-hoods in the clean white truck, with its tinkling bells and its emblems of various types of ice cream glowing like colorful stars on the vehicle's pristine sides. To unlatch the icy vault and pro-duce desired treats, as if by magic, from the lush bed of frost within, and to give a kid his heart's desire—that was a job that brought real good into the world, surely, a job I could hold with genuine pride, and if nearer access to the ice cream itself were a sideline benefit of the trade, that should not have been seen to compromise the altruism that motivated it. In truth, though, my commitment to the profession was only moderate, so much so that even the seasonal nature of the occupation, which should have been obvious to anyone sufficiently concerned to grant the matter a moment's thought, had never been present to me as a possible limitation upon means of livelihood. When a grown-up asked once what, if I were an ice-cream man, I would then do in the wintertimes, I reasoned for a minute and, thinking on my feet, answered somewhat crossly that of course in wintertime I would be a fireman. But the fact was that the real answer to this most predictable of grown-ups' questions was that I did not want to grow up; or that, alternatively, I wanted to grow up just enough so that I would be freed from the obligation to answer such inane questions, but never enough so that I might be in danger of being stricken by whatever numbness of the mind, universal among the grown-ups of my acquaintance, instilled the compulsion to ask them. The answer that I wanted to be an ice-cream man was at bottom little more than an expedient. I'd learned that grown-ups thought that answer was cute, as much for its maverick pluck when it was new as for its ritual durability as the years went by and it came to be so redundantly honored by time's passage. By seventh grade, though, the cuteness of the old answer was starting to wane. I'd keep reciting it, seeking vengeance for years of persecution by craftily provoking the mounting alarm the old answer now appeared increasingly to incite. But growth seemed inevitable after all, and there was a new answer, a truer one: I wanted to be an actor. It was all too clear that my principal appeal among grown-ups, cuteness, would soon be a thing of the past, if it were not already; but it was not at all clear what quality, if any, might rise up to replace the elapsed one. On those rare occasions when I gave the new, honest answer to the old question, it too spurred alarm, a different kind of alarm from that generated by the old answer. Day by day, I could *feel* it happening: the cute, winsome boy, turning into a willful, gawky parody of a man. And I knew it would only get worse.

Drama met in the cafetorium. In its capacity as *auditorium*, the cafetorium was a big open room of three split levels, across the hall from the gym. At the end of class, the custodians would start to roll out the tables for lunch hour, and when I came back for lunch after gym, my next class, I was constantly struck by the room's transformation. At lunch, the atmosphere in the cafetorium was noisy, dazy bustle. In Drama it was concentrated, introspective energy. Drama was metamorphosis, and the room's transformation attested daily to this truth. We'd start our warm-up acting exercises each day in the pit in front of the stage, a sunken plane bordered by steel rails that supported thick planks of wood. At lunchtime we were forbidden to play on those beams, but in Drama we were encouraged to make use of them—for why should a thing exist, if not to be used, taken for what it was, or made into what it could be? Drama was improvisation; it was making things up, or letting things be what they really were by imagining that they might be otherwise. Anyone could predict the future; only an actor could make up the past.

"*Be* something!" the Drama teacher cried, in her characteristic spirit of enthusiastically moderated abandon. "You can be whatever you want, but be *something!*" Feet planted on the floor, hands spread into the air, she swayed from side to side, and made a whooshing sound with her lips, her eyes closed, and her face calmed in an expression of beatific, sleepy reverie. "Ooh, I'm the wind!" she chanted. "I'm the wind—what are *you*?" "I'm a monkey," answered Bobby Adams, hanging from the beam, wrapping himself around it with a gymnast's methodical passion, exulting in the freedom at last to hang from the forbidden beam; and I, a tree in early autumn, rooted to the ground amid my hyperactive classmates in a performance that made up in inner intensity what it lacked in outward show, cringed. He was no more a monkey than I was a monkey's uncle, and, brazen opportunist that he was, he would have claimed any half-baked identity, so long as it gave him an excuse to swing from that beam. But Drama was equanimity, and all things were equal, at least to the extent that one could be any of them, and I was a tree. So I closed my eyes, and put the triteness of Bobby Adams out of mind. My branches were hale and stout, the slightest quiver only to acknowledge the coming decay that was the fate of all things. My own restraint was deeper than my peers' exuberance was loud, and the resignation with which I, a tree, awaited the melancholy onset of fall, and tolerated all the while the lesser lights of my surroundings, was an ennobled one.

The Drama teacher's name was Mrs. Henning, and I was in love with her. Most of the time she taught English, but one hour a day she taught Drama. She wore fuzzy black sweaters, and flowing black skirts, and dangly black earrings so exotic I would be able to identify their shapes only years later, when I studied Geometry. She told us we could call her Betsy, but only in Drama, because in Drama we were equals. At the start of the day's exercises she would snap off the earrings and hold them in her hands as she closed her eyes and began slowly to sway back and forth, her long silken hair waving, the dream of Drama about to descend on her, to reveal to her what she should be. As the exercises intensified, she would place the earrings on the edge of the stage and move quickly, muse-like, among the dancing or writhing or vegetating or spastic students grouped in the pit, imitating their motion or lack of it, mirroring their own simulations. "Be deep inside yourself," she would intone. *"Now leap out!"* And we would, on cue, all freeze, and open our eyes wide, and spread our arms and look around us, seeing the world anew. "Now go back in!" she'd say, and we would hug ourselves and close our eyes and lower our heads, burrowing within. "Now out! Now in—out, in, out, in!" It was needful that we come to know the exhilarating permeabilities between the self and the larger world. She'd flit from student to student, not fickle, not promiscuous, but all-embracing, and when she came to me, my heart leaped up as she faced me, moving her hands in synchrony with my own, up and down against an invisible wall, so that the wall became a mirror, and the wistful vivacity of her expression as she gazed at me through the imaginary mirror reflected my own. If only she would have me, then she alone might save me from a fate—the one I longed to avert, but could never put aside—that seemed more certain by the day. When I was thirty, she would have lived for half a century. But I had a better secret than that in my heart: When a century was past, then we two, in a life where we would mingle everlasting with all the world's redeemed mortals, would be the same age at last.

This fancy came to me largely courtesy of the heartrendingly sad, beautiful ending of *Candida,* a play by George Bernard Shaw that I had just read. I had come to the work quite by accident: I'd decided if I was going to be an actor, then I needed to read plays, and at the time a spirited popular song of the same name, by Tony Orlando and Dawn, happened to render Shaw's play, by circuitous association, an object of possible interest. In the play, the poet Marchbanks falls in love with the earthy, ethereal wife of a stuffy but humane pastor; in the end, with little in the way of the tiresome dramaturgy of romantic triangles—in fact, nothing much happens in the play—Candida tells the poet that she will remain with her husband. The play's tragedy lies not in the unjust or absurd disruption of a society's order, as in most tragedy, but in its very endurance. Conventionally speaking, the play is not a tragedy at all. Nobody dies, and there are no betrayals, no desperate intrigues. In fact, without exception, everyone in the play behaves perfectly well. The poet is right to love Candida, and Candida is right to stay with her husband, and she does so, miraculously, without spurning Marchbanks. Their final parting comes not out of rejection—Candida rightly refuses to initiate the silly game of unrequited love, and Marchbanks refuses rightly to play it—but from the acknowledgment, sadder than any murderous rage of jealousy, or any jeering endangerment to coupling, that everything might well have been different. She might have loved him—a fact more tragic, even, than the fact that she *does* love him, and cannot bear to hurt him—just as anyone in the world might have loved anyone else. The profound contingency of desire, this play teaches, is the most tragic of circumstances, not because of whom we might end up with, or what we might miss out on, but simply because it makes being human so hard a condition to take seriously. Candida and Marchbanks are able to take it seriously, though the end of the play smacks of neither triumph nor failure, because they recognize the problem; the rest of us—how could one such as Shaw not know it?—may not count ourselves so lucky.

Swept up in lyrical zeal, and fantasizing a smash production of *Candida* storming the boards of MacArthur Junior High, featuring myself in a dual part as both the poet and the preacher (it would be a daredevil feat, but if Hayley Mills or Patty Duke could pull it off, then so could I!), and none other than the teacher herself in the title role, I brought this most beautiful of plays to the attention of Mrs. Henning. "I said you could call me *Betsy,* hon," she said, patting me on a cheek inflamed with an anticipation soon to wither. "Remember? But only here in Drama: out there in the big bad world they might not understand!" Then she turned back to the other kids, in the midst of their warm-ups. On the whole, Betsy preferred to the classics skits selected from a series of little pamphlets called something on the order of "Let's Have a Play!" These skits, for the most part, concerned the everyday doings of people much like ourselves, scenes of adolescent home life or schoolhouse wranglings, predictable dramatic situations conveyed in tones of cheerful whimsy. In a typical skit, a likable new boy in school, due to a series of farcical mishaps, is deemed conceited and snobby by the spunky, decent girl he has his eye on. After much comical but tasteful hurly-burly, the girl comes around to seeing that she has been wrong about the likable new boy, and by the final curtain she agrees to go with him to the prom. Inferior as the role of the new boy was to that of the poet Marchbanks, still I coveted it as a fit vehicle to prove myself on the stage; I thought I could assay the role with real élan since I was so soon to be a new boy myself, and Drama was about nothing if not the link between imagination and real life. In the end, the part went to Bobby Adams. I was cast as one of the new boy's friends, Classmate Three, with a paltry two lines.

Bobby Adams could barely read his lines, let alone memorize them, and one day when he broke character to shout a greeting from the stage to Boomer Watson, who'd wandered in from the gym across the hall, I felt ultimately vindicated in my bitterness. Clad only in his soiled gym shorts, his back slick with sweat, Boomer Watson imbibed lustily at the drinking fountain, in uncouth gulps so loud you could hear them reverberating across the whole cafetorium. "Hey—Boom*er*!" shouted Bobby Adams, and

Boomer Watson turned his dopey gaze and his thick gut in the direction of the stage, wiping with the back of a thick hand the residual water that slobbered down his face. He was one of those types whose mouth hangs open, in a constant state of dullard's suspension, apparently in readiness should some grub requiring quick consumption turn up suddenly; and the empty eyes over the gaping mouth filled up with a recognition so painfully slow that it told why to keep the mouth permanently open was all in all a sound instinct, since speed of reflex could apparently not be relied on to stimulate it when necessary. "What the heck ya doin' up there?" Boomer Watson blubbered, causing unswallowed water to slosh out of the open mouth. "Drama," answered Bobby Adams, with a mildly sheepish shrug, at which point Mrs. Henning intervened. In spite of her praiseworthy permissiveness, she could still be stern when it was called for. "That will be enough," she said sternly, "from the Peanut Gallery."

It might very well be wondered why so coarse a figure as Bobby Adams should have chosen to invade the refined precincts of Drama, rather than to seek a milieu more hospitable to his nature, such as that of Shop. The answer was to be found, no doubt, in Drama's reputation for requiring little work. Even the risk of being thought a sissy—a risk I was well past, myself—was apparently worth the evasion of industry: Shop, which posed no such risk, was officially known as "Industrial Arts." The rationale behind Bobby Adams's whole curriculum, it would not have been unwarranted to conclude, was founded on the avoidance of effort, and the reason he was in only four of my classes, instead of all six, was probably that he had chosen remedial courses where I had chosen advanced ones—the notoriously simple "Life Science," instead of the notoriously hard Chemistry; or a History-for-Beginners, where they spent the whole time playing games with flash cards, instead of one for veterans, where the real turmoil of history was confronted head on.

But, like me, Bobby Adams was past being thought a sissy too, if for different reasons. I was only beyond the worry; he was beyond the taint itself. Something had happened to him over the summer. I'd noticed it right away: a new heightening of the brow, a new sturdiness of the frame. The year before, he'd been the same rude, scrawny boy he had always been, with the same rangy limbs, the same blank stare that would break off suddenly when his attention could no longer sustain it, the same overbite disclosing snaggled little teeth and making his chin recede, like a chicken's lower beak. His dumbness, his crassness, his puerile immaturity had always found a counterpart in his physical aspect, even if I had always been glancingly drawn by a passing glint of his eye, or by the paradoxical elegance (considering his character) of his long, supple fingers. But that summer changed him. The limbs were fuller, the chin stronger, the fingers lithe as ever, the teeth straighter, and if the stare was blanker, it was also longer, the glint persisting, and cloistered with a new ineffability, as if he were slowly awakening into the truth or the mystery of himself. I was still only, if anything, a parody of a man; he was coming more and more to resemble the genuine article, and even if the transition was distinct, it meant an elevation of his former features, not an abandonment of them. You could still see what he'd looked like as a boy—it was all still there—and you could see what he would look like as a man; which suggested that this transport was most prosperous not as the scrappy sequence of fits and starts I felt myself going through, but as a smooth, unbroken continuum. It was the same Bobby Adams, with his idle jabber and his juvenile sloth, but now he was suddenly beautiful: *beautiful*. His locker in gym was next to mine, and I saw day by day the ripening of the muscle of his arms and back and legs; I saw the growing definition of his chest, as if it were being molded by unseen hands more perfectly by the week. If the sight itself was coarse, still it came to me as beauty; if he himself, still, was crude, he was still beautiful. The evidence of my senses, and the freedom of inspection that was gym's only privilege, would not be denied. Once, he caught me looking, but he went on undressing, as if it did not matter.

Drama was metamorphosis, but gym, for all the hurdy-gurdy motion it decreed, was bleak stasis. In space, the gym was right across the hall from Drama, but in spirit it might have occupied another world. Congruities between Drama and gym—both convened in big, echoey rooms, both diverged from the typical routines of school, both called for energetic activity—could never bridge the real distance between them. Executing toilsome calisthenics on the hard floor of the gym, I'd try to convince myself that these exercises were really no different from the warm-ups of Drama, which I loved. Why then could I not coax myself to love these too? The answer, of course, was that Drama's wonder was to release one from the body, gym's burden to return one to it, irrevocably. Push-ups exacted a direct and ineluctable relation to the cold, hard floor, sit-ups to the high, unreachable ceiling. In both cases, a vexatious repetition, strictly enforced, mimicked rigor. Over and over, the ground pulled you back down, but the lofty, raftered ceiling did nothing to raise you up: all space was against you, but there was no escaping the brute fact that space—base, physical space—was exactly and only where you were, pushing yourself gracelessly up off the floor, or straining upward toward that far-off ceiling, or at least to a partly sitting position, and colliding at every turn with gravity's blunt, mocking hostility. The Swann twins circulated among us, gruffly vigilant, as we did our calisthenics, and every so often they yelled, "Bend those knees!" or "Down with that butt!" Calisthenics humiliated, all things considered, not so much in the unendurable strain that proved the terrible inadequacy of one's own strengths, though in that too, but in the whole callous, confining ethic of the corporeal, as if it were the only thing that was real, as if anything else were only a sissy's subterfuge.

Gym entailed games, but its atmosphere could never have been mistaken for that of play. The games were brutal and primal. The ones who loved gym—Bobby Adams, for instance, who seemed to have been born to it—loved most this worship of the primitive that was so intrinsic to the dogma of gym: the stripping away of street clothes, the donning of the shorts and the tee shirts, the choosing up of sides, as if tallying a binding list of the fittest apt to survive, or as if, leaping into the ferocious carnage of the game, making ready for that inevitable time when the false veneer of civilization would crumble, and we would be restored to that primordial condition, of which gym gave a taste as tantalizing to some as the tang of the enemy's blood, that was really our natural state. The romance of the corporeal was one thing, but this rhetoric of the "natural" that permeated all quarters of gym was really too much. For all the blather about the team spirit and self-reliance that were gym's putative educational justifications—a crude sanctimony—I knew it was really all about self-gain and self-righteousness, and another of its congruities with Drama, its highly theatrical dimension, revealed exactly how this was the case. Drama was for sissies, went the conventional wisdom, because it turned on pretense; gym made us real men, because it repudiated pretense. What was clear to me, though—but still couldn't be called on to overcome my loathing of gym—was that, in a very direct way, gym *was* theater. The shorts and tees were costumes, the games intricate, ragtag performances, and the whole arrangement depended on an elaborate system of learned codes and artificial conventions. Success or failure in gym depended not on the ability to learn these codes, for everyone knew them implicitly, but on the ability to enact them as if they were natural. We were supposed to call each other, in gym, only by our last names, as if who we were were only lineage; but some could shout these names with the wild, savage inflections of real conviction, while others, like myself, when they could muster them at all, could summon them only tentatively, preferring the individual stamp of the first name to the prototypical standard of the last name. Even the shouts of encouragement were like litanies in a foreign tongue: *"Good hustle, good hustle!"* or *"Way to toss, way to grab!"* By the same token, some could master, say, sit-ups, or push-ups, as if they were really innate functions of the body, not aberrant, unnatural exercises, while others could never, say, recite the potty-mouth diatribes the ones who were good in gym spouted spontaneously and incessantly in the midst of the games, with that berserk rage that proved they really meant it. Drama enabled you to perform another identity as your own, while gym compelled you to perform your own identity as another; and if, in gym, the self was a trap, in Drama it was a door.

For Halloween, our Drama class was going to perform "The Legend of Sleepy Hollow" for the whole school. I spent the week before auditions perfecting my Ichabod Crane, fine-tuning the prissy, nasal voice and rehearsing the lopey, lurching walk and the sour, effete expression of the face and the muliebrous curl of the hand, thumb and forefinger touching tip to tip, and pinky finger upraised with a milksop's disdain. It will not, I trust, too greatly violate modesty to say that by the time of the audition, that was exactly what the character had become: *perfected*—in every nuance and in every detail. My audition was nothing less than a triumph, my nervousness channeled brilliantly into the character, bringing a tremor to the voice that only enriched it, and simply by virtue of the whim of concurrence, my own performance could have been credited with substantially improving the rather pedestrian Katrina Van Tassel of Deborah Lick, my costar in the audition. I'd contrived to give one of Ichabod's seemingly innocent lines—"Let me get my tuning-fork!"—a comically lascivious spin, and in performance the line prompted a burst of uncoaxed laughter from the audience. So certain was my triumph, especially by contrast to the pale Ichabods of my rivals, that the vexed expression on Mrs. Henning's face as she led me backstage to the makeup room after the audition puzzled me. The makeup room was a cramped little chamber in the wings of the stage, and the teacher sat me down at the spindly-legged vanity with its dirty mirror circled by unveiled light bulbs, filaments glowing.

"You *definitely* have talents!" said Mrs. Henning, biting her lip.

It was a bad sign, for her to be stating in such neutral, objectively appraising tones what anyone could have seen perfectly well, but a show of modesty was called for. "Thank you," I answered.

"In fact," she continued brightly, "you're really one of the best students in the whole class. . . ."

The signs were not getting better. *One* of the best? And only in the class? In light of the triumph of my audition, it would have seemed more appropriate for my work to be judged on a global scale, rather than on the merely local one that she proposed. I gulped, trying to swallow the lump that was forming in my throat. "Thank you," I repeated.

"And that's why I'm going to be very, very honest with you," she went on. "The *trouble* is, you're just not right for the part— well, *physically*. . . ."

I blinked at her.

She produced a copy of the script and showed me the description of the character. "See what it says here? Look: 'tall and exceedingly lank.' See? *'Exceedingly!'* For gosh sakes, that's why he's even *called* 'Ichabod *Crane*.' And it goes on: 'loose frame . . . narrow shoulder . . . long arms and legs . . . hands that hang a mile out of his sleeves.' " She bit her lip again and looked at me. The evidence spoke for itself.

"Couldn't we just make the costume small," I suggested, "so I *look* taller?"

"But you're not even as tall as Deborah Lick, and she's playing Katrina." She closed the script in her lap and sat back, with an air of finality. "Physical types are very important in the world of the theater, so it's very, very good for you to have the opportunity to learn that early on. Now, we have a fine part for you, as one of the townspeople. . . ."

"But Mrs. Henning—"

She held up a finger to stop me. "Betsy," she said. "We're all equal on the same exact footing, here in Drama!"

As Ichabod Crane, Betsy cast the lankiest boy in the class, none other than Bobby Adams, who was all of an inch and a half taller than I was. Height being the deciding factor in the end, it was unclear in retrospect what had been the point of the auditions, and even Bobby Adams himself, not known for niceties of perception, seemed puzzled by the outcome. In the locker room the next day he told me he thought I should have gotten the part. Whatever satisfaction this admission offered could not alter the fact that the Ichabod Crane of Bobby Adams was irredeemably stiff, stilted, wooden. He was as hopeless on the stage of Drama as I was on that of gym. Volleyball was the sport of choice that week, and Bobby Adams had picked me for his team, probably, I mused privately, out of guilt. But I couldn't serve, or spike, or return. At the end of the week, all the classes would compete, with the winning team matched against the best team from Flint in a district championship the week after. Bobby Adams made it known that there were high symbolic stakes to be achieved in a victory of my old school over my future school, but his hopes dimmed after the first game. Our team won, but it had become clear that I was a liability, not a charmed mascot.

"You know what?" he taunted in the locker room after the game. "You stink at volleyball."

"Well, you know what?" I retorted, slamming my locker. "*You* stink at *acting*."

He slammed his locker too, but in the moment of the slam, a new cognizance dawned in his face. "Wait a minute," he said. "That gives me an idea."

"*That's* a first," I scoffed.

His idea was a swap: he'd teach me volleyball, and I'd teach him acting. We would meet after school and exchange lessons on the sly, so nobody would ever be the wiser. Grudgingly, I agreed that it wasn't such a bad idea; secretly, I couldn't believe my luck.

In memory these lessons take on the luminous sheen and the seductive rhythms of an emotion-laden montage out of an inspirational TV-movie of the day—say, *Brian's Song*—combining a boy's fantasy of camaraderie with the exuberant lyricism and the mellow sentiment required to express it, with stirringly lackadaisical slow motion to convey the ritual redemption and the terrestrial glory in the ever-deepening bonds of a friendship that exceeded the bounds of the earthly. We met three times after school. He was, perhaps, my complement, the element long sought to complete me, as I would complete him. When halves of the same whole come finally together, the alchemy of union brings anticipated ease: the lessons succeeded, beyond my fondest dreams. The boyish skill of Bobby Adams flowed into me, blessedly fertile; thus emboldened—a crack initiate—I slammed the volleyball over the net in a clean, pure arc, and watched in awe as it sailed, smooth and beautiful, a white blur coasting perfectly, into the opposite court. Bobby Adams howled his delight and his pride—pride, I marked, in *me*—pumping a triumphant, virile fist over and over into air newly charged by my spanking new skill. We would teach one another the names of all things, and their wonders. The Drama lesson went less smoothly than the volleyball lesson, but that was testament only to the greater profundity of what I had to impart, and the privacy of the setting, alone in the makeup room, was hearteningly more conducive to the intimacy of our mingling. Had there been music, it surely would have swelled.

We began with line-readings. I repeated my line from the audition that had garnered such thunderous response, and instructed him to say it after me.

"Let me get my tuning-fork," he said—a bland, uncolored rendition.

I repeated the line, twisting it even more garishly, more leeringly.

"Let me get my tuning-fork," he repeated, a little louder, but in the same flavorless monotone as before.

"Don't you get it?" I said. "Ichabod Crane's got the hots for Katrina Van Tassel, see, so when he says he's getting the tuning-fork, see, he's *really* just making an excuse to get closer to her because—*get it?*—he's *warm* for her *form*! Now say it again."

"What the heck *is* a tuning-fork, anyway?"

I heaved a sigh and placed my hands on my hips. "You're not even trying."

"I just don't want to sound like a homo, that's all."

His eyes flashed at me. He was saying something real. I turned away. "Thanks a lot," I said.

"I didn't say *you* sounded like a homo." He patted me on the back. "Just, *I* would, if *I* tried saying it like that, you know? I just can't do it like you, that's all." He stepped in front of me. "No," he said, "you're good. You're really good." Then he took me into his arms.

The moment when fantasy spills into reality has often been recounted as oceanic conversion, negative to positive. But I had had no fantasy of ever being taken into the arms of Bobby Adams, and so—scarcely a possibility—this moment seemed only to be a surprising inevitability, light shading over imperceptibly into light—inevitable in its very unlikelihood, surprising to the extent that it was inevitable, and straightforward, without ceremony. In the light-bulb-bordered mirror, I glimpsed us, holding each other, my face floating above his back, but I turned away, not wanting to be yanked out of the moment by the random exigencies of reflection, and pressed my face against his neck. "You're good," he went on, his voice lowered to a whisper. "You should have got that part. I can't believe you're moving. Why do people have to move? Do you know I've known you all my life? I've known you practically my whole life. Remember Frankie Holleran? He moved in fifth grade. He was my best, best friend, and I never saw him after he moved. What do people have to go and move for, anyways?" We held each other for many, many seconds. I was afraid for it to end, and afraid for it to go on, because a thing was starting to open inside me that I wanted to open but did not want to open all the way. When we separated, we acted shy with each other, quiet, but the next day, after another wildly successful vol-leyball lesson—the ball taking the air, high and gliding, and kissing the net as it whooshed over—as soon as we got backstage for the Drama lesson, he took me in his arms and we held each other again. I kneaded his back with my hands, pressing him into me, and what had begun to open in me the last time opened the more. Over time perhaps it would open all the way. Intimations of the pleasures and the dangers that might burst forth then were already foreboden. "I've known you my whole life," he whispered. "What do you have to go and move for?" He went on whispering under his breath as he held me and stroked me, something that sounded like, "You're good, you're good," as if I were in need of comfort, or assurance. The embrace went on and on, and he stroked my hair as I ran my hands up and down his back, pressing his shoulders into my shoulders, his chest to my chest, and—my hands at the small of his back—his belly to my belly. The indentions and recesses and flanges and protuberances of our bodies seemed somehow to match each other's, so they did not seem like bags or bulges; but he breathed out as I breathed in, so I held my breath a moment on exhale, and then inhaled in time with him, to bring our breaths like our bodies into synchrony. I shifted my head from his left shoulder, where it had rested, to his right, and as my ear grazed his face, he kissed it. It did not seem an intended aim. The time passed, nothing thought of, and we did not look into each other's eyes. We stood on the stage, holding each other, in the wings, behind the curtain, but had no thought to hide. I don't remember parting.

We did part, though, and the next day, everything was different. He didn't look at me when he showed up for the lesson, and he spoke gruffly. His distance threw me off. Though the volleyball lesson was not the unalloyed triumph of past days, I still pulled it off with mild success—not a grand slam, but a respectable grounder—but at the end he didn't praise me, as before. Instead he said, "It's only *volley*ball," to let me know it wasn't even a real sport I was so deficient in. Then he added, "You should know how to do all this stuff already, anyways." In the cafetorium he adopted a posture of exaggerated expectation, waiting on the stage, and I shrugged and ventured, "Well, what now?"

"What do you think?" he said sharply. "Teach me how to act. That's what we're here for, ain't it?"

We had made little headway on that score, but though he still hadn't even approximated the shrill Ichabod Crane voice, or the epicene Ichabod Crane walk, or come even close to imitating a single gesture that might remotely have been associated with Ichabod Crane, or indeed with anyone except Bobby Adams himself, I decided there was no putting it off further. We would have to jump right in with the biggest challenge the role presented—that of the final scene. The last scene brought Ichabod Crane into climactic collision with the Headless Horseman, and provided for any actor worth his salt ample opportunities for highly exaggerated displays of comic terror, especially when Ichabod Crane's pitiful effort to vanquish the Headless Horseman collapses into sheer pansy cowardice. I demonstrated: "I defy you, you unnatural creature, in the name of Christian purity!" I wailed at the imaginary horseman, waving unhinged arms over my head with deliriously flitting fingers, and stomping my feet with sissy righteousness to ward the horseman off, only to recoil at the onset of the relentless horseman's advance. Then, in the irresistible grip of the conjured person of Ichabod Crane, I screamed—squealed, blundered, screeched—a demented, earsplitting howl, both funny in its craven battiness (so I imagined) and genuinely horrifying in its naked fear, and I sank to my knees, which banged against the stage with an abandon that might have pained, if the knees were not more Ichabod Crane's than my own, if I were not consumed so fully by the harsh demands of my art. In the wake of the performance, spent, I looked up at Bobby Adams. In anyone else the performance would have inspired awe. Bobby Adams was watching me from the other side of the stage, with his arms crossed and his legs crossed, dramatically unimpressed.

"If you think," he said, "*I'm* going to do anything like that, then you need to get your head examined."

I stood back up. "What's the matter with it?"

"For one thing, I'd look like the biggest homo in the school. The *second* biggest, I mean."

I crossed the stage and stood near him. "You're missing the whole point," I said. "It's *acting*. It's not you doing it, it's Ichabod Crane."

"Oh, yeah? Well, it's not Ichabod Crane that's going to have to take the razzing from the other guys, for looking like such a homo. It's me."

"What's more important—Drama, or a bunch of chumps?"

"It's bad enough I have to wear that dumb costume. She knew I was bad when she gave me the part, so nobody has any right to expect anything from me."

"*That's* real mature." I stepped closer to him.

He looked at me. "It's different for you," he said.

"Why?" I reached for his arm. "Why is it different?"

"*No.*" He pulled his arm away. "We shouldn't do that stuff."

"*What* stuff?"

"You know what I mean." This time he held my gaze.

"I liked it," I said. "I didn't start it."

"The lesson's over," he said.

In truth, the lessons might just as well never have happened, since Bobby Adams's performance as Ichabod Crane remained wholly unmarked by any sign of my tutelage, and the enhancement of my volleyball skills proved untranslatable onto the court, in practice. Drama and gym were still at odds after all. I missed a particularly easy volley, and Bobby Adams, seized with rage, shouted across the court, "Can't you do *any*thing right, you pantywaist!" We lost, and I followed him into the shower after the game, deliberately standing near him and watching him out of the corner of my eye as he washed himself. I followed him back to our lockers, and we dressed slowly, lingering as the others were leaving.

"I'm sorry we lost," I said finally.

"I don't think you're a pantywaist," he said. He stepped past me, as if to leave. Then he turned back, suddenly, and grabbed me: one last, quick hug. "I think you're a homo," he whispered, "but I don't think you're a pantywaist." Then he was gone.

— — — — — — —

At my going-away party, he gave me a card that showed a dog carrying a cane and wearing a bowler hat. The card said "Good Luck!" in bold print inside. Under these words he had scrawled, "Signed, Bobby Adams." Unfolding the card, I felt a stray pang of loss, but in truth it was only one card among many, each laden with its own emotional weight, and I was swept away in the bustling romance of my imminent leavetaking, so my sadness was held off. These were the people among whom I had spent my life so far, and I tried to see myself as they saw me, now that I was leaving them. To learn how others love you, you have only to announce your departure. The party acknowledged that they realized at last how they had taken me for granted all these years: I was a figure of reverence to them now, whose departure made him elect, a pioneer of the spirit and the soul, going off in quest of wider realms. How would they do without me? Near party's end, Bobby Adams met my eyes briefly across the room. His lips were thickly coated, stained by the grapeade he had been drinking, and he looked like a clown, a beautiful clown. I burst out laughing. He looked puzzled, and sad, until he turned away.

For my part, I had calculated exactly how *I* would do without *them*. In the days leading up to the move, I felt myself returning to the love of family as greatest sustenance. To move, after all, is to realize the family as one's real society. They are those who will always be with you; and might the solicitation of other society be nothing, in the end, but evasion of that truth? My mother and father and older sister were absorbed in the last-minute logistics of the move, though, and paid little mind to the lugubrious, dirge-like renewals of my affections, so their burdens fell mostly upon my little sister. She was then only a year old, a captive audience, and she spent the bulk of her days standing at the front door, peering out into the street, spellbound in fascination with the things of the world that streamed by outside, every one of which was new to her. Even she grew quickly impatient with the elegiac attitudes the impending move brought forth in me, and so as soon as I swept her up into my arms from her usual place at the door, she began to squirm. I held her fast.

"We're moving!" I said. "We're going to *move*. Do you understand what that *means*? It means you won't be able to stand at that same exact door, looking out at that same exact street anymore. We're going to live in a whole different house, and start a whole new life, with a new school, except it won't be new to you because when you get to school it will already be old. It's very, very, scary, but there's really nothing to be scared of, because we'll always have each other. Do you understand?"

"Down," said my sister, wriggling urgently. *"Down."*

I clasped her to me more tightly, kneeling in a patch of twilight sun streaming through the window: that tiny body, so vulnerable. The intensity of my own love pierced me. It had been immediate, from the moment I'd laid eyes on her for the first time, only a year before, in this very room, this room we were so soon to leave, but it, this love, would never leave me. She was the purest, tiniest thing I had ever seen, with a fresh relation to the world that proved over and again how everything we know, we learn. Now she was learning to walk, and her walk, in her little orange jumpsuits frilled with lace around her baby-fat thighs, was a halting, exploratory bounce, each step a discovery. To hold her was different from holding Bobby Adams, except in its intensity, but it was that intensity, not its manner or its matter, that overwhelmed. I did not love Bobby Adams, surely, but maybe it was only, I thought, because I had not been given time. Would those feelings, too, always be with me, and could I ever make of them, too, as everything shifted around me, a weave to hold me up? My sister went on squirming in my arms, at the mercy already of desires of her own, and repeated, *"Down, down!"*

Time has no stop, and change is the surest rule, and so I let her go, released her to the demands of independence, which could only sadden me—that evanescence that alone brought growth. She ran back to the door, and pressed her nose against the smudged, smeared glass, burbling with excitement and bouncing up and down. I had not heard the bells, but now I did hear them, and saw, even so late in the season, what my sister saw through the glass, what had drawn her so irresistibly back to the door. In the street in front of the house, the ice-cream truck was whirring slowly past.

9

HOLY TERROR

He has come far. A question burns on his lips. Far from a near place, homeless, sightless; near to a far place, boneless. Eager to arrive, and to find and to speak, but when he comes—it is winter, it is cold, he is scared—he does not rise, and does not ask, and does not listen, and does not hear.

The boy dreams. In the dream he is alone. A road winds before him. A somber sky looms above, smeared with gray clouds. A few trees line the road. They are bare. The sharp, many branches claw the bottoms of the clouds. The road is rutted, still water pooled in the ruts of the road. Is someone behind him? No: someone is before him. The figure stands shrouded on a cliff, hooded, faceless. From the sleeves of the dark cloak protrude bony limbs, fingers like gnarled branches of the bare trees. Still he is alone. Another is there, pointing, to a near distance. Still he is alone. It is not raining. It has not rained. Nothing here an outcome of past cause. There is no present where the past might rest. The boy does not move. Nothing moves, yet the bony hand points, persists. A stone. A tree. Beneath it a hole. A grave. The hole is deep and wide and dark. It is for him. The sky flashes. Only a moment to fear, but every moment creates its own infinity. To leave being would terrify only in the moment of severance. Then nothing. Nothing: no need to reach, no need to grasp, all effort gone. The hole another infinity. Yet another, endless. It is dark, and his. Mine. Oh, give up to it, surrender, relinquish, it will not be rest—it will be nothing, *nothing:* imagine it—but it will not be labor. Nothing left. I fall. He falls. The boy falls. He falls, and does not wake.

Here. Gone. In, out. Tomorrow, today. One ear, the other.

A trap door come open. Seen only then. Is there any good in talking? Make an end of it, open the door. Bound to believe not to believe. A time after when the body lightens. But then, for the body, there is no time, and no weight.

The many dead. First: the child in the open casket. The casket small and plain, white. A sussurous murmur in the room, like the hum of a conch pressed still to an ear. She is at peace, say the voices, she is at peace. Let that knowledge temper grief. A body in death: is it more or less a body than one in life? Life the condition of embodiment—the body without it no longer a body, but a corpse, a husk. Or is it that the body comes into its own at last only in death, revealed as it must be, without the air of spirit. Sheer matter that it always was. The vapor fled. A mark on the clean white cheek the sign of perfection, of purity, not of blemish. Weavers that spin a flaw into the rug to honor God. It would be the humility of fault finally accepted, if death came simply, and were welcomed. Others remembered dead: a girl, playing on a hill at the roadside, fallen, run down by a car. A boy, shut in an old freezer abandoned in a field, the door fallen shut. How must they have looked in death—mangled, smothered? Broken body, twisted face—fought, fought, before giving in. I hold my breath. This, this is what that boy felt in death: the absence of air. But it is only willed: I can release, breathe again. He could not. Close your eyes: How would that sightlessness enlarge if you could believe it were permanent? You cannot enter the place where you are not. Death unimaginable. Whose hand shut that door? *She is at peace.* Why were they born, only then so soon to die? Why was he himself born? *She was so beautiful God wanted her home.* I must feel what they felt, but cannot, except in a death of my own. Is death one's own? I *must:* close your eyes, hold your breath. Death unimaginable. Don't think of it, don't think of it. She *is* beautiful. The pure cheeks, the frilled frock, the tiny hands, delicate fingers like porcelain. Only months of life, and a peaceful death, no more. No sound, no motion, no force, no breath—the quietest thing the boy has ever seen or imagined in the world, in his life. *Is* it his life? Can it be, if it too will end?

Hunger and thirst the chief sufferings. Regret that we escaped. Our hearts sunk within us. Perils less dreadful. Console yourselves with the hope of a new day. Hope of escape. Chafing the limbs. Good fortune, a gentle breeze. He came to himself. Evils that might happen: Bear them with fortitude.

What is there in life except ideas, air?

Age, and then the only end of age. Natural cause—but a child's death surely gives the lie to that faint hope. To carry the dead. Heavy wood, oaken planks. Carried to the grave. How peaceful they look, say the voices, how peaceful. But it is not peace the boy sees in the stopped, molded faces. It is stillness, vacancy. Only

the body left, the life of the body unimaginable. Death unimaginable. Six entreated to carry the coffin to its last place. It is
heavy, made heavy to defy substance, the body within impalpable.
Death not the end of birth, but its slough. The human has no
cousin in the sky. Panic in the face of the sun. Look away; carry
the terrible load as if it were no burden. Generations here gathered, the children of the living and the dead, and I am one. Say
nothing untrue. All eternity in a minute. What we carry the rem-
nant of what we have loved. Up, up. An illusion that we ever
lived. Birth of sight. At the top of the hill there stands a canopy.
It hides the grave from the sun. A dark cloud shrouds the sun
further. The discretion of elements, not to mock the gravity of
rite. All things conspire in respect, the world's apology to the
living for having taken death as its fundament. Grandmother,
grandfather: Rest well. Not enough to cover rock with leaves.
Years will pass. This will stand.

Drear: dread: read—the world the place where people lied, books
where they told truths. He loved the substances of them, pages
against fingers like skins, the books heavy in the lap like flesh.
The books not animate, but not mortified. They carry signs of
life. He does not understand all that he reads but does not read
to understand. It is communion, and self-presence, not meaning,
that he seeks. Once he glimpsed a graveyard, and thought the
stones were books, upright and overgrown, fanning out around
him, on successive hills, as he was hurried past. He was only a boy,
and could not know. Before understanding there is poetry: metaphor—a way to understand without knowledge, and in the influence of error. The words weave before his eyes like a ground
beneath his feet. They form a ribbon that suspends him. As he
learned more he would take greater pleasure in incomprehension.
It persuaded him that there was more to know, a future, and a

time before knowledge, a past. But to read was a present, a present of matter and self, and it would last. He could make it last. Later he saw the tablets of rock for what they were. Reminders of the dead. Harbinger of all mortality. A child again. An infancy of blue snow. There too must I go.

Not leaves enough to cover the face it wears. At last declaim our end. Difficulty to think. Twilight. To be, in the grass. Nothing left, except light. Wideness of the night. Self touches all edges. In the peacefullest time.

Love springs not from a notion of beauty they desire to uphold but from an impalpable sickness. Shun one another. Seek out those unlike oneself. Moved to ecstasy by their patronage. Brought back by exile to the company of their own. The disgrace alone makes the crime. All end the same.

To prove an independence. A terrible freedom.

Make an end of it. No pain but in the interference of others. No loss but that claimed for oneself. How must that end have appeared? Gun's barrel: little circle of darkness. Look into it. The darkness will take you. To want death. Is it something you take in, sustenance, or something you cast out, excrement? Sweet annihilation take us harrowing all. You must make yourself porous. Split skin, let blood run. Blood and pus and tears, bile. Fluids that give life. What does it violate, to spill them? How must it have appeared? Questions without voice, blood channeled: vitiate. Blood that stays in veins. (For the blood is the life.) Hands shackled, ankles. Failed in the effort to end, strapped, still in the world. Happy once, in a time that has been lost. Never again. Oh, help him to come back to himself, bring him back. Overcome doubt. The mighty rule the weak. We the living, weak, in thrall to the powerful dead. Is it weakness or strength, to want death? He lies still. Will not meet my eyes. Stillness shows no effort to break free. Defeat; resign. I, he, young, old. There is power in the silence that withholds, weakness in the silence that desires. No desire more. Death unimaginable. A great pain in consciousness. Snuff it. Those names. Soon, old. If he wanted death then I am surely lost. He who made me, bring him back. See light again. The dark little hole. Expand, fill the corners of the earth with a darkness that quells reason. Turned to light. Take it back. Here is proof. A mercury of darkness. A chosen death dark, a given one light. To want death: you must see the ugliness at the bottom of everything. See through. Those gone. It is because they saw truth that we cannot hate them simply. The ugliness everywhere. It is in me. If I think it is they who have done this to me then I can only fail. I must find it in myself, the ugliness, and bring it out. The ugliness in me to meet the ugliness of all the world. To be as they were, to see what they must have seen, and still go on.

Rivers of flame from the sky. Only sunset. A mother's caress. Weary of the sun. Stillness stoked the heart. Lulled. Dew from apple boughs. Notes somewhere, a dog's bark. You might hear a sudden cry. To lie and face the sky. Infinite deeps. Alone, alive, after, still. In all my life I have known no quieter time.

The secret wound of mind. More uniformly present. The consciousness of morbid sensibility. The longer this humble familiarity. Its influence. Things as they are. Life a theater of calamity. I

could not escape. I have not deserved this treatment. My improvement greater than my condition. An education free from the usual
sources of depravity. Somewhat above the middle stature. Sub-
orner. Hasten to conclude. The phantom of departed honor. The
idea of vindicating character. I have now no character I wish to
vindicate.

Diller. Dollar. Ten o'clock scholar.

He has come far. Nobody knows him there. Nobody knows his
name. The welcome he receives is benign and blank—he weary,
cold. Struggle of undoing. The place is strange. The mourners
weep their comforts. Mysteries rehearsed in darkest minds. Due
to tepid breaths (or lack of its). Whose grief is fuller, theirs? His?
Whose emptier? Between grief and nothing, nothing. Remember
him dancing. A way of touching the earth. Of reaching the sky,
while staying bound to things as they are: were. He danced, and
lured me, who never danced afore, whose swellest leg was still and
stern. Sing hosanna hey with a hey nonny nonny! In a room
bursting with light and limb I was happy once. All at once, him
there: *there*. Then came time he slipped shod on the crystal road
with the crystal trench and the crystal sledge on the crystal night
of the crystal morn, then nevermore again. They who knew him
know not I. Secrets not always vast or vagrant. Can mean other,
still again other. Not quite yet my jimmyboy a darlin', not quite
yet my filigree a love. Awash a wish a wish awash. Gone over.
Him dancing. Grace, grace. But nobody knows my name. Light
of foot. Heart's in the wind. There is a kind of riverrun swift
with undetermined mane but its lazy lazy currents scarcely ever
wane. Keep shut a mouth. Hey diddle diddle, the hemp and the
riddle. Hey diddle diddle, my wary young man. Cat's in the fiddle;

nary a hand. A question (round the bend): Were you a friend, a friend, a friend—a friend of his, this frabjous day (calloo callay)? On Orion on holy night he made a something bargain. Something something something something, something all the way. Road with no end, souls in busy flight. Think not the cause. I felt in my flying, genitals cold. Insulted body. Speak again, and better, else this domicile be rent. Another chance I'd tell him what he longed to hear, and I to say. But answer came there none. Being dead and all. Cold, cold as any stone. I'm not whats I seems. Incense and cotton, penny a pound, dance away, dance away, pricky old songs. Rise again, and learn you should of could of would of stood in bed. Stop, unless to make a go of it once for all. I not you. He not me. He not you. I not he. They have a many speak to shay, and will right sling it. Meanwhile there lies he, forever beyond reach, that once I happy touched. Oh, don't forgive me ever, but raise up voice, and let me mine, in heavy sorrow, holy terror. Too late blues: death unimaginable. Here, but not here. This time the coffin closed. One mercy.

All over. Now given leave to rest.

IO

THE INFERNAL TWONESS

*Be sure to mention the Supernal Oneness. Don't
say anything about the Infernal Twoness.*
—Edgar Allan Poe, "How to Write a *Blackwood's* Article"

Two jesters, dunce-capped and spatterdashed, perch side by side
on a stinted ledge. One bites the meaty end off a long sausage.
"It's pork," he pronounces gnomically. The other bites the same
sausage. "It's not pork," he counters. "It's pig!" The first jester, the
fat one, slow-burns: buggy eyes, puffed cheeks, steaming ears. The
other, the thin one, rests prim hands on crooked knees, his long
thin face flowering in a heedless, beatific grin that pinches his rosy
cheeks, narrows his muzzy eyes. The fat one's contortions, going
on right there beside the thin one, but utterly lost on him, can
be understood only as the culmination of a lifetime's frustration,
frustration at the irredeemable dimness of his clod-pated mate;
but it is a culmination without advantage of termination, for he
is condemned to reenact it again and again, always with no awareness on the part of the thin one, who is ever too dumb, too
genially addle-brained, even to notice the seizures his very being
inflicts upon his partner.

What brought them together, then, and what kept them

together? If the fitful agonies of the fat one were really so unendurable as they seemed, would not some spell of divorcement have been the best proper remedy? And yet the two never part. Scene after excruciating scene, the fat one and the thin one remain wed inextricably, rehearsing endless variation upon the same themes, their very names—Laurel and Hardy, a lilting pair of trochees—married in rhythmic necessity. To reverse these names—Hardy and Laurel, a sequence jarring as the inverted billing of Sullivan and Gilbert might be, if it were even conceivable—is to hear natural order violated, and so to infer how intimate is the inevitability of this coupling. There is something primordial and unspoken, perhaps unspeakable, that keeps them together, an edict so deeply seated as to exceed simple desire, or mere need. So eternal seems this affinity, it is impossible to envision the moment in time of their meeting, as it is to imagine some span of time before they met; yet it is, by the same token, inescapable to conclude that, had they never come together, something in the world far greater than themselves—but what?—would have gone unfulfilled.

Comedy was one apparent object of their pairing, and play thus a part of it, so despite the rounds of excruciation that bound them, pleasure was not absent among its qualities. Indeed, these rounds of excruciation were themselves meant to exact laughter. The fact that they were supposed to do so met, bristling, the fact that they could never really do so, to determine my own reactions to the antics of such figures as Laurel and Hardy. What most characterized these old-time comics was not that they were funny—they weren't—but that they were somehow presented, on a vast scale, as if they were. Perhaps, coming as they did from an earlier era, and lacking the effortless contemporaneity of the truly funny spectacles on TV—like *Laugh-in,* or *H. R. Pufnstuf*—they had very well *once* been funny. But now their fascination could only be seen to reside in their making visible the base anatomy

of the comic. One watched their rituals—the gestures, the prat-
falls, the double takes—in a state of analytical engrossment, enabled to perceive the underlying valences of comical attitudes,
without being flustered by the distraction of actual laughter. Their
antics placed on view the structure of the comic, detached from
its substance, so that one could absorb its features at a distance,
without being forced to take part in it. Their routines were about,
not participation, but understanding, which required estrange-
ment, not engagement. Still, it was a distance that came before
nearness, perhaps, if I were ever to become one of a pair myself,
as it seemed impossible to imagine that I would not, since everybody, everybody, was.

The frenetic energies of the Marx Brothers or the Three
Stooges, or the little-seen Ritz Brothers, told by comparison the
distance between the two that was fallow company and the three
that was a lumpish crowd. Quartets or trios neutralized the mystery and sway of the duo, each in the trio with a role to play,
none of the quartet joined in too much congress with any other,
all united in one explicable, diffuse brotherhood of slapstick. You
did not have to wonder why they all stayed together, and maybe
they could not even really have been said to be "together" to
begin with. Their interactions were on the order of a haphazard
relay: Larry's broomstick bopping Moe inadvertently on the head,
prompting Moe in turn to deliver blithe Curly a swift kick in the
rear—the risible persistence of chain reaction, a booby trap made
out of dominoes. This slapstick turned on self-protection and
vengeance, a gouged eye for a gouged eye, but for the trios or the
quartets, the joke was always in the short-circuit of reprisal, a slip,
a bungle, a mere accident generating the instant answering violence of misdirected retaliation. The ferocity of the Stooges' fights
could never be accounted for by direct causes, since those were
slight, but could always be understood as a lifetime's pent-up anger; and that ferocity vanished, anyway, as quickly as it had come.

The basic truth about families, I was already aware, was that the family's members were stuck with one another; the Stooges, like the Marxes or the Ritzes, were families—the names alone said as much—and the stern fraternity of aggression did not always over-rule, and sometimes even invited, forgiveness. If the curiously arid and loveless world of the Marx Brothers was free of violence, it was also empty of real contact, physical or (miscommunication being their comic métier) otherwise; and if these Brothers es-chewed the scrubby, rowdy skirmishes of those Stooges, then maybe it was because they had failed, in some unimagined past, to care for one another very dearly, and so could never really hurt one another very deeply.

Experience relieves all you need of theory until it teaches you that the world is bigger than you can ever hope to know, and then returns you, chastened, to the sphere of theory that must thenceforth compensate the lack. I—like every child in the world but the orphans who were objects of my deepest pity and rashest envy—was a member of a family, and did not need the comical Brothers or the rambunctious Stooges to teach me the lessons of families. But what could I, single as every child in the world, know about couples, except what I might have learned from Laurel and Hardy?

The solo acts, in their way, held fascination too, as evidence of a possible *solitary* adulthood, and even on rare occasions when the stories the comics acted out were tales of marriage, the joke was always the insufficiency, incongruity, or woe of the solo thrust into a duo. Even if its objects were arbitrary, and could turn on a dime, desire was apparently irrevocable, or else such a thing as marriage would not be portended in the first place. Chaplin, Kea-ton, Fields—all holdovers from a mysterious past, hangers-on in a diminished present, where all their jokes were already known, var-nished with the predictability of the classical. They were nothing but overgrown children, clinging to the balmy irresponsibility of solitude that one is supposed to relinquish when one gives up innocence, yet beset with the longing to mate that reportedly comes with experience—overgrown children, regressive in their persons as they were atavistic in their lingerings. To my own childish eye, Keaton and Chaplin were the more primitive, if only because they could not or would not speak, but no less childish than the elfin Chaplin or the matter-of-fact Keaton—who reminded me, precisely, of one of those brisk and businesslike kids you meet, who won't joke with you, who have never learned, or thought, that the world might be supposed fun—was the fat, sour, bulbous-nosed Fields, whose famed hatred of children and dogs was transparently motivated by his wish to supplant them, to devour for himself all the attentions they might demand. In his awkward, many-layered, ill-fitting clothes, with his drawly, twangy, but uninflected voice, W. C. Fields seemed, fatherlike, incapable of pleasure, and yet the seeking of pleasure and the avoidance of pain were, childlike, his only goals; and when he played a father, as in *The Bank Dick,* the posture was always presented as nothing but a bald-faced joke. Like Chaplin or Keaton, Fields was definitively *alone*—a grown-up orphan—driven by desires he could only satisfy on his own, and though dissatisfaction and frustration were part of his repertoire, they came most often not from the lack, but from the presence, of companions.

Laurel and Hardy, meanwhile, could be thought of only in relation to each other, even if frustration or dissatisfaction was the insoluble glue that yoked them. The misanthropy of a Fields derived precisely from his solitary nature. The corrosive mumble of his speech (which I taught myself to imitate when I was eight) never really seemed to be directed to others, but rather to be marked by the autistic, eccentric mutedness, the off-handed mutter, of a man talking to himself, and his wish to be alone often seemed to be the root of everything else he wanted. Paired, as in *My Little Chickadee,* with Mae West, Fields loses what most characterizes him, that idiosyncratic loneness, too melancholy to be proud, but too staunch to be really sad, and the erratic barbs spewed from the corners of the mouth, mercurial monologues, become toothless, compromised, in dialogue. Overall, W. C. Fields gave the impression of being wise to everything, of knowing that fellowship was only the suffering of fools, and of having elected, in that knowledge, solitude, even if it meant loneliness. The bumptious naïveté of Laurel and Hardy lay in a lack of such conviction. The fact that they remained together, despite every premonition that they might have been happier apart, was the only proof of their commitment, and the only hint that it obtained, precisely, out of their fears to be alone. If nobody wanted W. C. Fields, it would devastate no dearly held intention, because W. C. Fields wanted nobody; and even if the latter refusal were only an outcome of the former deficiency—a bulwark—it was still so trenchantly formed that it could not bring pity. But who would want Hardy, if not Laurel, and who would tolerate Laurel's overwhelming idiocy, or his blubbering repentances, but Hardy? I knew enough from glancing observation in everyday life to know that mates could live forever in a constant state of discord, giving no hint of any love that might have married them. From my own experience, I also knew that vows of allegiance or resolution were always followed by obtuse breadths of time that made those oaths hard to keep, and that this very phenomenon was what life was mainly about. But the child itself, I'd been told, was the only proof needed of the parents' love. If that were true, though, then might not Laurel and Hardy, childless, be held by a higher love, one not in need of proof?

If I ever doubted the love of Laurel and Hardy—and one does not doubt, or even really know, what one merely assumes, even if assumption composes all one's deepest knowledge—any question vanished when I saw a famous photograph of the two of them likened to the traditional masks of the drama, comedy and tragedy. Perhaps predictably, considering Laurel's role as rube in the duo, and Hardy's as foil, Hardy performs tragedy in the photograph, while Laurel mimics comedy. The straight man's nobility lies in his willingness to play second banana, and the comedy of duos typically turns on a clash of egos, jockeying for superior position or a lion's share of plaudit—especially in teams whose humor depends on awareness of their own celebrity, like Hope and Crosby or Martin and Lewis. But the most prominent feature of this photograph is a certain tranquil equitability. Laurel looks like Laurel, with that amiable angularity of face, the horizontal, abstract smile elongated well beneath the sparkling, bedeviled eyes. But Hardy looks nothing, really, like Hardy, perhaps because one is unused to seeing him at such close quarters. His head is tilted toward his companion, as if to rest on his shoulder, but his eyes seem trained on a sad distance that must finally be interior, and his mustache looks moist, as if wet with recent tears; his mouth is crinkled in a frown still with wryness in it, one that brings more than ever to the roly-poly cheeks and arch brow the nuance of sadness. It is as if, stricken with grief, he seeks consolation from his mate, who remains as ever unaware, and as if he gets it, somehow, miraculously, all the same. In this picture, Hardy is unmistakably consoled, whatever the source of his woe, and for all that its traces remain, though Laurel seems to take no note of Hardy's causeless grief—tragedy knows comedy, after all, but comedy must stay innocent of tragedy. Though Laurel does not knowingly give this consolation, Hardy intimately receives it, and it is just such comfort, perhaps, that keeps the two together.

Fat and thin: these were the poles of affinity that wed Laurel to Hardy, Hardy to Laurel. The mysterious likeness between them was eased by this difference, a difference that spoke richly of reciprocal correlations. In the quartets or in the trios, trade ruled the order of things, and dominance was a commodity to be usurped, the upper hand contingent upon resource and craft, but theoretically available to any or all. Even among others, the duo remained beholden to the unspoken bonds between only themselves. In a marriage of man and wife the dialectic of superiority and its opposite may have been determined by sex itself, if balanced by the influence of character, but in a partnership of men, it remained to be decided. Still, the irreducible weight of body swayed the verdict, and no pairing can progress in the absence of hierarchy: Hardy, fat, was the dominant, Laurel, thin, subordinate. This ranking was evident in every transaction, whenever Hardy's greater savoir faire clashed with Laurel's perpetual blockheadedness, wherever Laurel's churlish disregard triggered Hardy's fickle wrath. If Laurel's strength as prize buffoon earned him the preponderance of the laughs, this was the test of a self-sufficiency surrendered to dependence. Hardy was the bigger and the stronger, but he needed Laurel more than Laurel needed Hardy. Though such separation was truly unimaginable, without Hardy, Laurel could still be funny—granted that either of them could ever be funny to begin with—but without Laurel, Hardy would be deprived of his only fertile stimulus. The fool has a whole world of absurdity at his beck and call to reckon with, but the straight man has only the fool. Perhaps the blunt lassitude of Hardy's oddly tender rage—you could tell that Hardy, like the Skipper on *Gilligan's Island* pummeling his skinny mate, pulled his punches—acknowledged this strange equilibrium.

The rule of power was governed predictably by the body's changeless gravities, then, but even this edict allowed the flux of ambiguity. Dominion seemed as constant in most pairings of fat with thin as the inevitability of thin wedding fat was itself unremitting, but sometimes that dominion was harder to measure than at other times. In most cases—Gilligan and the Skipper, for one, or Fred Flintstone and Barney Rubble, or Ralph Kramden and Ed Norton from *The Honeymooners*—fat ruled thin as surely as rock crushed scissors or paper covered rock. But the rules changed. Movies on TV from the 1940s, for instance, that paired lithe, feline Peter Lorre (who, at other times, was fat) with robust, leonine Sydney Greenstreet, of the jutting belly and the rumbling, wheezy laugh, complicated the given patterns. In my favorite of these films, the gothic melodrama *The Verdict,* a playful coopera-tion emerged buoyantly behind the appearance of pettifoggery as the principal model of relation, but usually Peter Lorre played a fey, cowering functionary to Sydney Greenstreet's sternly affable authoritarian. At the climax of *The Maltese Falcon,* in a moment that always provoked in me (and still does) spasms of delighted, involuntary laughter, Peter Lorre as the prissy, retiring, perfumed Joel Cairo turns unexpectedly on Sydney Greenstreet, shouting at him furiously, *"You bloated idiot!"* Whether Greenstreet's zonked, affectless reaction to this assault means imperturbability or shock, the abrupt retaliation showed that aggression need not be a con-stant quantity. The top one could give up dominance—though perhaps not without some due of humiliation—and the bottom one could turn the tables. To movies of like vintage, I often found myself bringing the pretext of fat and thin, top and bottom, even where it did not appear visibly merited. Hope and Crosby, for instance, were comparably endowed in bodily dimension, but de-spite Hope's yellow-bellied, recreant simperings, because of his irrefutably superior wit (or maybe just because he seemed to be the more famous of the two) and because of the relative self-effacement of Crosby's presence, despite its cool poise, I viewed Hope as fat, Crosby as thin. In Hope's solo movies, he was ren-dered thin once more, or else simply beyond the grasp of the categories, while Crosby, when paired with the elegantly scrawny Fred Astaire, or with the finespun, wiredrawn Danny Kaye, in *White Christmas,* and driven to a crooner's folly, turned fat. What this meant was that the gauges of fat and thin were not intrinsic, immutable, but neither were they capricious. They were amenable, and changed each only in relation to the other, but steadfast.

Abbott and Costello presented the fraughtest challenges to the rule of the duo—fat and thin—but these only availed in the end to clarify it. Closest of all the duos in temperament, spirit, and figure to Laurel and Hardy, Abbott and Costello were furthest from them only in the most pertinent respect. The fat one was the nominal follower, the thin one the putative leader, caller of the shots. Costello's confusion, in their most famous routines, redoubles Abbott's brisk certitude, which disguises question as assertion: "Who's on first?" It is Abbott who knows the ways of the world—and he typically begins his unctuous dealings with the world at large by gabbing mealymouthed apologies for his lowbrow cohort's latest boners—and Costello who helplessly relies on this superior bearing. Thin reigns supreme, in this case, but fat still traffics in melancholy need. Costello's sadness is balder, more naked, than Hardy's, since it is never masked by tyranny, and his signature plaint belies infantile shame: *"I'm a baaaad boy!"* If Abbott is sexless, and Costello curiously ambisexual, it may be because thin boasts conjugal stringency, and fat polymorphous perversity. In the movie that made the pair famous, *Buck Privates*—a title, like *The Bank Dick,* that readily lends itself to pornographic reverie, borne out in the films' obsessive resort to double entendre—the two, unlikely warriors, are drafted, and the comedy derives from their slap-sticky efforts to ascend to the soldierly apex of proper masculinity. Abbott has less trouble adapting to this imperative than Costello, who jumps on other soldiers' backs, willy-nilly, as a call to arms, and who guilelessly asks the commander for a date when they tangle in maneuvers. By instinct, if not by declaration, Costello recognizes the sexuality of aggression, the feckless aggression of sexuality—in one scene, he's meant to box with a sexy young man, and seems strangely eager to put the gloves on, but at the last minute, a tattooed hayseed butts in as substitute, and Costello blanches—and if his subordinate demeanor dooms him forever to be only the object of this aggression, it is in the preemptive recognition itself that he might seize the prerogatives of the subject.

Abbott almost never has a love interest in their movies, but Costello, in one way or another, often does. In *The Time of Their Lives,* one of their most unusual films, and one of my favorites as a boy—second only to *Abbott and Costello Meet Frankenstein*—Costello plays the ghost of a soldier from the Revolutionary War who, in modern-day America, must clear his name of treason to be united in heaven with his beloved, and Abbott, who'd played a scheming traitor in a fanciful wartime prologue, returns later in the film as one of the living moderns, unwillingly recruited to help in the ghost's cause. In the movie's crass, garish last scene, Costello arrives at the pearly gates, liberated from his imprisonment on earth, and coos through the bars at his gold-locked ladylove, now so soon to be ransomed, only to find that heaven is closed in observance of Washington's Birthday. Did I only imagine, watching this scene, that Costello's heartsore double take subsumed a measure of relief, repreving a slighted troth to his one true mate? The two, Costello and Abbott, work within a whole ensemble in this movie's cast, with little real direct contact between them; yet even here, where they are not properly teamed—perhaps especially here—their status as couple remains unassailable, so vivid is the charge that still passes from one to the other. Affinity abides, then, at the level of soul, not in opportunity or mere proximity, and to see Costello without Abbott—in *The Thirty-Foot Bride of Candy Rock*, where the oafish marriage plot only punctuates the absence in question—is to experience the desolation of an unsung divorce. If—fat and thin—these two were not *made for each other,* as one of the many canards of coupling that made us take coupling so for granted would have spelled it, then maybe whatever marriage they might have hoped for could *only* be made in heaven.

Flatland University in 1978 was a modest settlement made up of a few 1950s-style buildings strewn across modestly disproportionate hills and running lawns in a region too rustic to be called suburban, if still too near the city to be called properly rural. Its bucolic quaintness and alluring nearness were its chief selling points, appealing to customers who liked their educations easy and safe and fast and cheap. Its disinfected simulations of the archetypal features of a real university were wide enough to persuade the pliable skeptic, and broad enough to placate the already sold, perhaps disinclined to enhance their pragmatic investments just for the sake of the picturesque. One wall advertised a dense muddle of ivy overgrowing its prefab brick, while a miniature moat with a jerry-built bridge arcing over it snaked around one of the "halls" (as real universities dub their constituent structures). I'd visited the campus for one day in third grade, at a Young Writer's Conference in which I'd won an Honorable Mention, and the ivy, the moat, the bridge, and the agrarian scope of the place had all lingered as fond memories. Considerations of money, that old bugbear, prevented me from going away to college, as all my friends from high school had done, and rather than yield to these considerations as real worries, I chose a local school, with an acceptance too rigorously cheerful to be called resignation. Flatland University had its countrified charm to recommend it over the schools of the city, after all, and knowledge was knowledge, no matter where you found it. The site of an early victory, revisited, might well open the inlet to future success.

The return to a childhood bedroom that finds it stunted and shrunken, by contrast to the grander, brighter chambers recall yields, is a familiar rendition of memory's cheat, and the day I arrived on the campus of Flatland University as a student was the very day I saw through my juvenile ideals to the depressing actuality of the place. In fact, I'd been there many times since the triumph of my Honorable Mention, because my sister had gone there too, ahead of me, and when I'd visited her on campus, it had still seemed a respectably august institution. Now that I was matriculating myself, I saw the collegiate trappings of the place for what they really were: bush league—the ivy wilting, the shallow moat polluted. There was, quite suddenly, no *there* there. How could I have failed to see it sooner? I felt like a hapless newlywed struck by the predictable thunder of coming to his senses the morning after the honeymoon. Matriculation points in more than partial homonymy toward matrimony: our proudly unschooled father made no secret of the fact that, if college was unfortunately necessary in my case, to make me a good provider, it would be justified in my sister's case only if it landed her a prosperous husband. I'd participated in the perpetuation of such received wisdoms, I now gleaned, simply by following my sister to Flatland in the first place, continuing the familial pattern of copycat enrollments, giving in to the impoverishments of tradition instead of forging my own path. And the whole question of college remained intertwined, densely as the tangles of ersatz ivy, with the matter of mating. My worst fear then, oddly enough, was being stuck with an unsuitable mate, and now, when I had to grow up once and for all if I were ever going to, I found myself stuck with the wrong college—a bad portent. College was maturity's last vehicle, mating merely its ultimate proof. Failure in the domain of the former summoned a fear worse than the worst I'd imagined—the conjunction of grave new superlatives, undreamt of, with the futility of all human endeavor. Maybe I'd never marry.

It was all too much to bear, and came down upon me all at once, and so I went to the movies. Orientation was a three-day affair before the start of classes, a protracted bureaucratic obstacle course, lorded over by two upperclassmen, a perky Business major with wooden barrettes impaling her thickly braided hair, and a sullen, pimply Engineering student with dark ink blotched along the bottom seams in the pockets of his polyester shirts, where the numerous pens he had carried there had burst. Some dozen of us, a dazed, dillydallying pack, were herded by these two through seemingly endless tours of the campus. I set myself instantly apart from the group by dint of my superior recognition of the uselessness of it all. I could even bring myself to see a certain poignancy in the earnest, hopeful attitudes the other members of my group all wore along with their confused expressions. Good citizens, starry-eyed at the start of what they took to be an auspicious enterprise, they all sported their name tags, as I would not deign to do, and in the sloppy scrawls of their names, composed in the vibrant green of a Magic Marker that bled profusely when it wrote, and in the disheveled posting of these slatternly emblems, affixed off-kilter upon their dowdy, optimistic breasts, one could see at once how much they all hoped for a better life—for the tags were badges of pride—and how little this hope availed. By midmorning, bored and unhappy, I knew for sure what they did not—that it was all for naught—and I fixed my face in a wry scowl. Another member of the group, consuming candied almonds by the handful from a big bag, rattled the bag at me peremptorily, as if it were a maraca, and wiggled his eyebrows when our eyes happened to meet. I looked away at once. That afternoon I shook the group and took flight. I went to the movies.

The movie was *Dear Inspector*, a French comedy with murder-mystery overtones, starring Annie Girardot and Philippe Noiret, whom I'd never heard of but whose very names I loved. I chose this movie over countless American blockbusters—it was the season of *Star Wars*—because it was foreign, and because it was playing at the Prudential Town Center. The Prudential Town Center was a new office building far across town, as far away from Flatland as my '73 Ford Gran Torino would carry me. It was the closest the suburbs could show to a skyscraper, towering amid the gimcrack, prostrate lairs of groundling business that surrounded it, with a pattern of gold-plated windows arranged diagonally from floor to floor to make a giant gold X across the majestic side of the building, galvanically aglow when the sun struck it. The cinema was nestled in a corner of the concourse, next to a lush arboretum traversed by cinder walkways and roofed with an angled wall of steel and mullioned glass, like the ramparts of a greenhouse. What I hated most about the suburbs, in that age when they were a little harder to despise because they did not yet seem ubiquitous, was their obeisance to complacent segregation, and what I loved about the Prudential Town Center—not knowing its erection was just another phase in the suburbs' conquest of the world—was its disregard of the usual barriers. Here, business mingled with leisure, and both with nature—the theater lodged among offices, beside the arbor—and the effect was not inapt, or chaotic, but elegant, urbane. The movies they showed there too were apart from the common run. They came from far off, where other languages were spoken, and they could transport one far away. They proved the existence of other states, of place or mind or being, to which, however the deliverance might be delayed, one could someday finally escape.

That the vehicle of these visions of liberation was really little more than a frivolous caper movie suggests, perhaps, the fragility of the fantasy. Foreign movies were to become for a long while my conduit to a place where, I imagined, stood beings akin to myself— a holy plaza of the mind—but I could never completely dodge the nauseous intuition that the reason I was stuck in suburbia was that it was where I really belonged, and one day, when I was trapped in a loveless marriage, that too would be a just desert. What if my utopian thoughts of kinship were, after all, just delusion? I loved slick, superficial French farces, and sought them out, because I fancied myself foreign, in my way, and I took my ability to enter into their genial spirit as authenticating evidence of my own sophistication, which was what set me apart. Whenever I saw a foreign film I did not understand, like the serenely, magisterially puzzling *That Obscure Object of Desire,* by Luis Buñuel, shown just the month before at the Prudential Town Center, or Ingmar Bergman's *The Serpent's Egg,* with its illegible horrors and its overwrought twists and turns, it could only mean that I was not really equal to the task I'd laid myself, to rise above the banality of my surroundings and take my proper place in the better world of my imagining, where I would finally be embraced. It could mean only, in fact, that banality *was* my proper place.

But *Dear Inspector* presented no such vexations. Sunny, high-spirited, with a sharp wit that redeemed what could no longer be considered, by virtue of its redemption, its occasional corniness, the movie married a comic love story—female cop meets ivory-tower egghead—to a murder plot that cheated a little, but still featured a satisfying crop of intricately cross-referenced clues. Annie Girardot, thin, and Philippe Noiret, fat—fused despite apparent incompatibility—were like a Gallic version of Laurel and Hardy, gaily bisexed in reincarnation. In the easeful darkness of the theater, where I was one of only five patrons, not one of us coupled, I watched the film in a state of ravishing contentment, happy that I'd chosen this gadfly pleasure over the tiresome responsibility of my educational future. Near the end of the film, there was a random shot of a city street at dawn, slowly coming back to life in the morning. It had nothing to do with the plot, this passing, lovely shot, but the beauty it captured of the luminous pink light of daybreak stirred my soul. Beauty sometimes lay in the margin, then, so would have to be watched for. I pitied my other self, the one who had stayed behind, and who was even now trudging through the dutiful march of Orientation—who would never learn such lessons about beauty. The next afternoon, for a second time, I shirked that other self, who was probably too dull to be worthy of my pity, and returned to see *Dear Inspector* again. But this time I was not alone, and would not be again, for a long season.

"And where have *we* been?" a boy asked in a stylized simper when I reappeared at Orientation again the next morning. It was the boy who had shaken the bag of candied almonds at me the day before. His name tag read NICHOLAS. His wide, green, hooded eyes, flanked by high cheekbones and thick, black eyebrows, always looked fraught with extreme emotion because of how big and bright they were, but this effect was undermined by the set of his mouth, curiously small in spite of the fullness of his lips, which suggested a good-humored skepticism. He held another bag of candied almonds.

Nobody at Flatland University had as of yet seemed in any way to notice me, so I was taken off-guard, and had only the truth to fall back on. "I went to the movies," I told him.

"Hmm." The wide green eyes narrowed slightly. "A *renegade*." He plucked a candied almond from the bag and, still fixing me with his moody gaze, tossed the almond into the air and caught it in his mouth, with only minor decrease of dignity.

That day Orientation was even more tedious, if so inane a quantity could lend itself to measurement, than it had been the day before. We were paraded into the library, where the sullen Engineering student and the perky Business major presumed to acquaint us with the complexities of the card catalog, a venture that served only to reveal their own insufficient mastery of that intricate index. ("Oopsy!" chirped the Business major, when advised of a breach in her grasp of the decimal system.) In the margins of these fruitless sessions, I commiserated with the boy with the candied almonds. He was as bored as I was, and when I told him I planned to escape to the movies again that afternoon, he asked if he could come with me.

We were the only people in the theater. He sat to my left, and I was very aware of him beside me, this boy I hardly knew, munching his almonds, as the movie, shot by shot, mechanically but still magically, ran its well-known course. It was known to me, that is, but not to him, and I felt myself trying to see it afresh, through his eyes. When the lovely shot of the daybreak recurred, with its breathtaking pink light, I heard him sigh. It was a sigh of contentment, not of boredom. Was it possible that he, too, saw the beauty of it? He had not thought it odd that I was going back to see the very same movie I had seen just the day before, nor had he seemed to be put off by the foreignness of the film itself. He did not try to talk me into seeing a more ordinary film. Could that alone be evidence of affinity? As we sat side by side, I felt some uncommon accord arising between us, and somehow already, right away, it seemed to differ from the sundry accords I'd sensed before. There was none of the tempered agon that usually accompanied the habitation of movie theater seats—the battle for the armrests, or the muffled fight for leg room. He sat with tranquil composure, arms at his sides, the big eyes wide and gleaming in the dark, quietly receptive to the quiet spectacle of the film, and he consumed the almonds noiselessly, careful not to crinkle the bag. He tilted the bag only a little to offer me some at intervals, and I was struck by the adroitness of the gesture, showing generosity without unduly disrupting my attention to the film. Even if these practices were only evidence of an elegance of personal habit or manner, they still seemed to demonstrate a real consideration of me—a way, somehow, already, of making me known.

Maybe, I reflected soon after, trying to make sense of what I thought, or feared, might be starting to happen, that was the true condition of mating: not to find oneself in another, or another to complement oneself, but to discover another with the capacity to make one known to oneself, in whom one's acknowledgment prompted the same capacity.

That is what happened.

Contingency, proximity, opportunity—these had come to seem to me, all through high school, the spurs and the detriments to mating, what made it possible but what made it odious. As anyone could see, the tool that paired boy with girl in the inglorious milieu of high school was principally instrumentality itself, the need, in a province where the trivial was always granted the weight of the ultimate, for a date to the prom. For those who would allow such coarse norms to rule them, as if they could not see that there might be better life after high school, I harbored nothing but contemptuous pity, and apart from a few groping, laggard make-out sessions with girls in the dark basements of dank parties, I eschewed the given rituals of mating, all the while chancing randomly, breathlessly, on far more opportunities with boys, pursued far more enthusiastically, than one who sought to rise above those temptations, too, could ever have hoped to resist. These couplings, also furtive, but never public, were simply not conceivable as preludes to real mating. They were sins of flesh, brought on by undeniable needs of flesh—mere convenience, but more honest, I thought, despite secrecy, truer than the same convenience that paired off my peers—and they could be absolved, if never redeemed, only by the thought of that need's origin outside myself. In one way or another I had always felt it, so surely it could not be mine alone. Whatever I made of it, it had to have been lent me—a gift, or a burden. The long route of the love of boys—Joey or Luke, or Bobby Adams, or Kevin or Craig—ended with sex. Even if carnality had been a real end, unknown, and never reached, of those loves, I could not love the boys, now, whose bodies were so known to me. I could only be fond of them, deeply fond, for what they gave me, and what they wanted of me, since their want, in its way, approved me, made me as real, in its way—I was stubborn then, and unwilling in the face of all evidence to count myself worthless—as girlfriends made boyfriends. Others mated to achieve maturity; I would first reach it, to better know the mate who would surely follow. But someday soon, when I was at last a man, once and for all, I still hoped, I would transcend base desire, which seemed always a new hurdle, each time it was discovered. I would feel, not what I was supposed to—for I'd always scorned rank conformity, and always would. No: transcendence then would mean rising above tendentious time or provincial place, *supposing* what one *felt,* feeling it truly, and finding it in oneself, not in another, but *through* another.

Memories of lost love flirt with elegy just as tales of first love tease idyll, but idyll and elegy flatter memory far more handily than they can ever honor loss. All that fall our friendship grew with an inevitability, outside effort, that rendered idyll, refused its temptations, much as vintners render the essence of grapes. It is only in memory that this season stays as idyll. In the reality insatiable memory devours, it was just an appointed lot. After the movie we went back to his dorm room. He'd loved the movie too, and we spoke of it with the passion monks might have brought to bear on talk of consubstantiation. Some recognition of the film's basic unseriousness may have hovered under our talk. Our appreciation of it lay not in the wish to elevate it, but in the details that mattered for their own pure sakes. We were two boys, turning men, unaddressed by the place or the time we lived in, who would have to find peripheral patronage in what we regarded, if we found it at all. That was what our avid chatter concerning the movie's costumes, and settings, and stray implications or half-baked epigrams was about: not a dawning consciousness, but one fully awake, though it has been given no space. A half-baked epigram is better than any well-done bromide. The only real furnishing in his dorm room was a big purple beanbag chair, big enough for two so long as the two did not mind passing contact, and we flopped into the plush pillow that whizzed under us like an overgrown whoopee cushion. We jabbered and laughed until, as noon gave way to night, our voices grew soft and drowsy, and we fell asleep together.

At Orientation the next morning, the perky Business major, getting a bit frazzled, told us that our absences had been noted, and informed us further that we should not expect to succeed at a place such as Flatland University if we were not willing to buckle down and put nose to grindstone and shoulder to wheel.

"Let's hit the road, Jack," said Nicholas, and we were off.

We went to see *Dear Inspector* again.

It could not have been an effort to recapture the day before because the spirit of the day did not seem to have fled. Our friendship started in refuge and never really left it. In these months we escaped together, not into each other, but only from what had no claim on us. It was shared discovery, not shared disdain, that was really the object of our flights, and though we spent almost all of our few months entirely alone together, pointedly *not* doing whatever we were supposed to be doing, that was out of elected affinity, not resisted society. I never met his family, and he never met mine. We both had groups of friends, but never once spent time together among them. The charm of our relation was that it was not a part of any larger social unit, nor did it ever seem cut off, unintegrated. The whole point, right away, was its integrity, and the reason I'd spoken of him so seldom among others, I told myself after, was the same reason I seldom spoke of myself. He'd become at once a presence within me, yet our relation had none of the smirky coquetry or the pouty doubt or coy, lovey-dovey solipsism—all that *Wuthering Heights* jazz we both hated—of couples. Proximity had brought us together, and opportunity given us time, and even if these forces were the instruments of utility, that could not dim real affinity. To accept them would perhaps not only let that affinity stand, but keep it from trifle.

He was eight months older than I was, almost to the day. His parents had divorced when he was ten. His father lived on a ranch in Wyoming, where he had spent a month the summer before, and he lived with his mother in a big house in the hills of Rochester, just off a winding road named for a favored constellation. His parents were rich. They did not understand him. They did not understand anything except money. He loved to dance because, he said, he loved the idea of being able to talk without words. He played the guitar, probably for the same reason. He was a terrible driver, and he had already been in two bad car accidents. There would be yet one more while I knew him, before the last one. There was a mixture of attention and distraction you could see in him, especially when he drove. Poised in the driver's seat, he would remain fixed on his passenger, holding the steering wheel with only one hand and glancing sidewise through the windshield, as if the wheel were just a minor diversion and the road ahead only one of the wearying obligations he prided himself on neglecting. Sometimes you felt he did not notice you, but then, when he spoke, his words, not cautious or careful, but weighed, showed there was really nothing he had missed, and when he danced he seemed to leave the apparent behind, to concentrate only on the perceptible; he ignored the trivial, but still saw the importance of the minute. He loved the feeling of traveling, but hated the thought that he was conveying himself willfully through the world: progress should be free of will. He was tall, and thin. He wanted to be an actor, and practiced mime. There was a love of silence about him. He had come to Flatland because he wanted to waste his parents' money without spending too much of it. He had come because the theater department had just hired a minor celebrity, whose claim to fame was having played Tiny Tim, many years before, in a movie version of *A Christmas Carol*. He loved the tackiness of this: to study Shakespeare under Tiny Tim. He loved candied almonds. The bones of his delicate wrists flared from the sleeves of his colorful shirts, and his Adam's apple bobbed prominently, his neck long and curved, in a manner that should have made him look gangly, and gawky; and the truth was, I did not think he was beautiful, at first. But I did not think I was beautiful, either.

Week after week as the term started, we would cut class and go to the movies. It was a terrible year for movies, which was a good thing for us, since it left our truancies uncondoned by uplift. The films we scoffed at the most were also the ones we prized the most highly, because that proved that value exceeded mere objects. Transport may have been the final goal, but not the easy one, beloved of the masses, that was always at hand. That transport was poignant, evidence of sad delusions we knew, but still hoped, we did not share. But the road to real transcendence was rough, never easy or smooth. Over entertaining baubles like *Heaven Can Wait* or *The Cheap Detective*, or weightier affairs like *Pretty Baby* and *The Deer Hunter*, we preferred—when there were no foreign films to be seen—innocuous, arty, out-of-the-way failures like *Comes a Horseman, Once in Paris,* or *Slow Dancing in the Big City*. Whether these movies were good or bad was not the point, since quality was only the veil of sanctimonious respectability. Even if they were touching in their failures, these movies revealed the sources of sentiment, so you could see why people wanted it, but they also expressed its flaws, so you could see why it had to be resisted. In this they were like the old-time comedies that Nicholas knew nearly as well as I did. They let you see what was supposed to be funny, or sad, but did not make you participate in it, and in that was their real tragedy, or comedy. Movies—even our beloved *Dear Inspector,* even *Star Wars,* even *The Deer Hunter* with its sprawling, interminable wedding scene, and despite its manic-depressive machismo—were so much about coupling, but if that theme lay under everything, its tireless excavation equaled its repudiation. It was in seeing through the imperatives of relation that we were joined. It was in a *sensibility,* invented by being shared—the things we liked together differed fairly from many things we liked apart—but granted a weight of its own. I wanted to be queer without being gay, or gay without being queer; so it made a certain sense that if when young I'd conjured romance without substantial bonds, I should now seek bonds, if I sought them at all, without substantial romance.

I never met his parents, but one day, when he was sure his mother was away, he brought me to their house. It was a big house in the hills, gambrel-roofed, relatively modest for a mansion, winged and turreted but sparsely and leanly so, and set far back from the road that wound up to it. The house was sumptuously decorated, all the rooms stocked with expensive, well-tended imitations of antiques, and he seemed embarrassed by its fey opulence. The place looked abandoned, unlived in. We wandered through the big, airless rooms, crammed with expensively tasteful furnishings but empty of life, as if we were making our way through a museum, a gloomy showplace, dedicated to the display of vulgar abundance. I searched in vain for mantelpiece photos of him—I'd have loved to see what he looked like as a boy—but the cavernous rooms were as devoid of the simulation as they were of the solidity of human presence. We moved about like ghosts, our footsteps echoing along with the hollow ticks of stopless clocks in the deadened space, and we did not stay long. He gazed around the costly, well-kept rooms, like me, with an air of detached curiosity and distaste, as if he were seeing the place for the first time, and were as much a stranger there as I was. "They think I'm away at school," he said. He always spoke of his parents as an anonymous entity—"They"—even though they lived apart. "We could rob them blind, and take it on the lam to Tahiti with the loot, and nobody would ever be the wiser. How's about it?" I demurred.

On the drive down the hill, his mood soared in a giddy recklessness that made me decide that his careful reserve on the way up had been prompted by apprehension, not by caution. Maybe he'd wanted me to see where he came from, I thought, so that he would not have to tell me. As we headed down the steep, tortuous road, brakes whining and tires screeching in the curves, we did not talk about what we had seen there. "From now on *I* drive," I shouted above the noise, but he waved off my stuffy alert. He sang with the radio—"Lost in Love," by Air Supply—reaching his free arm into the air through the window and catching the wind in his open palm; and although I did not think he was singing to me, I thought I had seen what he had wanted me to see—how little solace that home gave his well-being—and felt something new, maybe, even beyond accord, rising between us. It was only away from home, together or apart, that we would come into our own. Back in the comfortable squalor of his dorm room, he danced in pink fuzzy slippers, Donna Summer blaring on the radio, his felted feet sweeping across the floor, as if he were suspended above the ground, not flush upon it. From the beanbag I stared, mesmerized, but then he drew me into the dance, his odd, unforeseen joy dousing my reluctance, and as the feverish wail of Donna Summer gave way to the cool drone, once again, of Air Supply—the synchronicity seeming less, for once, a note of crassness, the usual recurrent hiccup of a puny culture, than a good omen—we danced together.

What could I know of marriage, then, except what I could learn from all that daily surrounded me, or from every movie in the history of the world? But what could I *ever* know of the joining together of men, except what I might have gleaned from Laurel and Hardy, or else could teach myself?

As the fall shaded over into the winter, and the air grew colder and trees gave up their leaves, I started getting fat. It was a mystery. I stopped sharing his candied almonds. I tried to eat less and less— but ate more and more, no doubt, of the diminished portions— and still the mirror threw cruel, unceasing light on the thickening thighs, the expanding hips. Too aware early on of the pitfalls of narcissism, I had never found any particular fascination in mirrors—sameness is not reflection, and reflection too can show difference—but I'd begun spending a fair amount of time in front of mirrors in the weeks just before I started getting fat. I'd gaze at the fair, freckled skin, the pale, shallow chest, the sunken, featureless belly, the knobby knees, wondering how it was possible to appraise what was simply ordained, and I'd think—without ever framing it so bluntly, so crudely—*Could he* want *me?* It was as if the rediscovery of my body made me fat, or as if fat alone could turn me back to my body. Our bodies—his tall and thin, mine short and, now, fat—were not at issue between us, but if the gravity of the body was among the powers we escaped together, it might also be the one that followed us, that we would have to come back to. As any two-bit shrink will tell you, fat insulates body from sex: I did not want to get fat, but if I was going to get fat anyway, fat would likely put off those boys I could not love, so that I would not have to gather the resolve to spurn them myself; and then I would be truly free to follow my one true heart, and be true at last to this boy, this man, whom I could, perhaps, truly, love.

But was he—or I—a boy, or was I—or he—a man? If we were boys, then I could still love him, perhaps, without its meaning something final. But if we were men, and if I loved him, then there was no going back. All that would remain to be seen was whether I would be Hardy to his Laurel or Abbott to his Costello. The wonder of us so far, the enchantment, was how little our relation approximated the system of dependency and sufficiency, of dominations and unrequitements and reciprocations that—we knew mutually, without ever talking about it, beyond the liabilities of the mutual—was marriage. A marriage between us was unthinkable, a coupling barely conceivable. This was not because we ourselves could not conceive it, or think it, but because the times and the places we lived in, the ones that otherwise paid us so little mind, made it so. When we fled to our afternoon matinees, or our other fugitive excursions, it was not responsibility we were shirking, but falsehood. If we were a couple already, and men, then maybe I got fat to realize the only way we could be one—to settle the questions of who was what to whom, of thin and fat, that would need to be settled, since the determinations of masculine and feminine could not be counted on to settle them. If we were boys, and were not a couple, maybe I got fat to insure that we couldn't be. Either way, our bodies were not yet at issue between us, except to the extent that we went on inhabiting them. But not long before the end of the term, as the holidays approached, and we fell into elegiac moods because we thought days might go by where we would not see each other, he remarked that he noticed I was getting "pleasingly plump."

The fate of enchantment is to dwindle back into real time, since that is where it came from in the first place, and all that fall, as I got fatter, I failed one class after another, with an attitude not even of resignation, since the classes held so little charm for me, so small a place in my attentions, but with the unblinking acceptance one brings to a foregone conclusion. I failed Logic. The wonderful idea that rational abstraction authorized any concatenation of terms in a premise so long as they would tally—accounting nothing to prohibit such thrilling propositions as "Ollie loves Stan" or "Bud loves Lou"—could retain its fascination only in the hours of enchantment. In real time, where knowledge was not hailed, but tested, I failed Logic. It followed (to fail a subject does not even bring the consolation of freeing one from its hold) that I would fail Math too. It did not necessarily follow (though that hold extend its compass into unexpected reaches) that I would fail French, but apart from the basic stuff I remembered from high school, I could summon only a few words in a private colloquy in the professor's office, where I was supposed to show off my vocabulary. These words were *gross,* which meant fat, *pommes frites,* which meant french fries, and *ignominieux,* which had been uttered by Philippe Noiret at a particularly memorable moment in *Dear Inspector,* and was much the same word in English. In fact, I'd been counting on my love of *Dear Inspector* to open up some magical access to the language for me, one more fecund than the drudgery of study could produce. No other hayseed in this rinky-dink class at this Podunk college would ever have seen *Dear Inspector*—an actual French movie!—and that must have counted for something. There was nothing flawed in the theory, but in practice the few words I could summon did not make for fertile combinations. The only viable one was a censorious comment on the ignominy of fat french fries, rasped in harsh reply to nearly every parry, in what was supposed to be a devilishly French accent, complete with guttural vowels and rolled *r*'s. It was a disgraceful performance. I never went back to the class. After that, it probably followed (I'd know for sure, if I'd passed Logic) that I would fail Literature, so I stopped going to that class too.

And where was Nicholas, during all of this? I did not spend enough time with him, not nearly enough, but he was there, with me, all the while. We saw each other a few times every week during this time, and that meant I was often alone, but somehow I was never lonely, because of him, and though, in spite of him, I must have been unhappy—I was getting fat, after all, and flunking all my classes—I never felt it then. I did not go back to French after my failed colloquy, not because I was embarrassed, but because I did not want to have to be, and with Nicholas, somehow, I never had to be. We talked little of the mess of daily life, much of the pith of higher things. Kindred intellects, we were more inclined to meditate on the *concept* of defeat, its inner structure, than to acknowledge the fear, if we held it, that it might overcome us, ourselves. It was in talking of the postulate, we knew, that one could know oneself. Fleshly, intimate: when our bodies soon *be-*

came matter between us, it still did not have to mean that I was gay. It could mean only that I wanted to know him more—beyond the measly pairings of thin or fat, bottom or top, tragedy or comedy. *This*, this *beyond*ness, is what would change, nothing less, from the loves of boyhood. He was what I'd never looked for, would not have known to seek—how could we ever know, with nothing to teach us, before we taught each other?—if I had not found it first. It was so, so clear: it was possible to love another, and another man, without fancy, and, maybe, without shame. At first I had not thought he was beautiful, but now I knew that he was, and knew that the bridge between thought and knowledge, therefore, was one that could be crossed. That too was boon change. Even if I lost him—for I'd started to overcome the basic prohibition, but I had still not unlearned its corollary, the hardest one to unlearn, that love between men is founded in lack, and must always return to it—this knowledge would always stay. I knew I loved him many weeks before he sat me down and told me, at last, that he had finally accepted the fact that he was gay. His wide, green eyes flashed with hope and sadness. I hugged him, and said it did not matter to me. How could it matter? I know he wanted me to say that I was gay too, but I was not, in spite of everything, unless I said it.

Driving home that night alone, I cried behind the wheel, not really knowing why, and I pulled over when the tears blinded me. The month before, together, we'd been in an accident. I had not held to my resolve that I should always be the one to drive, so he was at the wheel then, animated by a sudden idea that diverted his attention from the car he sideswiped. A crash, a crunch, a jolt, and then a dead stillness, with only the quiet sizzle of hot juices leaking from shattered engines—and after we'd gathered ourselves up, and found that neither of us, that time, was hurt, he moaned under his breath, *"Another fine mess . . ."* While we waited for the police, he hugged me—there in public, out in the open, with no sense of embarrassment—and told me he was glad I was there with him. "Some day, in Tahiti," he said, "we'll look back on this and laugh." I made him promise to be more careful, and though he scoffed at the notion, he did promise. He said he promised.

There, and not there—how I remember him: bodily, insubstantial.

All that talk, from every quarter, that yammering, about the mysteries of desire—as if they were miraculous, and not debilitating—but it was only such talk that kept desire mystified. That was its very purpose. But the truth was, Hardy stays with Laurel, Laurel with Hardy, because there is percentage in it, and he wants to. Where was the mystery in that? Nicholas wanted me to tell him that I was gay too, I thought, because that would mean I loved him. For boys like us, maybe being gay was, sometimes, the only affinity you needed—a rare enough one—and we had more. But I decided I would tell him, instead, that I loved him, and if that meant, in turn, that I was gay, then so be it. He was such a lousy driver, but if I really loved him as I thought I must, it had to mean I loved that about him too. Nothing lay apart. It was only the thought that telling him I loved him would mean that I was gay, with no going back, that kept me from telling him right away. But I knew already how quickly everything goes, so I knew I could not wait forever.

I decided I would tell him in the spring, but by then he was gone. The end of winter brought a hard freeze, and a long thaw. Bare trees withered and withstood, and dark, gray skies rained ice on the land, freezing the sea, crusting the ground. Even careful travelers, whose roads home were straight and sure, found the way treacherous; even the careless made wary. But casualty is indifferent to care. I would tell him in the springtime, I thought, and meanwhile I would love him, in a language definite as speech, and hope that he knew. It was not so long a time, and the innocence before experience has experience in it too, just as the fullness before loss has loss in it, and the loss after, fullness. The winter was cold, blistery cold, but even then, I recall, I thought I might remember it as warmth. I loved him, and I knew that would not go, but it would change—I would change it, in speaking—so something about it, though augmented, would still have to vanish. It is when you think something is about to disappear that you live experience as memory. That only, and the world, nothing but the world, stayed me from speaking: the world, that had made us what we were, and would not let us be what it made us, and made of us, in that hindrance, what we were not. But what of it. Springtime was famous for forgiveness and rebirth, and would come soon, sooner than it seemed. I would tell him then, I thought—in the springtime, come the spring.

But by then he was gone.

11

BROKEN FEVER

The doctors washed the blood from their hands. Steel sinks lined the blank walls of the room, and these sinks were elongated, like community urinals in a public latrine. Spigots spaced at intervals sent columns of water into the tubs, and the sound of water against steel was like the scorch of light in one's eyes. One was at once aware, even then, that none of these forces—water, light—connived to shock, and the atmosphere was calm, torpid, not subdued (for that would have implied an act, a vanquishing), but funereal. What little moved there cast stillness as its source and its goal, and any power to act seemed less to have been obliterated than never first to have been thought. There was water and there was light, but the stream of the water was impalpable, the merest glimpse of small, stagnant channels lodged between invisible oceans, and the motion of the light was impalpable, even as its substance prickled, like heavy, wet cotton, on the skin and on the eyes. Under the static shafts of thin water, the doctors' hands seemed paralyzed, and though the water took the blood away, it was not its charge to cleanse. There was no color—the white of the doctors' coated backs as vacant as the silver tin of the sinks, or the cold tan of the table where I lay. I opened my eyes to what might have seemed the very bottom of nothingness, if the view had not proved nothingness endless, bottomless, and when I screamed, I knew that the blood that crackled in my throat was the same blood that stained the doctors' hands.

In bad dreams I still see that room. Even in the worst of these dreams, though, where the room stands in as, say, a crematorium, or a chamber of more general horrors, it is always less oppressive than it is in my memory. It has, say, a window, through which gleam the hopeful possibilities of other worlds; or else one of the doctors—they are always there, a grim triumvirate with anonymous dead looks, like the three functionaries who come to call from Joseph K.'s office—turns a kindly look upon me, and I believe at once that a single gesture of kindness might redeem an eternity of oppression, and wake, crying. I have these dreams most often when I'm sick—fever dreams—and I don't get sick, now, as often as I did then. But if these dreams prove anything, these dreams of a place so terrible I know I could never have imagined it if I had not remembered it, it is the powerful sway of wish fulfillment. In my memory, by contrast to these dreams, the room is windowless, and the doctor who turns his face to me, after I scream for my mother, bears a cold, stern countenance, and he comes to me with his hands stretched out before him like a creature of the living dead, and he wraps his hands, still covered with my blood, around my scarred, inflamed throat. For all their horror, I look back upon these dreams, from wakefulness, as poignantly optimistic—there's a window, after all, and the doctor smiles— and when I can bring their measure to the corresponding memories, I can sometimes convince myself that what the memories prove is nothing but the indelible fineness of the line between memory and dream.

Something must have gone wrong with the anesthetic, a doctor explained later. I was supposed to have remained narcotized until long after the operation was over. My having screamed when I awoke on the operating table, the doctor went on, with disapproval, would most likely make it take longer for my throat to heal. The doctor who did the talking did not look at me as he spoke. The disapproval lay in that fact, and in the reproof of his even voice. The doctor's head was bald, but there were dense patches of black hair above both of his ears, and you could see flakes of dandruff in the hair, like sand in beach grass. His hands were not covered with blood, but his fingers were stained with nicotine, and as he spoke to my parents, he folded his hands together, bridged, and twiddled his big thumbs, the skin so dry and leathery that the contact of fingers made scratchy noise, like the craunch of sandpaper on sandpaper. He did not tell them that when I woke on the operating table I'd screamed for my mother, but I hoped he did not expect me to be grateful for this grudging discretion.

In my ten years I had not been inside a hospital except the one where I was born, and now I had to spend three nights in the hospital. The paradox of the doctors' wounding me in the name of cure—they claimed the tonsilectomy would make me less "sickly"—could not have been fully apparent to me then, but the fact that the hospital itself, the very seat of restored health, was a terrible, oppressive place could not be avoided. From a distance the hospital looked like a gigantic upended cinder block, monolithic and slablike. From within, it appeared labyrinthine and compartmentalized, branching angular hallways leading past windowed cells or closed-off chambers, hive-like, where the uniformed staff pursued their busy futilities under the kind of unceasing light, saturated but somehow unbright, that promotes ease of inspection over expansion of mood. Denial of comfort was the hospital's evident vocation, all the chairs stiff of back and lean of cushion, the mattresses thick but hard, the walls and floors unadorned but for painted strips or plastic stripes in dull colors, a different shade denoting each department, meant to lead valetudinarians to the proper wing, to enforce aim and restrict wandering. Bouquets of flowers vegetating at patients' bedsides, meant to lift the gloom, only mocked the general atmosphere of lifelessness and were, in turn, and more oppressively, mocked by it. Bars of chrome, kin to those that braced the beds, girded the toilets, and the décor of the room combined plastic, metal, and wire in an environment that neither welcomed nor accommodated, but only anticipated, the worst possible injuries, the most advanced bodily deteriorations, the gravest imaginable illnesses.

The flowers by my own bedside languished after only half a day, as if they could not breathe in the hospital's stringent air. The next day a nurse whisked them away after she'd briskly fluffed my pillow—a routine that seemed less for the gain of my comfort than for the good of the pillow. The nurse was a big woman with gray eyes, buckteeth, and jowly chins. She tucked the flowers firmly under her arm as if they were fashioned of clipboard (since what she usually had clenched under that stalwart arm were the rigid boards of patients' charts), and she did not notice when a few petals fluttered to the ground. "Last thing we need around here," she commented with brittle harshness, "—things *dying.*" She disappeared behind the curtain that separated my bed from the next one, which had been empty the day before, prior to my surgery, and I heard her pounding on the neighboring bedding like a boxer working his bag. "But *your* flowers still look nice," I heard her say with a brisk cheer that still shared severity with her more typical dourness. "And," she went on, "looks like you're on the mend your own self."

A voice acknowledged her quietly. It was a boy's voice.

"Hi," I said, after the nurse had gone. No answer came, though I imagined a slightly zonked, quizzical inflection to the silence, so I repeated, "Hi."

"Hello," said my roommate. His voice was quiet, gentle, somehow modest.

"I'm Jimmy."

"I'm Joey." Breathy, careful, but still, I could tell, somehow open.

"I'm supposed to stay in bed."

"Me too."

"Is there a window? I can't see: this curtain."

"I think so," he answered, after a pause.

"We're on the sixteenth floor."

"I know." Sureness, but not, maybe, cockiness.

"How far down is it?" I asked. "Can you see to the ground?"

"No." A quality of regret, and not just for the occasion, I thought, but always—a quality, something sad. "I can't," he said. "My eyes."

I waited a long time.

"I'm here for my eyes," he said.

"I'm not really supposed to be talking," I said.

"Okay," replied Joey.

Agreeable; concordant.

Common sense promotes the knowledge that the human capacity for illness is inborn, but even the most meager experience counsels that the art of sickness must be learned. Disease troubles the category of the "natural." It is a force of nature, presumably, yet we understand it as a deviation from the bodily norm. Its prevalence reveals the ability of nature to encompass the purportedly deviant, just as its many grievous triumphs deride the very idea of norm. Illness stands in dialectic with wellness, makes us aware of the possibility of loss, forces the sufferer to engage with the body, which could otherwise be denied, left to its own devices. Watch a baby stricken with fever, earache, sniffles, chest cold; witness the spastic helplessness of the cries, the shock of the coughs, the instinctive rub of the baby's own hand against the sore ear. A baby would sooner rip off its own ear than subsist in such pain, but the baby's violent, destructive remedies could be called impatience only if patience itself were part of a baby's wordless lexicon. The graceless scratch, the brutal grab of the offending ear, the convulsive rub—all perform the baby's reflexive self-therapy, and the well-known need for custodial intervention should be sufficient to prove that the curative reflex is liable to harm. A baby's slow, painful ease into illness as a known quantity is like the topple into language. It is only when we understand illness as temporary that we learn, as children, to stop damaging ourselves by trying to exorcise disease immediately, physically, and can even begin to comprehend the paradoxical directive not to scratch an itch; it's only when we accept the fact that language is permanent that we finally agree to speak.

A "sickly" child, I first learned to bear illness, then learned to love it. Quite young, I became aware of the widespread cultural association of illness with arrested development, probably through such sources as Frances Hodgson Burnett's *The Secret Garden*, a book I loved. With its neo-Dickensian atmosphere, the book replaces Dickens's Miss Havisham, who stops time on the day of her failed wedding, with a tubercular little boy, Master Colin, who lives in regal stasis, wasting away in a grand Gothic hall. This boy also has associations with Rochester's mad wife in *Jane Eyre,* a story I knew, not from the book, whose paragraphs were too long and forbiddingly empty of quotation marks (and what is the use, as Alice asks, pre-Wonderland, of a book without pictures or conversations?), but from the dark, lovely, soberly sweeping movie with Joan Fontaine and Orson Welles. Like the madwoman in the attic, the sick boy in *The Secret Garden* is kept hidden but craves exposure, and as in her case, there may be some connection between the enforced concealment and the construed malady. The boy, at any rate, gets well, and my heart swelled so oceanically at the final scenes of the book, scenes of springtime, renewal, rebirth, that I could not see why the world should so conspire to fuse sickness with decline and decay, rather than with revival or recovery, especially since, in my experience (very limited then, of course), far more sick people got better than succumbed. Indeed, if the will to cope with pain confers some measure of maturity, and if the relative brevity of sickness grants experience with manageable pain, then why shouldn't we take illness as the paradigm of accelerated growth?

Though I suppose my reasoning as a boy could not have been so lucid, I know I experienced my many illnesses as cherished interludes, wonderful respites, during which time seemed, at once, to stall, and to open itself to the aspect of eternity. A sickness meant two or three days away from the irksome, noisome toils of school (much as I loved getting sick, I hated getting sick on weekends), shut away in the peace of my room with lengths of measureless time as fully in my possession as the quiet of the room was, disturbed only by the low trill of the morning game shows, the low hum of the afternoon movies. Sickness spun its own kind of time, in which the hours could no longer be quantified but the days gathered their own distinctive rhythms, and each illness had an atmosphere of its own, from the druggy torpor of the head cold to the queasily pleasant inertia of stomachache. If, on occasion, pain ever became so great as to overwhelm the myriad liberties of sickness, then I promptly lost my zeal for sickness altogether; but usually whatever pain was entailed by the minor afflictions I suffered was theoretically grave enough to let me think I was confronting the malaise that defined the true nature of being, yet mild enough to permit the continuance of peace, rest, play.

The bright, welcoming voids of sickness never seemed to me to reveal an emptiness, but rather a freedom, the yielding of a permission to go into oneself; and even its supple boredoms prompted discovery. Fever dreams came like welcome revelations, and because whenever I was sick my mother rolled into my room on its spindly stand the rabbit-eared TV, a late-fifties space-age black-and-white RCA job, with a protuberantly convex gray-green screen, these dreams sometimes became intertwined with the mild drone of the afternoon movies as I dozed. Those presentations were hosted by a minor one-time actor in B movies named Bill Kennedy, who took viewers' questions over the phone ("Who was the first Tarzan?" "How many Lassies were there?") in the breaks of the movies, and who alternated between mannered, self-effacing disparagements of his own failed film career and sudden, florid bursts of bitter, diva-like temperament. Over a period of months one autumn, when three bad colds came along in succession, I was amazed (but not really, for the state of sickness brings such equanimity as to preempt surprise) to find the same movie being shown every time I stayed home from school. The movie was called *The Unsuspected,* and all I remember of the plot is that Claude Rains, a respected radio personality, is driven to murder, perhaps to protect a beloved niece played by a bland ingenue (Joan Leslie?). He must then scale ever greater heights to hide his crime before finally, trapped, delivering a dramatic on-the-air confession: "*I . . .* am the Unsuspected!" Details of the movie's plot escape my memory, but its atmosphere is etched there: the ashen grain of its black-and-white world, the wry twists of gentlemanly skullduggery, the subtle range and baffling consistency of Claude Rains, gingerly and good-humored, but then suddenly sinister, caught in a disproportional, shadowed, chiaroscuro-graven close-up, the lordly face, with its ironic, querulous brow, turning ratlike. Like Bill Kennedy, the Claude Rains of the movie hosted a broadcast—a radio show about, as I recall, famous murders—showcasing features of his knowledge and his personality, which was as mannered, self-satisfied, and contemptuous, narcissistic and self-hating at once, as Bill Kennedy's. The effect of these correspondences was to throw open a portal to a willed, dreamlike condition of infinite regress, worlds within worlds, each, by referring to the other, showing the congruity of all things, and I—mysteriously addressed by the fated recurrence of the movie, as if I were the recipient of some cosmic message—was somehow a part of this strange, complicated pattern.

I'm trying to give a picture here of the eccentric, rarefied realm of experience I felt sickness enabled me to contact, a kind of heightened sensibility, a shimmer of transcendence, when things settled into momentary but intoxicating logic. What I saw in sickness was the form, not the meaning, of this logic. I saw only that it was there—that was all I wanted to see—and had a shape, and would perhaps someday be apprehensible; and I was implicated in it—for every illness had a beginning, a middle, and an end, its own pattern, that even if indifferent to intervention, still went on inside me, marking me as special, elect. The lure of illness was that it was ultimate without being final.

If the near-pathological grandiosity of these conceptions is not fully apparent—the crisis of scale in their conscripting implications so large from stimulations so small—it is perhaps because the locale of their emergence has yet to become fully visible. The sickroom is a little rectangle of nine feet by ten feet, with a single bed in which a boy (myself) lies supine in a state of delirious passivity, waiting to be anointed by rays of light beaming from the television, which is pulled so close that its rays touch the hot skin and enter the memory without pausing in the conscious mind, while wads of Kleenex accumulate on the floor, like exploded ordnance. It is only my bedroom, but it is transformed, as everything is transformed, by the illness, and the bristling atmosphere that would likely strike an outsider as rank odor is, to me, holy aura. There is a desk, a lamp, a window; but it is the presence of the TV, usually holed up in the kitchen, that changes everything with its ethereal light and its news from the larger world beyond. These experiences of transcendence, to be sure, had everything to do with the TV. When I was sick I got to watch movies on TV, and my attraction to illness may have come down to something so simple as that, though it would have been hard to say whether I loved movies because I loved sickness, or loved sickness because I loved movies. The two loves were intertwined, but movies themselves, at any rate, appeared altered from the throes of sickness, subject at once to a heightened inner awareness and a dulled outward perception. In sickness, I did not attend much to the plots of the movies but, in my druggy state of receptivity, tuned in only to their sensory surfaces, their looks and their sounds. *The Bill Kennedy Show* was on a UHF channel that often suffered airwave interference, and when I wasn't sick, the interference troubled me. When I was, though, I welcomed it as a gauge of the films' mystic link to my fevered dreams: the slow, cyclical invasion of the screen by quietly buzzing dots, swarms of static that threatened to overwhelm the picture (and, as background white noise, strangely intensified my doze) until, suddenly, they vanished, leaving the picture clear, until a while later the process of invasion recommenced. Often, when sick, I would search the whole UHF band, slowly turning the big knob on the control panel, pausing on stations so distant they were only barely received, plagued by pointillist throngs of dots, louder and angrier than those visited upon *The Bill Kennedy Show*. Sometimes, when sound was audible above the harsh murmur of the static, the people on these stations could be heard to speak in foreign tongues, and I'd fiddle with the rabbit ears, seeking subtle improvements of sound or picture, trying to get closer to this distance, and sensing the perverse, oneiric thrill of discovery, so intimately connected to sickness itself.

A conduit to other states, sickness interrupted the daily rounds of the ordinary, with an intimation of eternal return. Alone in my little room, with an achy belly or stuffed-up nose, I felt connected to an empyrean of illness, despite my solitude, since I could imagine the millions elsewhere who shared my fate, a mysteriously linked community of blessed sufferers; or maybe it was *because* of my solitude, since I could imagine equally the millions who were also alone.

The sickness originated inside of me, but channeled its social dimension, its character as a shared, known condition, and even when I saw that its origin was perceived as the deviation from a norm, it still reassured me, because it proved I was not empty.

In a little paper cup filled with water, next to my hospital bed, floated the petals that had fallen to the floor when the nurse whisked the flowers away. I'd furtively gathered them after she left. It was my second day in the hospital, and somehow I still hadn't gotten a glimpse of the boy on the other side of the curtain. That lack pained me almost as sorely as the dull ache in my throat, and as I drifted in and out of sleep, still benumbed in the wake of the operation, I longed to be left alone with him, to be able to strike up another conversation. All day the room bustled with the comings and goings of our families. My parents alternated between badgering me nervously about how I was feeling and frantically ordering me to rest, while my sister sat glumly in a corner, casting me baleful, resentful looks, sullenly consuming dish after dish of ice cream, her share in the benefit of this time-honored remedy for tonsillectomy still apparently doing little to compensate for the corollary loss of attention.

The balm of ice cream had been the restitution held out to me before the operation, the pledged abundance that was supposed to ease my convalescence, and though I'd been at pains to display some of the courage in the face of surgery that the promise of ice cream was meant to extort, in the aftermath I was utterly indifferent to the pledge, the promise, the courage, the display, the abundance, the ice-cream, and anything else that offered miserably false hope to relieve a pain so severe, so unceasing, that it swept away any expectation of indemnity. If, before, sickness had brought me into a fuller contact with the delicate contours of time, this pain threw me back upon the rack of space, at the mercy of time's creep—in which I'd never felt the power to intervene, but now no longer felt the ability to grasp—that alone would bring cure. They'd claimed the tonsillectomy would make me less "sickly," and one of the reasons I had dreaded it was that I feared it would deprive me of the pleasures of illness, but if this pain was really what it meant to be sick, I thought now, then I wanted no part of it.

"Nothing personal," Joey said quietly from the other side of the curtain, some time after visiting hours had ended, "but I really can't wait to get the heck out of here and go home. This place gives me the creeps."

Outside the room a muffled voice repeated a doctor's name over the public-address system, and a mechanical tone, like a grim parody of music, sounded several times. Joey had referred to his home, and I took this as an opening. "What's it like, where you live?"

"Just a house," he answered.

I tried to imagine the house. His mother and father had smiled at me as they'd passed by my bed, moving to and fro, and I tried to picture these people, and the others who had come to visit him, all grown-ups, inside the house of my imagination. The father was a burly man who had never taken off his heavy coat during visiting hours, and who had clutched a fur cap in both his hands, nervously turning it round and round by the fuzzy rim, and the porous ridges of his forehead wrinkled upward over the top of a balding, spotted head, with clumps of oily hair, some strands gray, others brown. The mother was petite and pretty, with dark hair and eyes, and she had smiled less readily than the father, who seemed unusually nervous for such a burly man. Whenever he'd met my eyes during the long, hectic hubbub of visiting hours, he had smiled bashfully and looked away, as if he were scared. But why, I wondered, should he be afraid of me?

I imagined all of them inside of the house, where they would not be afraid, and from this tranquil tableau I tried to conjure an image of Joey himself.

"What do you mean, 'What's it like'?" asked Joey, a new edge of sharpness entering his voice.

"I was just wondering," I said.

"It's just a house," he repeated. "What's yours *like*?" He gave a slight spin to the word 'like,' as if it were odd to wonder about what things were like.

"Just a house," I answered.

From beyond the curtain came a bright, twinkly laugh, breezy and strangely uninhibited, without a trace of the derision I'd begun to fear was creeping into the conversation. "That's good," he said. "I'd hate to think you lived in a barn."

I laughed too, and when the nurse came in, she told us this wasn't a party, it was a hospital, and we'd better settle down and get our rest. A second after she left, we both broke into laughter again at the same time, on our separate sides of the curtain, and we mocked the nurse, and imitated the ludicrous monotone of the public-address system, and made fun of the bland, barely edible hospital food, until we were both helpless with laughter. The laughter scalded my throat, but it was clear to me already that to establish some connection with the boy on the other side of the curtain was the only goal that might speed recovery, whatever immediate harm it seemed to cause.

"I'm here for my eyes," he said, "but my patch comes off tomorrow."

He said this last with a perky, hopeful cheer, and I fancied he took heart, not just in the thought that he would be able to see again, but that he would be able to see me. The excitement this fancy stirred loosened my caution, and I asked, "What's wrong with them?"

After a long silence, he answered quietly, "Nothing, really."

I cursed myself; I should not have used the word "wrong." How could I, so versed in words, still use them so stupidly? "I had my tonsils out," I said, eager to return the subject to my own losses. "I'm not really supposed to talk."

"That's too bad," he said.

A silence followed, lengthening like a shadow, and I fell asleep. In the night, I woke up, and caught my breath because of the strangeness of the place, but the ubiquitous pain in my throat reminded me a second later where I was. I slid out of bed in a darkness that lay upon the room as heavily as the coat had lain on the shoulders of Joey's father, and I shuffled cautiously forward, my arms stretched out in the darkness like the arms of a sleep-walker. On the other side of the curtain, I did not pause at the bedside but went to the window, so that if Joey were to wake he would not think I had crossed over to his side of the room only to see him. But he did not wake. The window was so far above the ground that the cars parked below looked like miniatures, a neatly arranged collection of Hot Wheels, and it was too high up to admit the light of the lamps in the parking lot, so the light that faltered through the window must have been moonlight, though it had the glazed cast of electric light, of the hospital light I'd come to know so well. It fell on him obliquely, like a meshed, silken veil askew across its wearer's face. Both his eyes were bandaged. His blond hair, matted, gathered in sprigs like bunched, delicate thorns across his forehead, and the nostrils of his fine, straight nose flared slightly with his breath, lips parted just a little, dry, but showing the silvery wet glimmer of tongue in his mouth. His cheekbones were high, as if stretched by a slight smile, and one cheek was pressed against the pillow, flushed with contact, and one of his elbows was crooked in trussed bedclothes, the forearm

upright in front of his face, the white, long-fingered hand dangling in heedless salute. Either my eyes adjusted gradually to the
light, or he grew paler, more limpidly fair, as I looked at him. This
palpable change in my vision confirmed the dawn of feeling,
which warranted in turn what I'd felt as we'd talked and laughed
between the beds, the obscuring curtain separating us. It came
with dread as well as with exhilaration, though, for I was leaving
the next day, and that meant I would have only another morning
to make him love me back.

Can it be an accident that E. M. Forster's only novel about homosexuality, *Maurice,* unpublished until after Forster's death, is also
about illness? Early in the novel, Maurice's friend Clive falls ill
with influenza, and Maurice helps to nurse him back to health,
caressing his fevered brow and emptying his chamber pots. Later,
Maurice himself resolves to see a doctor, and the reader realizes
only gradually in the course of the halting consultation that it is
precisely himself that he wants to cure. "I am an unspeakable,"
he confesses suddenly, with forthright self-contempt, to the addle-
brained doctor, "of the Oscar Wilde sort."

The tone of the scene, as of the whole novel, is difficult to read.
It is mired in a faintly arch, comedy-of-manners whimsy, drawing
delicate attention to characters' minor foibles, and it satirizes the
doctor's oblivious moralism, but it also satirizes Maurice's weakness and self-doubt and harbors paradoxical undercurrents of bitterness and rage. None of these factors is inexplicable in itself, but
their clash is that of the aesthete and the activist, of a robust dan-
dyism and a rather wan polemicism that wed, in this book composed a mere twenty years after Wilde's trials, a cult of refined
infirmity to a very modern doctrine of in-your-face identity politics. Such tensions are typical of gay literature before Stonewall,
of course. Finished in 1914, *Maurice* was published in 1971 (the

year after my tonsillectomy!—though it would be another decade before I would read it). What distinguishes *Maurice* is the passionate confusion roiling just beneath the novel's carefully composed, epigrammatical surface. The novel proposes a romance of illness, to the extent that the vulnerability brought by Clive's illness is what enables Maurice's love. That proposition troubles what appears to be a quite explicit political agenda of the novel: to overturn conventional societal associations of homosexuality with sickness. Maurice wills Clive's sickness so he can cure him with love, and the novel idealizes illness, in its way, as a bastion of contemplation that brings greater receptiveness to what is already contained within one. If love is the cure, the novel instructs, then homosexuality may still be the illness. Maurice's ruminations participate in a strain of virile lyricism on the subject: "The diseases still simmered. . . . He knew his own strength. Presently he would put it forth as love, and heal his friend." Such passages suggest not so much a wholesale rejection of the oppressive identification of homosexuality with sickness as a call to glorify illness as a phase in the rise of self-consciousness, or even as itself a form of therapy.

Homosexuality and illness have in common, in fact, a single feature, one that is intrinsic or endemic to neither: both are feared. The evangelist wailing from the pulpit of inherited belief would surely adduce shared reason for such fear: Sickness brings mortality; gayness, sterility. Gayness stirs morbidity; sickness fulfills it. Sickness punishes solipsism—the famed hypersensitivity of the tubercular, or the notorious repressions of the cancerous—while homosexuality sanctions narcissism; and both pervert the norm, which despite its endless history of untold misery and unimaginable brutality remains apparently the only force that need never be feared.

Maybe because dominant social constructs of male homosexuality still current postulate a paradoxical relation of surface to depth, of inner to outer spheres, they find vexed correspondence in typical constructions of illness. In such constructs, the gay man is all prettified surface—male beauty always provokes suspicion in a culture where beauty is decreed as the possession of men, who still define its terms, but the province only of women—and empty core. Gay sex cannot be certified as real, because there are no offspring to evince it, and gay love cannot be validated as true, because there are no rituals to legitimate it. From this vantage point, its allegiances are thought to be strictly to surface and to instant, to the compulsive, immediate pleasures of male flesh, and it is deemed sterile, bereft of any outcome that could connect it to a legitimating lineage. The cultural assumptions that produce these narratives are much the same, it is worth noting, as those that continue to generate ideals of male sexuality as potent, productive, and active, female sexuality as reticent, reproductive, and passive. Nothing but biological complacency produces such notions; every schoolchild knows, and wears the penis envy or castration anxiety to prove it, that a boy's sexuality is visible on the body, hard, erect, straightforward, a girl's concealed, soft, invaginated, mysterious. These conceptions are, of course, as natural as the ebb of the tide and as unassailable as the flow of the capitalist growth economy, shared profoundly, we are given to believe, even by those who would conspire to deny them. It is to the extent that gay desire is a species of male sexuality, albeit an "inverted" one, that it is construed as definitively superficial. Only if we can see how traditional patriarchal notions of gender are what give rise to stereotypes about gay men will we admit the cultural alliance of misogyny and homophobia, though homophobes will routinely invoke their reverence for women, by contrast to the alleged scorn of gay men, as the motive for their hate. This alliance is nowhere more apparent than in the familiar rhetoric of abomination, the injunction against lying with man as if he were woman. Hence the paradox. Too much sensitivity in a boy, a morbid inwardness, is the dread omen, but the symptom's outcome, the production of the fully fledged gay man, is a condition deprived of any interiority whatever, while the objectification of gay sexuality necessitates the complicated nexus of interiority, the gay man's transgressive mimicry of the projected feminine, that alone could substantiate the attribution of sin. In other words, gay men cannot have insides, for that might make them real, yet they must, in order that they—*we*—remain ghostly.

In these terms, it is more than possible that the reckoning of homosexuality as "sickness" is indeed an effect of correspondence rather than the function of an enforced causality. I don't believe it was my love of sickness that led me to contemplate my inner life as homosexual, nor was it any felt sense of the prelude to that life that made me "sickly." I *do* believe I was *taught* to love sickness. It was the analogue, the outer manifestation, of what was really there, "inside" me—an indenture to mindfulness, a readiness to sentience. An unusual concentration of attention (hours spent watching an ant cross the driveway, observing the shifting patterns of sun reflected on a wall, reading and rereading the same page of a newspaper), a heightened need for solitude—these were my symptoms, the attributes that cast me as sickly. It made sense that if I were going to love them, and not fear them, I would have to love sickness, and not fear it.

What I feared, indeed, was having it taken away from me, and in the days after the tonsillectomy I felt the nearly unbearable pain in my throat as a measure of my rising resentment. They had reached inside me and torn something out, something they diagnosed as the cause of the sickliness they imputed to me. They had torn it out, to deprive me of what I loved, and only they feared. But even though it was a taking away, it left in place of the purloined element a pain so grave, it exceeded any that sickness had ever endowed, even when I'd had pneumonia some months before, when the redoubling of my typical discomfort when sick was only barely made up for by the longer stretch of time I was able to spend in my room. I could not now even properly be called sick—can it be sickness when one consents, as I nominally had, to the curative infliction of pain?—yet not only was the intimacy of my connection to illness potentially severed forever, but I felt worse than I ever had before.

On the morning of my last day in the hospital, I awoke feeling unutterably changed, as if the climate of my body had been altered for good. I'd never been conscious of thinking my body had a core—the intensity of my attentions was usually directed elsewhere—but now that it had been so torturously liquidated, it seemed proved by the fact that it had vanished, replaced by a blazing knot of pain too far from the center to be thought of as a core, but too vehemently fixed in my throat, a housing that would not before have seemed big enough to contain it, to be thought of as anything else. Joey was not in his bed, and the hallways were quiet, the light sickly, and there was a terrible, terrible smell in the room. The floating sense of failure, of clammy anomie, that hovered, and may have accounted for the smell, came to me that morning as the awful feeling that there would not be time enough for Joey, that a wonderful opportunity would be lost. I knew nothing about him except the strength of my feeling for him, which may have implicated me more deeply than it did him. He didn't want to talk about himself, or about his affliction, and hadn't wanted to describe his house, and had told me nothing of his life. He had not even seen me yet, and I had seen him but once, and so our love, if it were allowed to grow, would have in it always an element of disembodiment. We had talked, on our separate sides of the curtain, not of ourselves, but of the world, at least the localized world of the hospital, and of its comical shortcomings, which we had agreed upon. We'd shared a laugh, a physical pleasure that had arisen mutually, and involuntarily. But if this bodily act, and our common infirmity, had brought us together, we were separated still by the curtain, and by the fact of our having each to imagine the other, to fashion an inner picture with only the sound of a voice as epitome. Our love would be selfless, I thought, if only given room, and it would be incorporeal. That, in turn, might make it pure.

On that ennobling thought, I expansively threw aside the bed-cover and swung my legs out of the bed. As I did so, I saw that the backs of my legs were covered with flakes of shit, and the bed was filled with shit.

It is a wonder, in retrospect, that my first thoughts, on seeing that the bed was filled with shit, were not thoughts of disgust, or of shame, or of expiation, but simply of the practical necessity of concealment. I did not even wonder, at first, where the shit had come from, or how the bed had come to be filled with it, or how I had slept so soundly in its viscid embrace. Instead, I flung the cover back over the bed, and scampered into the bathroom to wash my legs. It took most of a roll of toilet paper, balled in thick, damp clumps, to clean the hard, scabby shit from the backs of my legs. When I came out of the bathroom, the nurse was at my bedside, inflicting her usual violence on the pillows. My mind raced: Were there routines in her daily consuetudes that might compel an unseemly revelation? She shot me a stern look. "You— bed!" she ordered, pointing a long, straight finger. She would hear no protests, and it seemed preferable in any case to return quietly to the scene of the crime than to risk prompting inspection through a display of suspicious behavior. With the daintiness of a noblewoman skirting an unshielded puddle, I hoisted myself cautiously back into the bed, careful not to disturb the cover for fear of permitting a view or distributing the pungency of what it concealed. "Cover up," the nurse demanded. I lifted the cover slightly and slid myself under it, like a bather descending into the cold shock of a full tub. I found that if I braced myself on a far end of the mattress, pressed against one of the bed's braces, I was able to simulate a condition of repose under the cover, while avoiding further contact with the shit. The nurse watched my exertions, eyeing me with unkindly suspicion, and I imagined that she leveled an unspoken accusation when she grimly sniffed the acrid air, but she finally left.

All morning I was rolled in my wheelchair from office to office as the doctors examined my throat. But a helpless submission, not a delight in coddling, was the dominant note. The potential pleasure of the wheelchair's novelty, promoting effortless mobility and the sense that I was being served, akin to royalty, was completely undermined by apprehension about what might be going on back in my room. Would some busybody orderly happen by, and chance to reveal my disgraceful secret? Would my parents arrive for visiting hours and in innocent offer of succor, thinking to freshen my bed, find that it was filled with shit? Would Joey have come back from wherever he was, his eyes unblocked only so that—fate's cruelest gambit!—he could take his predestined place as witness to my shame? For, as impossible as it seemed to believe, the shit that filled the bed could only be my own. The disgust and shame that I had not felt initially redoubled themselves now in their delayed onset, and instead of feeling the injustice of the doctors' cold, unfeeling examinations of me as I was wheeled from room to room, I wanted them to probe harder, poke deeper, to spare me no hurt. The fact that I was not myself—that I'd had my tonsils ripped from my throat, that I was in terrible pain, and it was getting no better, that I was forced to wear a ridiculous gown with a gash in the rear, that I was away from home and was only a boy—may have been an excuse, but could hardly be taken as a source of absolution.

When I was rolled back to my room later that morning, the pertinent circumstance remained unchanged. I'd allowed myself the faintest hope that random magic might have occurred while I was away, and the bed would be cleansed, the shit gone, and no one would ever speak of it. Now, however, as I resumed my precarious position balanced against the bed's brace, shunning the touch of the shit, but still occupying a proximity to it greater than any I'd have chosen in the best of all possible worlds, I cursed such sentimental naïveté. Then Joey's voice, tremulously, came from the other side of the curtain. "Is that you?" he asked.

"You're back," I said.

"It really smells bad in here," he observed.

I, the shamed, had no reply to make.

"I got my patch off," he said.

"That's really cool."

"Want to see?"

I heard him, learning forward on the other side of the curtain, straining to see past it. I heard a mild groan escape his throat, from the effort, and had a delicious impression after so long a time of incorporeality of a body's struggle. I leaned forward too. I bent, groped, strained, to see him past the curtain. I felt the shit against my legs, cold and hard, and it did not matter. He was seeing me, between the beds, beyond the curtain, and I him, for the first time. We looked at each other without speaking. Only one patch was gone. The other remained. He smiled at me faintly. He was the first to lean back. He disappeared again, behind the curtain. I heard a quiet sigh.

After a long while, he asked softly, "Did you fart?"

I answered, "No."

"It really, really smells." The sadness I'd noted at first had returned to his voice.

Balanced against the brace of the bed, I stared at the ceiling. My heart raced, but the substance it seemed to pump through my veins was a heavy, liquid peace.

"The other patch comes off soon," he said.

"Cool," I answered.

It had changed something: our seeing each other. When visiting hours began, the rush of activity brought a kind of mysterious surcease. My parents readied me to go home. The wheelchair would come for me soon. On the other side of the curtain, I heard Joey talking to his father, with an uninhibited note of simple whining: Why couldn't *he* go home? Why did it smell so bad? Why couldn't the other patch come off? I did not view his whining as a fall; I knew it was only because I was leaving and he was not. In the aftermath of whatever we'd exchanged, I saw myself as having assumed the implacable dignity of one who has glimpsed the greatest good but accepted, in the end, a lesser fate. Even if an evil-wisher had, at that moment, with a covetous flourish, thrown aside the bedcover to reveal the shit, I would have answered with the solemn, forgiving silence of those who have come to the knowledge that indignity is a common estate. My last act as a patient, before I left the room, was to flush away the withered petals that had floated in the paper cup at my bedside. They whirled in the vortex of the toilet as I watched, and then they disappeared. When the wheelchair arrived, we barely said good-bye. He went on talking to his father, whining, and his voice broke. He was starting to cry when I left him.

It was a bad year for illness. First pneumonia, then the tonsillectomy, the two of them combining to contribute to a disillusionment, an awakening resentment, I learned only gradually to welcome. Part of the lure of illness had always been, for me, to make possible an assumption of martyrdom without significant cost. A case of the sniffles made the depth of my suffering visible, without occasioning any really intractable pain. The severity of pneumonia, the irrevocability of the tonsillectomy, made me start to think for the first time that perhaps I'd been playing with fire all along in my private romance of sickness. Maybe mortality wasn't only a question of style; maybe in flirting with it so fervently, I had really been nurturing it, making it more powerful, rather than keeping it at bay. That year was certainly the first time I experienced disease in its literal sense, as the *opposite* of ease. The fever dreams of pneumonia, fixing a distorted lens on the world, revealed a dilution of color, a dilation of space, that threatened to alter forever how I perceived. Specters haunted me. A fanged simulacrum of Lon Chaney as the Phantom of the Opera, with a forehead stretched wildly out of proportion like the funhouse-mirror visages hyperbolized across a TV screen deprived of vertical hold, hunched at the foot of my bed, staring at me malevolently for hours and slowly squashing my marbles, one by one, into a kaleidoscopic pulp between his thumb and forefinger. A boy in a red hooded jacket floated across my vacillating field of view, the fervent red of the jacket the only color amid the general gray, and when I would call out feebly, he would turn in my direction suddenly to reveal that the hood shrouded a blank gray hole where the face should have been. Then, for a moment, I might come to, my fevered eyes stinging, wan, like the wicks of burnt-out candles. Even in the deadened calm of my sickness, I found the hallucinations as fascinating as they were horrifying, but I worried that they would never go away. What recovery is possible, after such vision?

If I still welcomed the heightened state of perception illness brought, then, I worried all the same that it might finally alienate me in material and permanent ways. This possibility came home to me most forcefully when, at the height of my pneumonia, my family had a pool party in the backyard. They had offered to cancel the party, but I—still the martyr—wouldn't hear of it. As I languished abed, though, while the loud, squally merriment of the party went on outside my window, I fathomed unhappily that such martyrdom was stripped of pleasure or use if I was its sole beneficiary and only witness. During the pool party, my father looked in on me, opening the door only a crack. Surprised to find me awake, he waved at me through the little crack, and then he closed the door and went away. If I'd been granted the power in that instant to shrug off my illness as if it were a fusty cloak, even if it meant I could never take pleasure in illness again, I would have seized that power. I would have strided into the midst of the party, pale and naked and healthy, and jackknifed into the pool, reveling anew in this dizzy thrill of celebration.

A few years after my tonsillectomy (though I would hesitate to assert a causal relation between the events), homosexuality was declassified as an "illness" by many of the nation's learned societies. A decade later, when the first friends were infected by a virus whose face seemed to change by the day, it appeared that the process of contravention would have to begin all over again. By then, I, who had so loved illness, had come without effort, and completely, to hate it. But a sick friend one day accused me: "You *can't*," Owen said, his clear eyes shining with anger. "It's *in* me. If you hate it, you hate me." I held him, so that I would not have to answer, and because I loved him; but as I felt his tears trickle down my cheeks, my neck, I still could not prevent the thought that this was an illness that manifested itself, not just in the blood, but in the tears, of those who suffered it.

In the wake of the tonsillectomy, I was confined to the sick-room for ten days, with a bell at my bedside to ring whenever I wanted anything, since I was also condemned to silence. In former days, that bell would have been a source of infinite delight. The fact that it now seemed little more than a utilitarian device was clear proof that the bloom of illness was gone. Every day or so, my father appeared at the door and repeated the gesture that had originated at the pool party—peered in through a little crack, waved to me across the room's distance, and then withdrew—and every time my heart leapt: I had not been forgotten. Many years later, I read in Kafka's letter to his father a description of the writer's joy "when, during my last illness, you came tiptoeing to

Ottla's room to see me, stopping in the doorway, craning your neck to see me, and out of consideration only waved to me with your hand." This memory Kafka proposes, in a buildup of quite extraordinary emotional density, as a "wonderful" exception to his father's usual hostilities. It is, however, difficult to imagine any reader interpreting the pitiful gesture of Kafka's father as anything but an instance of extreme emotional stinginess, and the over- whelming pathos of the passage comes from the completeness of Kafka's own blindness to this very evident fact. He sees as "con- sideration" what anyone else reading his report would see only as remoteness, or cruelty, or self-protection, and the disproportionate emotion Kafka expresses moves one to recognize how empty of affection the relation of father and son must have been, if so parsimonious a gesture could be perceived as an example of sur- passing kindness. "At such times one would lie back and weep for happiness," writes Kafka, "as one weeps again now, writing it down."

When my own father had waved to me from the hallway, when I was stricken with pneumonia, I knew why he did not come closer. It was because I might be contagious. But after my tonsil- lectomy I was not contagious. Strictly speaking, paradoxically, I wasn't even sick, despite the terrible pain. I didn't think my father was refraining from approaching me in my afflicted state out of consideration for me, but it was only after reading Kafka's letter, many years later, that I realized the truth of the matter. How terrified Kafka's father must have been of his sensitive son, capable of weeping with joy over a perfunctory little wave of the hand. It is not the fear of contagion that keeps the hearty father from the sickroom. It is the fear of inwardness itself.

In the cold light of a spring morning, leaving the hospital, I waited in my wheelchair at the entryway for my parents to bring the car to fetch me. My hands were folded in my lap, my eyes tilted slightly skyward. This was the disposition of the glorified

sufferer, whose acquiescent, dignified despair lies in having relinquished all martyrdom. In their resolve to deprive me of sickness,
the doctors had bequeathed a horrible perturbation of the body
hitherto unknown, and its repugnant evidence lay still under cover
in the sickbed I'd left behind in favor of the bright air of health.
My memory presents this to me now as the moment when another resolve took hold: the brutality of the doctors' taking away
would be met by the new equanimity of a giving up, which
would be my own. I would give up my claim to the love of
sickness. If it meant loss of contemplation, that too could be made
good by a gain in ripeness. Growing up, after all, was always a
leaving behind. Perhaps if I'd had the thought that I would never
see Joey again—as I never did—or if I had considered that I was
only embracing the plebeian standard I had previously scorned,
then I might not have looked with such composure on an imagined future of defiant wellness. But I held no such thoughts, and
at once, as I waited in my wheelchair beside the mechanical door
that slid to and fro, to admit the ill and eject the well, my sickly
past was bathed as I thought of it in the light of nostalgia, nothing
more than memories that would at length be forgotten, or put
aside, as memories of past life always must be, in the lives to
follow.